TIRED OF YELLING

Teaching Our Children
to Resolve Conflict

Lyndon D. Waugh, M.D.
with Letitia Sweitzer

LONGSTREET
Atlanta, Georgia

Published by
LONGSTREET, INC.
A subsidiary of Cox Newspapers
A subsidiary of Cox Enterprises, Inc.
2140 Newmarket Parkway
Suite 122
Marietta, GA 30067

Written by Lyndon D. Waugh, M.D., with Letitia Sweitzer

Printed in the United States of America

3rd printing 1999

Library of Congress Catalog Card Number: 99-60100

ISBN: 1-56352-531-3

Jacket and book design by Burtch Bennett Hunter

Dedicated to

My parents, M. C. and Agatha Waugh, who nurtured me,
taught me, and granted me the freedom to be me;

My sons, Derek and Branden, who were easy to parent,
who are still easy to relate to, and who are excellent young men;

And especially my wife, Sherry, who is loving and lovable
and who supports me in every way.

This book is not intended to replace appropriate evaluation and treatment by a licensed mental health professional if needed. Such professionals include an M.D. psychiatrist/child psychiatrist, a Ph.D. clinical psychologist, or an LCSW/MSW clinical psychiatric social worker.

If your child has sustained violent behavior, rage episodes, or any other significant emotional or behavioral problems, I hope that you will pursue professional help. Evaluation and therapy can also be very useful for marital and other adult conflicts and anger management problems. It is usually best to ask for a referral from your pediatrician, family physician, or a friend or relative who has had a good experience with a therapist.

Contents

CHAPTER 1

The Conflict Resolution Model

Tired of yelling, arguing, slamming doors? Had enough snapping, sarcasm, and angry retorts? Discouraged because nothing gets settled? Afraid someone will get hurt? Depressed by silence, avoidance, lack of intimacy, and resentment?

It doesn't have to be this way. You can change your family's well-worn patterns of dealing with conflict, and you can teach your child a better way.

I remember years ago I was treating a young boy who had a tendency to overreact to nearly everything, crying and having a tantrum over what should have been small annoyances. I encouraged him to think of phrases he could say to himself as an early reaction to a situation, phrases to calm himself. These phrases would replace the reflexive angry thoughts that had been his typical first reaction in the past. I suggested "no big deal," "whatever," "relax," "chill," "no sweat," and other expressions. Then I asked him to pick a favorite phrase. He thought a second and came up with his own: "No biggy piggy!"

We had a good laugh. I enjoyed the vision of a laid-back pig in a hammock sipping lemonade. The child resolved to try to use this expression as a better way to think before reacting to minor aggravations.

Not long afterwards, when I was treating an adult with a self-admitted tendency to overreact in anger, I told him about the child's "no biggy piggy" technique. The man adopted the phrase as his own reminder and found that it helped him. One day he brought me a stuffed animal as a gift, a pig with "No Biggy Piggy" painted on its bib. I displayed the pig in my office

and have passed on the phrase to many people. Consequently, my office now has a large collection of pigs — stuffed pigs, ceramic pigs, nested pigs, laid-back pigs of every size and description that people have brought me to join company with the original "No Biggy Piggy."

The "No biggy piggy" story is just one small example of changes in thinking that people of any age can make so that anger doesn't get in the way of resolving a problem.

One of the greatest gifts you can give your child is a set of attitudes and skills that allows him to manage his anger well and find a solution to conflict. If your child can resolve conflict well, he can have genuine intimacy, better overall physical and emotional health, improved productivity, and in general a happier, more meaningful life.

Children need to develop a mindset that favors peace, not by avoiding conflict nor by winning through intimidation, but by resolving conflict with others.

It is possible to teach your child . . .

* that the important thing, for both adults and children, is to shift from thinking that anger is about who's right, who's wrong, or who's to blame, to thinking of anger as a "signal" emotion — a signal to resolve a problem.

* to recognize reflexive first thoughts when angry and to replace them with more appropriate thoughts.

 The appearance of this icon signals a "real-life" story that illustrates conflict resolution.

* to learn perspective by asking oneself, "How big a deal is this really?" and by empathizing with the other person's point of view.

* how to "out-mature" the other person rather than "out-power" him.

* that admitting what you are doing wrong in a conflict is empowering, not losing.

* that conflict has two aspects: what the disagreement is about (content) and how you're going to handle it (process).

* that resolution has two aspects: a practical solution to the problem and a "resolved feeling." You have resolution when you have a plan to solve the problem that made you angry in the first place and when both people genuinely feel better towards each other.

So how do you teach these concepts to your child? How do you make them a real part of your child's life?

For years in my family psychiatry practice, I've used a three-part model of conflict resolution as a teaching tool and as a way to assess where children and parents have significant problems in managing anger and conflict. Many families have learned to resolve conflict better using this method. It's my belief that you, too, can experience success using the model, the teaching methods, and the age-appropriate language presented in detail in this book.

And what is success? If your child has a significantly better attitude towards resolving conflict or changes even one behavior pattern for the better, you have reason to celebrate. Better attitudes are contagious; better behavior leads to more goodwill.

Here then are the three parts of the conflict resolution model:

Think

Thinking appropriate thoughts before speaking or acting in anger is so critical and so often neglected that I call Part One of the three-part conflict resolution model "The Thinking Steps." The Thinking Steps not only help hold off the impulsive, angry behavior that could jeopardize reconciliation but also allow the angry person to become more open to resolving the conflict. Thinking things through is also respectful to the other person. After doing The Thinking Steps well, you will be less defensive, clearer in your ideas, and ready to empathize, solve the problem, and forgive.

Talk/Listen

Part Two, "The Talk/Listen Steps," is more interactive than introspective, although, of course, you still must think appropriately as you talk and listen. You state the problem as you see it, in resolvable terms. Then you really listen while the other fellow states his perspective. Both of you listen to and appreciate the other person's point of view.

Solve

Finally, we have Part Three, "The Solving Steps." This is the part most traditionally associated with problem solving: the participants in the conflict brainstorm solutions and reach a workable agreement. The problem is either solved, or, if it's unresolved, it drifts away and then circles back, coming upon the conflict participants again and again from behind, in the same or another guise.

Over the years, working with individuals and families, I have developed and elaborated on this three-part model of conflict resolution until it is admittedly complex, but you begin with these three primary, easy-to-remember concepts: Think, Talk/Listen, Solve.

Beyond the Basics

If Think, Talk/Listen, Solve was all you had to learn, this would be a much shorter book. But there's more. Each of the three big parts of the conflict resolution model has five steps. And three times five is. . . .

"Fifteen steps! I don't have time to teach my kid fifteen steps! I don't have the patience!" you may be thinking. Bear with me. If you spent fifteen minutes for fifteen days teaching your child these steps, how would that compare with the time you spend fussing about clothes left on the floor, arguing whose fault the sibling squabble is, nagging about homework, and dealing with the "my teacher/coach/playground bully picks on me" ordeal? These fifteen steps will not cost you time; ultimately they will save you time — and frustration. Many families report an improvement in their family dynamics within weeks of conscientious use of the model.

If you need further reason to expend the effort, think of the overall importance of conflict resolution in life.

In relationships, conflict resolution is an important source of intimacy. Knowing that anger and hurt can be talked about without destructive behavior enables couples, parents, friends, and others to bring up and get through problems that inevitably arise.

Unresolved anger underlies a lot of heart disease, depression, and other illnesses. Conflict resolution is important for health — physical and mental.

Resolving conflicts is a major factor in doing well in business and getting along with neighbors, classmates, and co-workers as well as family. We even use conflict resolution strategies to promote peace among nations.

As parents, we spend tons of time and energy trying to prepare our kids to have an economically secure life by education and career guidance. Your child may spend an hour a day on math, for example. Let's do the same for their attitudes, emotional reflexes, interpersonal habits, and conflict resolution skills. These are areas that contribute heavily to "emotional intelligence," the set of abilities that author Daniel Goleman (*Emotional Intelligence*, Bantam Books, 1995) describes as mattering more than IQ or academic achievement in getting along successfully in the world.

We also provide our children with hobbies and opportunities to socialize with groups. Isn't conflict resolution worth the same commitment of time and attention as scouting or Little League? If you think of conflict resolution as you do learning piano or tennis — as a project needing formal lessons and lots of practice — you can stay on track with the teaching. Work on reflexes toward anger as you do reflexes in tennis, encourage good habits in conflict resolution as you encourage good habits in piano, teach conflict resolution skills as you do soccer skills. Make it a family project and keep momentum going with approval and recognition.

You may not need to spend a lot of time on every one of the steps because you and your children already know and use some of them well. Concentrate on the ones you omit or do poorly. In a classroom or family with older children, you may want to sit down with the children and study the whole model formally, but in other situations you can introduce the steps more casually as the occasion allows.

While the three parts of the model should be used in order — Think, Talk/Listen, Solve — you have more leeway with the order of the steps within the parts, as you will see in the sample conflict resolutions later in the book.

Here's the expanded three-part, fifteen-step model. For each step, there is a short, easily remembered label and a brief elaboration.

PART ONE: THE THINKING STEPS

Step 1. Assess Emotions.

Anger is a signal to resolve a problem. Learn to recognize anger quickly, label it properly, and distinguish it from other emotions, realizing that several emotions often coexist.

Step 2. Accept Anger, Behave Well.

Tell yourself, "Anger is OK; it's how I handle it that counts." Separate feeling anger from acting out anger such as by hitting, yelling, or saying hurtful things. No one should be punished or feel guilty for feeling anger; however, you should control aggressive or hurtful behavior.

Step 3. Gauge Intensity.

Rate the intensity of your emotion on a scale of 1 to 10. Very low levels of anger may be ignored, while very high levels of anger must be reduced before a good resolution talk is likely. In the mid-range, it's okay to proceed with the conflict resolution process.

Step 4. Who and What?

Sometimes people get angry or in a "bad mood" and flail out at the nearest bystander (displacement) or complain about the wrong issue. Instead, learn to recognize what the real problem is and who is involved.

Step 5. Perspective Check.

Are you overreacting? Underreacting? Learn to keep anger in proportion to provocation, recognize your own contribution to the conflict, and try to see the other person's point of view.

PART TWO: THE TALK/LISTEN STEPS

Step 6. Time and Place.

Give resolution a chance by choosing the right time and place to bring up the conflict.

Step 7. Avoid Coalitions.

Limit the conflict to the appropriate persons. Don't try to get uninvolved people to take sides. Conflict is almost never resolved when it's a team sport.

Step 8. **Express Appropriately.**

Tell the other person in a reasonable tone and manner what you are angry or hurt about. Don't spoil your chances of a friendly resolution by hostile or inappropriate behavior. State the problem in a way that makes it a resolvable issue.

Step 9. **Listen Actively.**

Repeat in your own words what the other person is telling you so you both know you truly understand his point of view. Expect him to do the same.

Step 10. **Admit Fault.**

Acknowledge your part in the problem. Most problems are not all one person's fault. Admitting what you have done to contribute to the problem adds objectivity and helps gain the other person's cooperation.

PART THREE: THE SOLVING STEPS

Step 11. **Brainstorm Solutions.**

Exchange ideas without judging them. Be creative. Consider ways to solve the problem without pointing out the flaws in anyone else's ideas.

Step 12. **Pros and Cons.**

Decide which ideas have the most merit and assess the good and bad points of each.

Step 13. **Decide and Plan.**

Choose the solution that has the best chance of working, that all sides buy into. Plan how to put it into action and how you will monitor it. Set a time to review its success.

Step 14. **Do It.**

Follow through. Make a sincere effort to do what you have agreed to do and remind the others in a constructive way to do their part of the plan. Keep track of progress.

Step 15. **Review/Revise.**

Get together and talk about how well your plan has worked. What changes do you need to make? Celebrate success.

You may want to return to this section and read this model over several times until it's very familiar. The rest of the book is based on understanding, adapting, practicing, and teaching these steps.

HOW TO USE THIS BOOK

In the next chapter, I present some general principles and techniques for teaching children of any age. Included are ways to be a model of harmony yourself, to draw your child out, to get him to buy into the resolution of conflict, and to reinforce his progress. This is a critical chapter that I hope you'll read carefully and even study.

In Chapter Three, I address some special obstacles that you may need to tackle before teaching conflict resolution. These obstacles are defensiveness, noncompliance, and a behavior pattern called "getting your goat." A fourth obstacle is not related to the child's behavior; it's the reluctant adult. I offer ideas to the person who doesn't expect to be able to "sell" the idea of conflict resolution to the other parent or adult who is a major player in the child's life. Sometimes, in fact, the other parent or adult may be a big part of the problem.

In Chapters Four through Seven, I address teaching conflict resolution skills to four different age groups: infants through preschoolers, elementary-school-age children, preadolescents, and teens. At the end of each chapter, I run through a typical dispute for that age and how to resolve it, using the three-part, fifteen-step conflict resolution model.

To thoroughly understand the whole process and its rationale from an adult point of view, turn to Chapters Eight, Nine, and Ten. In these chapters I use adult examples, a greater degree of analysis, and a mature perspective.

Some readers may want to read the adult chapters first. Some may want to read Chapters One through Three and then skip to the age group chapter appropriate to their child. These are reasonable plans. Realize, however, that while reading the book from cover to cover will admittedly involve repetition of some of the concepts, it is one of the best ways to learn the ideas well enough that they become close to second nature. And you will find some ideas in one age group chapter that you won't find in the other chapters. You may end up adapting a technique meant for one age for use with another age, even a technique from the very young years to apply to someone much older, as the "No biggy piggy" reminder was passed on.

Moreover, if you go through the book in order, from teaching preschoolers to teaching teens and on into the more analytical adult model, you can learn the model as the child learns, from the simple to the more complex, from the more playful and incidental approach to the more intellectual and direct. You may observe how attitudes about anger and patterns of conflict are formed in childhood over time. You may also gain insight into how your own attitudes were formed. And, if you happen to be an adult who in childhood got some unhealthy ideas about the expression of anger and the way to resolve conflicts, you can relearn more constructive patterns from childhood up. I hope you will find, while reading this book, that you yourself are changing as you pick up the tools to teach your child.

You have reason to be optimistic. Years ago, I was doing a cognitive therapy approach with a bright young child. We were working on altering his habitually scary bedtime images to convert such thoughts to funny images. He was also confrontational and argumentative but wanted to be better. He came in one day and surprised me by announcing that he had "made a decision." He was going to throw out the window "I can't," "I won't," "I won't try," and "no."

Stunned with his understanding of the importance of such thoughts, I asked what he was going to keep.

"You know, of course," he said. "'I can,' 'I will,' 'I'll try,' and 'yes.'"

Fifteen minutes later, when his mother told him to clean up the toys and get ready to go, he said angrily, "I won't . . . whoops, I threw that one out the window. . . . Okay." He cleaned up the toys and departed happily.

CHAPTER 2

Teaching Our Children

Does your eight-year-old still leave no spaces between words when he writes, but he's reached the "Professor" level on the computer game "Gizmos and Gadgets"?

Is your teenager unable to learn six forms of a regular Spanish verb but knows the complete lyrics for 537 unintelligible rock songs?

Why is this?

MOTIVATION, OF COURSE

Computer games are stimulating and fun, and "rock rules." Composition skills and Spanish verbs pale by comparison.

It's not always "fun" that makes the difference, however. A kid will bring home an A on a science test but his interest in learning Psalm 23 for his Sunday school class is nil. Is science more fun? Not necessarily. More likely, the science test grade produces more parental approval, peer status, another good mark for his record for college admission, and maybe even privileges. Sunday schools usually can't compete in immediate payoff in this world.

We learn better, and the lesson sticks better, when we want to learn, when we need to learn, or when what we're learning is so interesting and fun that we learn without a conscious effort to learn. Motivation is as important a factor in learning as ability. It takes many forms. Children may be motivated to learn new skills, strategies, facts, and behavior:

* out of natural curiosity.
* to feel accomplished, successful, and responsible.
* because they understand it's in their self-interest.
* to please parents and keep the bond (or, in the case of teens, to displease parents and break the bond!).
* to get good grades or scores.
* for some distant goal like getting into college.
* to get status in the adult or peer world.
* to compete with peers or siblings.
* to avoid parents' disappointment or anger.
* to avoid anxiety.
* to avoid embarrassment.
* to avoid punishment.

What are the chances your child will be motivated to learn a better way to handle conflict? Of course, it depends on age, ability, prior experience, your relationship with him, and other factors. But a lot depends on how you approach the teaching and how well you use the motivators mentioned above.

Your child may have a little bit of curiosity and some desire to please. He may have a slight realization that he'd be better off if he learned how to resolve conflict. But you are competing with TV, his social life, sports, naps, and the comfortable inertia of doing things the way he's always done them.

What's more, let's face it, learning conflict resolution skills sounds a lot like a lecture coming. If you hope to teach, you'll often have to amplify your child's natural motivation to learn.

You can show children that resolution feels good . . . once you get there.

You can offer:
* relief from emotional pain.
* relief from "walking on eggs."
* relief from recurring conflict.

You should:
* lead them rather than lecture.
* draw them out.

★ give them a chance to participate in the lesson.

You can give:
★ positive reminders.
★ praise and approval.
★ "tests."

You can use:
★ humor.
★ play and toys.
★ literature, TV, movies, and drama.
★ reasonable levels of competition.
★ formal reward systems, such as points or stars.

And — this is important — you can show them that you are willing to learn new, better behavior, too.

All your efforts to motivate may seem to come up against their efforts to resist. Here's why:

Some children view any correction or coaching as a judgment or criticism, and they react defensively. Severe or habitual defensiveness is discussed more fully in Chapter Three.

Other children are resistant to your teaching:

★ because listening to a parent may not be as much fun as playing or talking with friends.

★ because they think it's too abstract and doesn't relate to their lives.

★ because a parent's teaching feels like an admonition to "be good" rather than an invitation to feel better.

★ because they don't like to be told what to do and consider you controlling when you try to teach.

★ because they anticipate your lessons are going to be long-winded and boring.

★ because they just want to figure things out for themselves rather than be taught.

To motivate a child, it helps to recognize her reason for resistance and devise techniques to address it. For example, if your child just doesn't like to be told what to do, you may be able to subtly draw her out by asking questions. The "drawing out" technique is discussed more fully later in this chapter. If your child can't see the relevance of your subject to her life, you'll need to avoid a lecture and choose a situation she really cares about to use as a demonstration. If she'd just rather be playing, you can make a game of learning the conflict resolution skills. You can also watch a well-chosen video with your child and make occasional short remarks about the good or poor conflict resolution skills the characters use.

IS IT CONTENT OR PROCESS?

Every conflict has two elements: the content — the facts of a disagreement — and the process — the patterns and style of dealing with disagreement. The content is "what" the argument appears to be about. The process is "how" we deal with it. The content is often easier to focus on and deal with than the process problems. Teaching our children to resolve conflict requires that we think about both content and process and teach them to recognize the difference.

A couple came to me complaining about incessant arguing between their two children. The boy, who was younger, liked to be a debater. He was incredibly persistent. The girl often reacted to him quickly and intensely. Each child told me readily what the other does that drives him or her crazy. The girl said the boy never gives up and always has to be right. He tells her what to do. The boy said the girl sticks out her tongue and treats him like he has nothing valid to say. She won't listen to him and she tells him to shut up.

I got the picture; the conflict was almost all process — the way they handled issues. I worked out a plan with this family, and, when they came back, they said they'd had a much more peaceful week. In the car coming to my office, however, an argument had broken out.

The girl had received a gift — a picture frame — from her cousin. In the frame was a photo of the cousin that didn't fit very well. The girl was going to take out the photo and put it on her bulletin board and put another picture that she liked better in the frame.

The brother told her that replacing the cousin's picture wouldn't be polite. If the cousin came to visit and saw that her photo was not in the frame, she would be hurt. The sister, fed up with his moralizing, yelled at the brother to be quiet and leave her alone. He then bombarded her with multiple reasons why he was right, and she countered every detail with an objection, then finally held her hands over her ears while he tried to pry them off.

The mother was a little bit on the boy's side regarding the content as she was telling me this story. Of course, the argument started up again in my office. I let them go on for a while so I could observe their process. I finally stopped them and reminded them that they had agreed to work on not always thinking it's the other's fault, our project for the week.

"What were you doing wrong in the argument?" I asked each of them, shifting our attention to the process.

After I'd persisted a while, the girl admitted she had overreacted, she had yelled, and she had been too caught up in countering her brother's argumentative points. The boy admitted that he was telling her what to do, judging her, and criticizing her. Then he added, "And I have another point to make . . ." and he started talking again about offending the cousin and changing the picture in the frame.

This was a great chance to point out that the frame was the content (a fleeting, resolvable topic), and we were not trying to resolve the content or we would have to get together every day for every new issue. We'd agreed to work on what was really bothering the family: the habitual dysfunctional process.

Once the children finally began to consider what they were doing wrong, they did a pretty good job of self-criticism. The lesson didn't take hold right away, but over time they learned and improved.

Distinguishing between process and content is very similar to determining "what are you really angry at," as in Step Four of the conflict resolution model. Many times what really drives a conflict is a process issue; it becomes the real substantive "what."

TIME, PLACE, AND MOOD
(YOURS AND YOUR CHILD'S)

Timing is everything, as they say. You won't be as effective if you teach when your child is tired, hungry, in a hurry to join a friend, or obviously irritable. You will probably be inspired to teach your child when she is extremely angry. Perhaps you could make some brief points, but it's usually the least likely time for a receptive attitude or solid learning. Warm your child up in whatever way works for you. Do something like read a story, shoot a few baskets, make cookies, or swing in the hammock together.

As for place, make it somewhere private where the phone won't ring and nobody will interrupt. Make it comfortable. Try the barn, the burger restaurant, or the hammock again, whichever works. Riding in the car has its pros and cons. A disadvantage is that you can't look at the child to read his expression and body language or to convey your feelings to him. On the other hand, your not being able to watch your child may give him a feeling of extra comfort. Choose a place and situation where the child is comfortable physically and emotionally.

In teaching a child, the importance of your own mood is paramount. If you're too light, silly, tentative, nonchalant, or pleading, the kid might not take what you say very seriously. On the other hand, if you're too stern, stubbornly authoritative, intense, or irritable, you're not ready to teach. You're likely to provoke more resistance and resentment than cooperation. Be upbeat and positive. You're probably not ready to teach if what comes to mind to say first is, "I'm sick of this problem with your anger and you're going to learn this model." You're more in the right mood if you genuinely feel like saying, "Wouldn't it be cool if we learned a new way. . . ." Your mood leads to your tone. Your tone largely determines whether your child is defensive or not.

TEACHING STYLES

Teaching may mean anything from making a meaningful remark in passing to assigning an exercise on paper. If it gets through, it's teaching.

Teaching conflict resolution lies on a continuum from being a model of harmony yourself to very formal instruction — making lists and checking them twice. Which end of the hierarchy works best? It all depends.

Modeling

In any case, for better or for worse, modeling is a powerful teaching method. A recent study concluded that whether children wear their seat belts when riding in a car is almost entirely based on whether their parents do. No big surprise to most of us. The "like-parent, like-child" effect holds true for other habits, bad or good, like controlling anger, being neat, smoking, or drinking.

But how many children set out deliberately to do what their parents do? In fact, fairly often I hear youngsters say of their parents, "When I grow up, I'm not going to be like them."

In spite of their stated intention, children turn out like their parents in many ways largely because they incorporate their family's behavior as a norm. Children pick up norms for all kinds of behavior: how often people sitting in the same room speak to each other, how many hours a day the TV is on, what the dinner routine is, when people raise their voices, or what happens when someone comes home. And, of course, how people solve conflict. They can at some point question the norm or go against it purposefully, but more often they unthinkingly adopt it.

The point is that the better you resolve your own conflicts, the better your child will likely resolve his.

A woman says to her husband, "Why don't you wipe up the orange juice you spill when you shake the container? It's simple enough, and I've asked you a million times."

The husband snaps, "For the same reason you don't quit shaking your hands in the air after you wash them." They both already know he wants her to wipe her hands off on a towel instead of shaking them "like a dog."

"At least, when I shake my hands, it's just water, and it dries clean," the wife counters. "When you shake the juice jug, it's orange juice, and it dries sticky all over the counter."

The husband marches out of the kitchen very annoyed.

There are a number of things this couple did poorly in their exchange. For one thing, the defensive husband replied to his wife's complaint with a counter-complaint, albeit disguised as an answer to her question. The wife

> **What does "winning" an argument mean to you?**
>
> 1. The decision went your way.
> 2. The other person cried "uncle" and says you won.
> 3. You believe you made the best points and you won intellectually, whether or not the other person was persuaded.
> 4. You achieved an emotional victory: You're the one who left the argument in the best mood.
> 5. You paid him back for what he did to you so he feels just as bad now as he made you feel — or worse.
> 6. Both people left the argument glad it came up. Your feelings were respected, and you had some input into the outcome. You solved the problem so that it is not likely to come up again soon.
>
> I like the last way, don't you?

then returned with a comparison of the severity of their two sins. Which one was worse? The exchange was obviously a competition; it was not an attempt at resolution. Nobody mentioned solving anything; nobody promised to do any better, nobody tried to see the other's point of view. And in fact, they both continued in their annoying habits.

The child, observing this interaction, sees a competition. He may decide who he thinks "won." He thinks that to win, you have to bring up the strongest points in the arguments, or he thinks the one who stomps off wins (or maybe the one who doesn't). He thinks that when someone accuses him, the thing to do is counteraccuse. What he misses completely is an opportunity for learning to solve a problem.

But this couple can stop the argument over the spattered orange juice by resolving it. *How* is what the fifteen-step conflict resolution model is all about. Let me add now that either the mother or father in this case could also have said to the child, "That's not the way I like to behave when we have an argument," or "We're going to have to talk about this soon and work it out." They need to label the wrong way when they recognize it so it will not remain the norm in the child's mind. After that, they need to learn, model, and teach the better way.

Modeling harmony in general is an important way to instill in your child the expectation of harmony and the desire to correct discord. Modeling conflict resolution in particular is a way to teach your child the skills and the language to deal with conflict well. But everything you do and say serves as a model on some level.

Modeling is the least formal method of teaching. Children rarely realize at the moment that they are learning from your example. There are other informal ways to teach that are more structured than modeling but still not so structured that your child sees you as a teacher.

Casual Comments

Nearly every comment you make has teaching potential. The fact that you don't require a reply doesn't mean your child isn't listening and taking in your idea. In fact, you'll sometimes hear your child repeat your comment to a friend or sibling. Then you know you have made an impression.

You can make casual teaching comments at the time of any conflict you observe and especially one between you and the child or between siblings. Also effective are casual comments about conflicts you observe but are not involved in, like a parent in a grocery store dealing with a child's temper tantrum, or two playmates vying for the same swing next door, or Aunt Katherine yelling at Uncle Jim. You can comment on how one person listened well and had his feelings changed by what the other person said. You can comment on how a child's anger at not getting something he wanted escalated from a 3 to an 8 because the mother yelled at him. Pointing out steps taken and not taken, process versus content, and good and bad ways to handle anger is an effective but low-key way to teach conflict resolution in real life.

Books, films, television shows, and even songs present conflict children can learn from. In spite of all the complaints about children watching too much television, television does offer some stories designed to teach good resolution skills.

On *The Cosby Show*, Dr. Huxtable, played by Bill Cosby, once offered a wonderful model of teaching a child perspective. Little Rudy tells her father that she doesn't want to go to school anymore because, on her first day, a little boy called her a name. Dr. Huxtable's gentle inquiry reveals that the classmate has called her Rudy Huckleberry.

Dr. Huxtable asks, "Did he say it this way?" and he screws up his face and gives as hostile an imitation of the insult as he can: "You ain't nothing but a low-down Rudy Huckleberry!" "Or," Huxtable continues, "Did he do it this way?" and he gives a more benign teasing version. He draws her out about how hostile the offending child's motives were — not very. He then tells her that kids sometimes tease other kids who have a big nose or some other perceived flaw but that it's evident that Rudy's tormenter couldn't find anything at all wrong with her so he could only twist her name a little bit. When Dr. Huxtable puts this positive twist on the taunt, Rudy is happy.

Of course, Bill Cosby knows exactly what he's doing when he presents a fine role model of the firm but warm parent who finds many occasions to teach his children. You, too, can do a fine job of teaching by pointing out not only the good examples like those from *The Cosby Show* but the poor examples. You can ask your child what is wrong with the way such and such a character acted and how, if he had acted better, the story might have had a quick, happy ending.

Warning: Don't overdo this routine or your child will see your efforts as lecture instead of moments of casual learning. And your comments will be more welcome if saved for commercial breaks.

Drawing Children Out

Drawing children out often works better than "telling" them about conflict resolution. In his book *The Seven Habits of Highly Effective People* (Simon and Schuster, 1989), Dr. Stephen Covey says, "Seek first to understand, then to be understood." This advice is the essence of "drawing out." It's often good to get your child's ideas before you give yours, especially if you can do it with genuine curiosity. You'll become more aware of the distortions in their thinking as well as delighted by unexpected insight. When you draw your child out, he can feel that his ideas are being respected and valued whether you agree or disagree with what he says. He will likely be more willing to listen to you later if he has been listened to first. Furthermore, while drawing your child out, you are modeling good listening behavior.

Drawing a child out is not like a game of twenty questions — don't pepper her with rapid-fire questions. Start with more general, open-ended questions: "What do you think just happened here?" "How do you see what just happened?" "How do you feel about what Tammy said?" You may not get very far, but give the open-ended approach a try. You will learn the most if your child will give you an unguided answer.

If that fails or if you need to go further, then get more particular: "How do you feel about Tammy calling you a 'creep'?" "What do you think Tom meant when he said you weren't fair?"

Well done yes-no or multiple-choice questions can be another approach: "Do you think Tom was right about you not being fair? Or do you think he said that just because he wanted to win? Or do you think there are two or more reasonable ways to look at what happened?"

If one of the choices you offer is correct, that shows you can empathize with your child. Ask multiple-choice questions with genuine curiosity, not putting the answer you want to hear in any particular order or tone of voice.

Then move on to expressing your opinion. "This is how I see it," you say. Ask if he agrees or disagrees with you: "Is this how you see it?" Leave room for his disagreement without your angry rebuke or put-down, especially if he is disagreeing in a reasonable and respectful tone.

If they do disagree with you, ask for their alternatives. Unless you think he's just being argumentative, actively listen. Respecting children's input doesn't mean you have to agree or do what he says. It means you listen attentively and let him know you heard him. Then say, "This is why I disagree." And here you can, if necessary, exert some authority.

Direct Teaching

Direct instruction — or just telling the child what's what — is the easiest route for some parents, especially if they've just read a book about conflict resolution. Unfortunately, this style of teaching carries with it the greatest danger of "lecturing." However, some children do learn better with the direct approach. Direct teaching also gives structure to what has been previously experienced and learned more casually. The child will have a framework to remember the material better. In direct instruction, you should still be mindful of timing and mood, how much and how long you teach, and how well they are receiving your message.

ASSESSING STRENGTHS AND WEAKNESSES

As you study and learn the three-part, fifteen-step model, you will become increasingly aware that you already do certain steps well and others poorly. You may balk at one or more of them. "I just can't do that," you think. Even reading the step makes you anxious or angry. If that's the case, it would be good for you to examine why you're not comfortable with the step. If you learn to be more comfortable with and competent at the parts of the process that are difficult for you, you can better help your child. You'll not only model conflict resolution better, you'll be more natural in teaching it.

As you read the age-related chapters, it will be useful to ask yourself at each step whether your child has particular problems with that step or whether he already does it well and needs only to be reinforced for that good behavior.

Once you know where you're going and what needs the most work, you can tackle the model. If the child's age and receptivity suggest that you can teach more formally, introduce the three parts. Then present the steps in order. Of course, it's unlikely that you'll discuss all of them in one sitting. You can draw the child out on each step and ask him to tell you how he sees each part of the process. Once you have presented the whole three-part, fifteen-step process, you don't have to teach the steps in order.

The first step you might pick to teach is the one your child is likely to do successfully. That way, you can establish momentum. Then pick a problem area and decide whether it's enough of a problem that you should agree to make a "project" of it.

REINFORCEMENT: MAKING GOOD SKILLS STICK AND BAD BEHAVIORS GO AWAY

Behavior that is followed by pleasant consequences is likely to be repeated. In fact, positive reinforcement is more effective than punishment in increasing good behavior. And it's certainly more pleasant to administer. At times, however, punishment is clearly necessary. Like other aspects of teaching, reinforcement falls into a hierarchy from natural to formal.

Positive Reinforcement

Children like for you to be happy with them. Positive reinforcement at its most natural is often just a matter of a parent's being friendly, in a good mood, and obviously enjoying the child's company.

Casual remarks of approval work well, too. Catch your child in an instance of good process behavior and say, "It seems you did that well," or "I noticed you got mad at first but you settled down and listened. That's a really good sign." Or, if you've had a serious talk, you could say you noticed they were listening well and you appreciated it. Or you noticed they kept an appropriate voice when they were telling you they were angry, and that made it a lot easier for you to listen. Opportunities for positive reinforcement arise often in the daily flow of life. The key is to notice and take advantage of them.

In one instance, eight-year-old Owen, a sometimes difficult child, got out the vacuum cleaner to clean up some spilled popcorn. He likes to vacuum. His two-year-old brother, William, seeing what was happening, ran to get a broom and came out to attack the same popcorn. His grandmother thought, "Uh-oh, trouble. Owen will see that William is about to sweep the popcorn that he wants to vacuum, and Owen will yell at William, maybe even push him away."

Instead, Owen said, "Oh, look, William is going to sweep the popcorn into a pile for me to vacuum." William poked at the popcorn with the broom, and Owen vacuumed it up.

His grandmother, pleasantly surprised, said to Owen, "I really like the way you acted when William came running up with the broom. You said,

'Oh, William is going to push the popcorn in a pile for me to vacuum.' Some big brothers would have thought, 'Here comes William to get in my way,' or 'Here comes William to take my job away from me.' Some big brothers would have pushed him away. But you had a better idea. You decided that William was helping." Owen did a great job at Step Five, the perspective check, by interpreting his little brother's behavior in a good light. His grandmother, her own perspective checked, reinforced his good attitude.

When commenting directly that a child is improving, it's useful to redirect the child's good feelings back to himself so he will be encouraged to do well for his own sake, not just to please you. Say, for example, "I think it's good that you . . ." or "I'm happy to see you are learning. . . ." Noticing, acknowledging, and reflecting on children's improved behavior and being "happy for them" (rather than "proud of them") serve as effective positive reinforcement.

The most structured positive reinforcement consists of rewards. It's useful to brainstorm, perhaps with your child, what your child would be willing to work for as reinforcement. I usually prefer rewards that are fun things to do together, rather than material rewards such as candy or money.

Every child is different when it comes to what she'd be willing to work for. Nine-year-old Stephanie loved scallop shells, which she had seen only in pictures. Living on the north shore of Massachusetts, she had periwinkle shells, clams, mussels, and Chinaman's hats, but she thought scallops were the ultimate in seashells. Her grandmother casually remarked that she knew where she could pick up scallop shells on the beaches of Cape Cod. Stephanie immediately wanted to go there. Later, when her grandmother wanted Stephanie to learn some new behavior, she offered to take her to a Cape Cod beach to gather scallop shells for the day as a reward for a month of documented improvement in certain habits.

What does your child really want? What would you be willing to provide as a reinforcement of new, better behavior?

Many children are positively reinforced by:
* getting to do what they want to do, that is, privileges and opportunities.
* your playing with them, that is, your time and company.
* your emotional attention, showing you care.
* recognition of success, symbols like stars or points on a chart.

★ material things, such as toys or money toward some eventual goal.

Concrete and specific symbols, such as points or stars on a chart, serve as their own reward to some degree. A classroom teacher I know once quieted an unruly class by giving each child a jar and, when a student was sitting attentively or working diligently, putting a popsicle stick in the child's jar. The class immediately became attentive and quiet without even knowing what the popsicle sticks meant or what behavior the teacher was rewarding. Just the attention of being chosen to receive a stick and the pleasure of accumulation transformed the class. The kids recognized immediately that some individuals got more than others, and it became a competition to get the otherwise meaningless sticks. They were changing their behavior for symbols of recognition.

At the end of the week, however, this teacher cemented the children's interest in the mysterious sticks by allowing them to trade them for bubble gum with trading cards inside. While points, stars, or popsicle sticks and the attention accompanying them are somewhat reinforcing, a tangible reward to be earned for the accumulation of a certain number of these symbols is likely to be even more reinforcing. Generally, however, I prefer the less material forms of reward.

> **Reward Junkies**
>
> Has your child disappeared completely behind a giant mound of gummy bears? Maybe you are doling the sweet rewards out too liberally. I periodically see children who I think of as "reward junkies." They have become so dependent on rewards that they try to manipulate me and their parents into giving them a material reward for any desired change of behavior. Judgment is necessary here. Does your offer of a reward have the feeling of a "bribe"? Does your child make demands and threats?
>
> It's possible to scale down rewards after behavior improves. You might say, "You're doing so well, you have moved up from AAA to the Big Leagues," or whatever your child would understand. Then offer a different reward for longer periods of good behavior.

Punishment

At times, a child clearly requires punishment to take the need to change seriously. Punishment ranges from a disapproving look to a formal penalty. In the middle is direct verbal disapproval.

The punishment should match the seriousness of the negative behavior. More forceful punishment would be appropriate for a seriously poor conflict resolution process such as hitting a sibling or yelling disrespectfully at a parent. Note, however, that if a child's yelling is an improvement over hitting, you might make note of the improvement while still disapproving of the yelling.

In meting out punishment, think also of the motives of the child. Was his destruction of property a pathetic attempt to look cool in front of a peer group? Or was he wantonly destructive, feeling entitled to harm property just because he wanted to? Drawing your child out on his motivation may give you some clue as to why he does what he does. Punishment then should relate to the motivation. If a child significantly misbehaves when he is trying to impress peers, you should punish him, but you also need to teach him better ways to impress friends, how to feel good about himself without impressing, or how to find a more worthy peer group. The willfully destructive child needs more severe punishment to show him in no uncertain terms that he is not entitled to harm other people's property.

Punishments that teach children how to think about what they did wrong, learn from it, and develop a conscience are better than those that are merely unpleasant or create fear and resentment.

I prefer punishment:

* that is calm, firm, and serious in style.

* that expresses your disappointment and concern at least as much as your anger.

* that is shorter and more intense, rather than longer and more easily "worked around" by the child.

* that matches the seriousness of the bad behavior and the apparent motives of the child.

* that occurs as soon after the negative behavior as possible.

* that has some logical relationship to the behavior, if possible.

* that develops some genuine remorse or guilt.

* that causes anxiety about damaging their relationship with you rather than just makes them fearful of you.

★ that makes them think.

Appropriate forms of punishments are:
★ You express disapproval in a serious talk.

★ You enforce a "thinking time-out."

★ The child expresses an understanding of her wrongdoing and tells how she will do better in the future.

★ When appropriate, the child makes reparation or suffers a clear imposed consequence.

The most powerful punishments include all of these aspects.

Your expression of disapproval may be minor — a raised eyebrow, for example. At other times, your disapproval may be expressed in a firm, brief talk in which you tell your child how deeply disappointed you are in her behavior and how serious the natural consequences of that behavior may be.

You usually then draw her out so that she expresses her understanding of the significance of her wrongdoing. You ask her about what she did wrong and why it was not good. You give verbal approval if she seems to understand. Then you draw her out on how she will do better in the future.

If the situation merits, you inflict a "thinking time-out" for her to spend examining what she has done and its consequences. The time-out ends when the child has prepared a statement of what she did wrong and how she'll make amends. This can be, especially for young children, something they say to prove they have thought through the ramifications of their deed and are therefore ready to end the time-out. Or you may require school-aged children to write sentences, paragraphs, or whole essays, depending on their age and sophistication. The time-out for serious issues may require a longer period for research or self-exploration and may take the form of a time-out from TV watching or a general grounding until their essay is complete.

For any wrong done, the child should try to make things right. For example, if they have taken something of someone else's, they should return it in good condition as part of the punishment. If they have broken something, they should offer their own as a substitute, work to earn money to repair or replace it, or even fix it themselves. Cleaning up messes made is another logical reparation.

One twelve-year-old named Alan repeatedly hit a tennis ball against the side of the house contrary to his parents' repeated commands. He usually did this when his parents were out. One day he missed the wall and smashed the ball through a kitchen window. Alan's mother didn't scold him for what was obvious. Instead, she instructed him how to measure for new glass. She checked the dimensions he gave to the hardware store clerk and deducted the cost of the glass and putty from Alan's allowance. Then she taught him how to set the glass. His mother found that the child was much more deft with the putty knife than she herself was, and the job was done smoothly. The result was a new windowpane, a new skill, and the self-respect that comes from restitution. Then Alan's mother handed him a bucket of soapy water and a sponge to clean off the tennis ball marks from the siding since he wasn't going to be hitting the ball there anymore. In most cases, supervising restitution is more trouble for the parent than fixing things herself, but the parent must take the trouble to see the child through this step.

In the most serious cases, a combination of a talk, thinking time, and reparation may be best. For example, when a child shoplifts, I suggest repaying the debt (even double or triple the worth) and writing a paper on honesty. I tell kids I can think of eight fundamental reasons that stealing and dishonesty are bad and I ask them to think of them all. It's the rare child who gets more than four or five. In other cases of serious or persistent bad behavior, I have sometimes recommended a "moral marathon." A parent takes the child on a camping trip or arranges another long period of uninterrupted privacy. The two spend the whole time exploring the relevant issues and coming to an agreement on how to prevent such behavior in the future and how to make restitution if appropriate.

Eight Reasons Not To Steal or Be Dishonest

1. It's morally wrong.

2. It gets you in trouble.

3. It hurts other people.

4. People don't trust you.

5. You get a bad reputation.

6. It can easily become a habit.

7. It's not a "smart" way to get your needs met.

8. You feel guilty and bad about yourself.

Withholding Attention

Your emotional attention or a display of caring is often a very strong positive reinforcement that your child will work hard to win. Getting your emotional attention encourages him to spend more time in a good relationship with you, helps him feel more loved and secure, and at times makes him feel appropriately important. Withholding emotional attention can be a sufficient punishment.

Much of the time children who are behaving well are ignored by parents. This is often appropriate, of course, but don't forget to give your child positive attention when she's good; this reinforces her good behavior.

Often a child will try to win emotional attention through bad behavior, even if it's "negative attention." For this reason, parents have often been advised to give no attention to a child behaving badly unless there's danger involved. This technique can be effective, but it's tricky. Paying "no attention" is hard to fake. Children are often aware that you are aware of what they're doing.

Moreover, when a child who has done something bad in hopes of getting attention finds himself ignored, he'll often escalate the bad behavior. If that's ignored, he does something worse. This pattern can get out of hand and turn into a full-scale power struggle.

If you choose withholding attention as a deliberate strategy and it doesn't work or you don't think you can persevere, return to other types of reinforcement, use distraction, or engage in a more full-scale conflict resolution effort.

A Point System

I have a lot of families on behavioral plans with a point system for reinforcement. While the system requires careful thought to set up, it becomes simple to administer. That's important because anything too difficult to administer is soon abandoned. This system works well when you're trying to improve several behaviors at a time. Here's the plan:

First, choose two to four goals — too many won't work — or even just one. The goals can be relatively broad but may include particular behaviors you have discussed with your child, such as chores or habits. Good goals are: being more cooperative, being more compliant, being less defensive and talking more reasonably, following through on responsibilities, working on controlling temper, and making more of an effort to get along with siblings.

A couple of hours before bedtime or at a defined time, parents get together and decide what points to award the child for each goal for that day. Zero is a bad day for a goal; one is a little bit better. Two is fair. Three is good. Four is super. If, for example, you are working on three goals, four points towards each goal, or twelve total points, represents a super day.

But you don't go through the day counting things, you just do the best evaluation you can at the end of the day. And don't threaten the kid with points during the day. The once-a-day accounting keeps the child aware of the project, but it's not nit-picking.

When points are given out, if the child argues about a point, he automatically loses one. If he accepts feedback well, sometimes he gets a bonus point. If, for three goals, he earns nine or more points for the day, he gets a minor reward. For fewer points he gets nothing. For three or fewer points, he gets a mild negative consequence such as no electronic entertainment or going to bed early.

Keep track of daily points on a calendar. At the end of a seven-day period — usually Friday to Friday — a certain number of total points — maybe sixty to sixty-five for three goals — gets a reward like having a friend over or going to a movie. At the end of the month, if they have 250 points out of a possible 336, they might get some material thing they have been wanting badly or a special trip with parents.

I like this system because it requires only five or ten minutes a day. Other systems I've heard of have more frequent or arduous rating schemes or else they are too vague to determine progress. This one keeps the issues alive without harping on them. It's a system that's respectful of the child and doesn't undermine the parent's authority.

HOW YOU SAY IT

It's not what you say, it's how you say it. How many times have you heard or thought that? Some communications experts say the words themselves carry the lesser part of the impression a person makes in spoken exchanges. Many times how you say it — your tone of voice and facial and bodily expression — is the primary trigger for beginning a conflict. And how you say the response is what feeds a downward spiral. Fortunately, how you say it — if you say it well — may invite resolution.

Your Nonverbal Expression

A speaker on National Public Radio's *All Things Considered* not long ago read a delightful essay on the use of the common Southern expression, "Bless her heart," which represents, on the surface at least, a positive thought. It can be an enthusiastic expression of admiration uttered, for example, when a child spells a word correctly to win a spelling bee or when someone has done a good deed. Through slight changes of inflection, however, the speaker demonstrated that "Bless her heart" could convey a whole range of deprecation from pity to condescension. And so inflection changes blameless words into something else — at times obviously critical and at times open to the interpretation of the listener.

People usually know when someone is joking by his voice and facial expression. Fighting words often become fun when said "the right way."

Facial expression adds to or changes the meaning of words. A sneer on the face during an "I'm sorry" negates the words; a raised eyebrow suggests doubt; an eye roll and slight head shake seek a coalition in putting someone down; a smile or look of concern makes a negative statement more appealing. Actors make their living interpreting written lines with the artful use of their voice, body, and face, and we emotionally connect with those who do it well.

The tone and manner of delivery of spoken words add meaning, and — here's the downside — they may be misread. For example, people's feelings are sometimes hurt when they read a joke as not really a joke, and they don't trust the person who says, "Just joking." Unlike words, which at least have a dictionary meaning, nonverbal cues have meanings that vary from individual to individual and family to family.

What is there to do about this nonverbal aspect when dealing with conflict or teaching your children? Of course, being aware of it so you can self-correct helps. But overanalyzing yourself or others can be unnatural and interfere with the goal of "open and honest" communication. So try to get your feelings to match your expression as much as possible, be open to feedback about how you are coming across, and give your child appropriate feedback about this component of communication.

Your Words

Words, too, carry some emotional content outside of their dictionary meaning. Some words and phrases are more inflammatory than others, partly because of the context in which they are usually heard or were usually heard during a certain time in a person's life. Here are some word choices that often play a role in how another person perceives what you say and how he reacts to it.

I Instead of *You*

Use the pronoun "you" sparingly when teaching your child to resolve conflict. Saying "you think" or "you do this" seems to point an accusatory finger at the other person. Many communications experts and therapists recommend using "I" statements about how the other person's behavior makes you feel. "I" own my own thoughts and feelings. People, including children, aren't as likely to feel unjustly accused when you make statements about your own feelings. Instead of "You keep on saying . . . ," say "What I hear is. . . ." Instead of "You make me so mad," say, "I feel so angry because. . . ." Instead of "You're so critical," say, "I feel criticized."

Here are some "I" statements that serve as openers to conflict resolution. Note how they focus on the speaker's feelings and not on the bad thing the other person did.

* "There's something I'm angry about and I need to discuss it with you. Is this a good time?"

* "Mom, I hope you don't think this is disrespectful because I don't mean it to be. I'm angry about something and I've been thinking about it a lot and I need to tell you."

* "You can probably tell I've been distant this evening. It's because I think. . . ."

* "Maybe you can tell I'm pretty angry, and I'd like to talk about it."

* "You know the little argument we had this morning? Well, I'm still angry about it, and I'd like to talk about it now. How about you?"

* "That thing that happened just a minute ago . . . I'm angry, but I'm calm enough to talk about it, and I'd like you to hear me out."

Another way of not leaning too heavily on "you" while instructing your child is to use the first person in telling a story about yourself, when you were in a similar situation as your child. For example, "Once I accidentally broke my mother's dish, and, when I heard her ask my father about it, I went to my room instead of saying I knew what happened. Later. . . ." Tell what you did that didn't work or what you did that resolved a situation. Telling a story about yourself, as long as it's not in a tone of superiority, instructs while taking the heat off your child. It also reminds the child that you've been in similar situations and that you were once his age.

The Impersonal Third Person: *He, She, It, They*

In the same way, it's less likely to make a child defensive if you say, "some people" or "kids your age" instead of "you" because the third person seems less accusatory. You can make a general point and let the child apply it to himself when he's ready. Say, "Some people find that making a list helps them . . . ," instead of, "You should keep a list and then you wouldn't always be forgetting. . . ." Or try, "I read about a kid whose anger skyrocketed whenever people criticized him. So he chose a calming phrase to say to himself the minute he heard criticism." Using those "other people" keeps the finger from being pointed to "you." You can also make a statement with the impersonal third person it. Instead of saying, "You should do this . . ." or "Do this . . . ," say, "It's better to do this . . ." or "It's a good idea to. . . ."

We Means *We*, Not *You* or *Me*

Don't speak for your child. Avoid saying, "We don't want to hurt little brother" or "We don't want to cause any commotion" when you mean, "I don't want you to. . . ." The use of "we" in this case is an attempt to trick the child into your way of thinking without his noticing. At times I see parents using "we" incorrectly as merely a bad habit. You should speak for yourself and encourage your child to develop his own voice and own his own thoughts and feelings. Instead of saying "we don't want," say, "I hope you don't want to. . . ."

Again, the "I" statement is more straightforward, honest, and therefore, less annoying. Moreover, when you use the word "we" inappropriately, it implies too much of an enmeshed quality in the parent/child relationship and doesn't grant your child appropriate autonomy. The same applies to adults when one spouse uses "we" to express feelings or opinions that the other spouse doesn't necessarily hold. The use of "we" is appropriate and desirable, however, when both parents have discussed

a subject such as curfew or rules and are presenting their united opinion to the child.

But, the Contradictor

"But" and its cousin "I know but" are frequently fighting words. Many a
comment that raises people's hackles begins with a robust "but." When
someone tells you what they think and you say, "I know but . . . ," you discount what they said even if you listened to it. Try making your point by
skipping over "I know but . . ." and beginning with your thought.

Often people say something like, "You did a good job with the dishes,
but you missed a few places when you mopped the floor." The "but"
clause says you don't appreciate the dishes because the floor mopping was
less than perfect. The cure? It helps to reverse the order so you end with
the positive: "You missed a few places when you mopped the floor, but you
did a good job with the dishes." Better still, omit "but" altogether, and
replace it with "and" or another less negating word. For example, instead
of saying, "I understand why you didn't want to go to Aunt Emily's house
but you should understand she needs attention now that she is alone," say,
"I understand why you didn't want to go to Aunt Emily's house. Still I feel
she needs a lot of attention now that she's alone." Given the same tone of
voice, on the hierarchy of contradictory expressions, "but" seems to be the
most annoying, while "still" and "even so" are the least, with "however,"
"nevertheless," and "yet" somewhere in the middle.

Take the eloquent and confrontational eulogy given by Princess
Diana's brother Earl Spencer at her funeral. In speaking of the future
upbringing of the young princes, Spencer said that his family appreciated
the traditions of the monarchy, but they wanted the princes to have other
kinds of experiences. See how different the statement would have been if
Earl Spencer had said the family appreciated the traditions of the monarchy, and they wanted the princes to have other kinds of experiences as well.
The first statement expresses appreciation for the royal traditions and then
negates it. The second statement suggests his family appreciates the royal
traditions and also wants to add other kinds of experiences. The second
statement has the same content but is less inflammatory.

Know-It-All and Commanding Phrases

Some adults have a way of stating things dogmatically as if they were the world's greatest authority. They say, "Here's the way it is, I know." They give orders, saying, "Do this, do that." Adults may be authorities on some subjects, but rarely do they know it all when it comes to their children's lives. And, while they do have the authority over their children, they would be wise to exercise it judiciously in serious situations. Education and persuasion are usually more powerful than intimidation in the long run and much less likely to backfire into useless power struggles. Instead of barking orders or making pronouncements, try saying:

★ "Could it be that you're . . . ?"

★ "It seems to me that . . . ."

★ "If I understand your situation clearly . . . ."

★ "I don't know exactly what you're thinking, but if I were in your situation, I'd want . . . ."

★ "I don't know all of your friends. Even so, it would seem that some of them. . . ."

Showing some appropriate humility about your knowledge does not undermine your authority; it gives you credibility.

Never Say Never

Avoid expressions that make sweeping generalizations like "never," "always," "everybody," and "nobody." Such absolute words are rarely technically correct and tend to engender and prolong conflict.

For example, when you're talking about your child's or someone else's behavior, say "sometimes he does . . ." or "many times she does . . ." or "you almost always do" instead of "you always do." Replace "they never do . . ." with "usually they don't. . . ." Say "Some people think . . ." instead of "everybody thinks. . . ." When you make

---

A Writer's Dilemma

A book by an expert requires the ring of authority. Moreover, editors like crisp, snappy language. The language I recommend parents use with children and which I often use in therapy, however, could be termed both tentative (because I use so many "sometime's," "often's," "It seems to me's," and other modifiers) and wordy. So, in this book, there are many commanding and definitive sentences that a big part of me wants to modify. Editors have rightfully turned my "it's good to avoid" into a snappy command: "Avoid. . . ." The book is peppered with "you should's." As a reader, please don't take them the wrong way. They are there to make it an easier book to read. The tone is intended to be encouraging and thought-provoking, not absolute and definitive.

strong generalized statements, using *always, never, everybody,* and *nobody* for emphasis or persuasion, you teach your child to think that way. Overgeneralization tends to amplify feelings. In the language you use, you're teaching your child. Remember this point when you hear your child say, "Everybody else is doing it, why can't I?" "Nobody else thinks that," or "You never let me do anything fun."

In addition, by using *always, never,* and *everybody* you're opening the door to an argumentative and defensive side of your child. When you tell your child, "You never do what I say the first time I say it," your child will likely reply, "Unh-hunh, I put on my coat when you told me to," or something similar. He thereby misses the substantive point you were making about his frequent noncompliance in order to correct his parent about the detail.

It's Hard to Be Hip

Avoid "hip" phrases that aren't really "you," especially with preteens and teens. In the first place, your attempts are apt to fail. Second, kids in these age groups don't generally like parents (or therapists) taking over their exclusive linguistic domain. It's artificial and unnatural if not downright embarrassing, and it looks as if the adult is trying too hard to be a buddy.

ZITS

ZITS reprinted with specialpermission of King Features Syndicate

Talking Down — or Up

While it's good not to talk over a young child's head — he's not as familiar with relationship words as you are — it's more likely that you'll offend an older child by talking below his level. You know this happens when the kid says, "What do you think I am, stupid?" when you tell him something he thinks is obvious. Choosing the right language level takes judgment, knowing your child well, and especially paying attention to verbal and nonverbal feedback.

Lighten Up

Use humor in your language, humor that says "I'm on your side" because it presupposes a common knowledge or appreciation and it reaches out to connect. Goodhearted humor reduces tension and shows you're not hostile. To use humor effectively, you have to cultivate a step-back-and-look-at-it-a-different-way stance, which is in itself helpful to objectivity and goodwill. I won't try to give you examples of humor; a lot of effective humor is the "you-had-to-be-there" kind. Humor is out there. Be on the lookout.

Least Favorite Phrases

Try to assess what it is about your language that creates resistance. Ask your child if there is anything in particular you say (probably repeatedly) that bugs him. I still get teased by my sons about saying, "It's time to turn on the afterburners" about their studies. I only said it a few times, honest.

There's a column called "Fresh Voices" in *Parade* magazine, a section of many Sunday newspapers, where preteens and teens express their feelings about personal issues. One boy said that when he and his father are having an argument, "My Dad tries to tell me what I'm thinking. . . . And then he'll go, 'I know you think I'm a bad parent and I don't help you.' But that's not what I'm thinking. . . . I've never thought that. He's wonderful to me." What the boy was thinking was something else that needed discussing, but his father's guessing his thoughts out loud got the discussion started on the wrong foot.

Other lines kids dislike are: "You won't understand this until you're grown up . . . ," "If I've told you once, I've told you a million times . . . ," "This is the last time I'm going to tell you," "Believe you me," "Mark my words," and other expressions that suggest a scolding finger.

Another common phrase that often causes resistance is: "Why did you . . . ?" when you don't like something your child did. For example, "Why did you put your coat there?" You aren't really asking why, you are criticizing. Instead, say simply, "I wish you'd hang your coat up when you come in."

These phrases are especially inflammatory when said in an authoritative, whiny, or accusatory tone. Probably the number one factor that triggers resistance is a parent's blaming tone of voice. Try to keep your voice calm, matter-of-fact, and low rather than high-pitched.

Some of the suggestions above might sound as though I'm asking you to be too passive and to allow your child to run the show or take advantage of your good nature. In actuality, using language and behavior that doesn't inflame the child demonstrates your maturity and control as a parent. This helps you to get your own genuine point of view across to your child, and he consequently becomes more receptive to hearing it.

Children don't have to be seriously afraid or secretly resentful of you in order to respect you. Nor do you have to be their buddy or their friend. You can be a respected parent in the best sense of the word when you are perceived as safe and supportive and at the same time willing to take charge when you need to.

As a parent, your job is not so much to "indoctrinate" your kids with your values as it is to give them the tools to think and evolve a value system that respects others and their own needs at the same time. Their set of values and good attitudes, their work ethic, and their competencies become the bedrock of their self-esteem.

CHAPTER 3

Four Special Obstacles
and How to Get Around Them

Maybe you read the first two chapters of this book with good understanding and high hopes for sitting down with little Mary and Billy and
solving everything. Then you found yourself asking, "Do this with my
kids? Are you kidding?" You realized Mary argues with everything you say,
and Billy jumps up and throws a tennis ball against the living-room wall
every time you try to talk to him. Besides that, Mary torments Billy by calling him names until he screams at her and hits her in the head with the
tennis ball. There's no way, you conclude, that you are going to teach conflict resolution to these two unless this book comes with a magic wand.

I don't have a magic wand for turning all children into docile beings. But
I do have ideas on dealing with three negative behavior patterns that often
stand in the way of teaching: reflexive defensiveness, noncompliance or dis-
obedience, and deliberate aggravation. I commonly see these patterns in my
family psychiatry practice. When they are a substantive part of a child's problem with anger they will likely need your direct attention before you proceed
to teaching the full conflict resolution model.

A fourth common obstacle is that the two parents don't see eye to eye
on how to evaluate their child, how to nurture and discipline their child,
or how to deal with anger and conflict generally. This, too, needs some
thoughtful attention before you proceed.

REFLEXIVE DEFENSIVENESS

"Well, everybody else was going twice as fast as I was," says a teenager explaining why he got a ticket for going fifteen miles over the speed limit. "It was just stupid for him to give me a ticket."

"You don't need to worry about the other people. Just worry about yourself. If you were going fifteen miles over the speed limit, you were, by definition, going too fast."

"Yeah, well, you drive much more dangerously than I do when you go fifty-five on the expressway and everyone has to go around you. It's drivers like you who ought to be off the road."

And so on. Teenagers would be shirking their duty if they weren't defensive. Children of all ages are often defensive when confronted.

Reflexive defensiveness — a conditioned, rapid, automatic response of significant resistance — is a big problem at any age because it limits communication and shuts down learning new things about yourself. Habitual defensiveness is so extreme in some children that I'm often tempted to call it "defensiveness disorder."

The Triggers

In my experience, defensiveness is generally triggered by:

* being directly criticized.

* perceiving someone is angry at you.

* being told what to do, especially in a bossy, nagging, or authoritative tone.

Some children are defensive even when you give them teaching, advice, or coaching, no matter how reasonably stated. They seem to be thinking — and they often say — "What do you think I am, stupid?" Some children even become somewhat defensive when you praise them. This seems contrary to common sense, but think about the fact that criticism, advice, and praise are all on the same spectrum — the spectrum of being monitored and evaluated. The children who are sensitive to this would rather be left alone than know their parents are thinking about their behavior and giving them a mental grade. Take, for example, the parent who says to her child, "I was so proud of you today." The child begins to beam. "You didn't interrupt my conversation with Mrs. Edmunds even once." The child's face sinks. Praise is sometimes just a reminder that the child has a problem.

Forms of Defensive Reaction

Defensiveness takes many forms:

★ quick denial ("Not me!" "You're wrong about that!" "I did not!")

★ quick projection of blame on someone or something else ("He started it!" "The dog ate it." "Sammy was the one who was playing with it.")

★ quick arguing back about a detail ("It's not turquoise; it's teal.")

★ quick name-calling or counterattack ("Well, you are, too.")

★ a quick, insincere acquiescence to get the other person to stop ("Okay, okay, I'm sorry.")

★ shutting down, blocking input, and not really listening ("Just leave me alone.")

★ shrugging off a valid criticism ("Well, it's no big deal.")

★ clowning around, making a joke out of your remarks ("You're right, I'm a major criminal.")

The Evaluative Atmosphere

I theorize that sensitive children who are difficult in temperament or children with Attention Deficit Hyperactive Disorder (ADHD) are more prone to defensiveness. They understandably get a higher frequency of criticism and ultimately get fed up with hearing it over and over.

Moreover, some parents are excessively evaluative no matter what their child's behavior. They seem to think that the main duty of parenting is evaluation. Almost everything the child does goes through a perceptual filter and comes out with a grade attached.

At one end of the spectrum, we find overt anger, direct harsh criticism, and an overly strict authoritarian style that meets a parent's need for control more than the child's needs. Next, there's lecturing and preaching. Then there's coaching, advice-giving, and teaching. At the other end of the evaluative spectrum, there's affirmation, praise, and approval. Of course, I'm not implying that you should accept all of your child's behavior. What's appropriate is the middle ground between managing every little thing and total lack of supervision.

Depending on their parents' behavior and their own sensitivity, many kids feel overly monitored and critiqued. Their antennae are almost always out anticipating evaluation. The longer their antennae are, the more likely they are to overreact, misinterpret, and display their defensiveness as they mind-read.

Some parents do have a high frequency of intervention. Such "eagle-eye" parents bring a child into my office and deliver a constant stream of directives: "Look Dr. Waugh in the eye when he's speaking to you." "Speak up, he can hardly hear you." "Keep your feet off the couch." These usually well-meaning parents are trying either to socialize their kids or to prevent any problem from arising.

"Eagle-eye" parents who create an evaluative atmosphere often have a child who is sensitized to criticism and quick to be defensive. This defensiveness begets further evaluation and renewed efforts to get through to the child. The intervention frequency and defensiveness escalate, cycling to nonresolution.

"Loaded for Bear"

When parents know that their children are defensive, they often gear up for it. They go into an intervention with more anxiety or more determination not to lose. They have their ammunition ready; they are "loaded for bear." "The kid is not going to get the best of me this time," they seem to be thinking. They are too firm, or the opposite — too pleading, rather than relaxed and confident.

Kids read the expectation of trouble and they think, "Oh, brother, here it comes." So they start off a little more defensive. The parents respond in kind, with their intervention becoming stronger. Then the kid's defensiveness goes up a notch, and so forth till the conflict has escalated into a full-blown war. It's hard to say who "started" such a cycle of escalation. It's more important to decide who will stop it or, at least, improve it.

In most cycles, it's better when both sides make an effort to change simultaneously in a teamwork fashion.

Breaking the Defensiveness Cycle

I don't have to tell you that it doesn't work well to tell a child to just quit being defensive. One thing about a child's defensiveness is that the person who triggers it has a hard time being the one to talk to the child about it. When a child gets defensive about being defensive, he creates an almost impenetrable barrier. "Well, you don't have to be so defensive about it," is a remark that makes some older children (and adults) go through the roof.

Nevertheless, there may be a time when you think your child will be receptive to a calm yet frank talk about his defensiveness. Or perhaps one parent with whom the child is less defensive can talk to him about his defensiveness with the other parent.

First, explain to him the concept of defensiveness and why it interferes with learning new ideas and maintaining good relationships. Draw him out as to whether he agrees it's a problem. Explain that it's a reflex he likely learned when he was very young and was trying not to feel bad about himself at difficult times.

Then try to teach him a "new reflex." Tell him that, when he feels that first rush of defensiveness, he should try to replace it with this new reflex: genuine curiosity. He can invite the person who is criticizing or bossing him to tell him more about the problem. Explain that he needs to be sincere lest he be seen as a "wise guy."

Drawing out a person who is angry with you is sometimes called a "diffusion" strategy. People aren't expecting this response so it tends to disarm them and make them express their criticism more succinctly and calmly. This strategy alters a blaming, criticizing, or angry confrontation and makes the kid feel mature. With practice the new response of curiosity can become more genuine and natural. Give approval to your child if you see improved process.

If your defensive child is not cooperative or not mature enough to understand, there is still much you can do. In the first place, pick your battles. If you evaluate too much, try not to be an eagle-eye. Intervene less often.

When you do tell your child what to do, be natural, confident, and assured that you are the parent. You can speak in a friendly, upbeat tone, a bit playful. Say things like, "Hey, kiddo, it's time to put your pajamas on and get ready for bed." Sound as if you're not expecting a battle. The "I'm expecting a battle" voice triggers defensiveness.

Just as the child cannot flick a switch and become curious instead of defensive, you may not be able to flick a switch and become convincingly optimistic and assured when giving a directive. If your child has a problem with defensiveness, you may need a "strategy," too.

At times it is appropriate to quickly call them on their defensiveness in a calm, direct way and remind them that they are displaying that old reflex and that they had agreed (assuming you have gotten this far earlier) to work on the project of keeping an "open mind" and being curious when they are criticized.

Also you can try saying to yourself, "What's the worst that can happen if I'm laid-back about telling him it's bedtime? He won't listen — so what else is new?"

Use humor. When a defensive child blames you for something, try making an exaggerated Steve Martin response: "Well, excuuuuuse me!"

I use a fair amount of humor in my sessions. Sometimes humor will crack defensiveness and break the cycle. It softens the mood. The humor shouldn't be biting, hostile sarcasm or a put-down. I use humor in reference to something going on right at that moment, something about their reactivity, for example. If my judgment says the timing is right and they're likely to take it well, I may joke about their bossiness or defensiveness or argumentativeness. Most of the time it works.

Occasionally, they don't smile or laugh. You have to be reading cues carefully to see if you're further alienating them. What commonly works is to say, "Sorry, I just made a bad joke" or borrow a late-night talk-show technique and joke about your lead balloon. Booing yourself will bail out many a joke that fails.

Anger can be funny . . . in retrospect. Be assured that it's possible to get even the defensive child to the point where he can look back and laugh at the way he used to respond.

NONCOMPLIANCE:
THE KNEE-JERK "NO!"

When Andrew's family was ready to get in the car and go home — whether from the mall or the grandparents' or a friend's — they called him: "Andrew, it's time to go home. Get in the car."

Andrew at that point looked around quickly to see what activity he could get involved in, and if no toy or game caught his eye, he started running in the opposite direction from the car.

His parents raised their voices and became more urgent: "Andrew, get in the car. We're about to go." When Andrew didn't come, his father went after him. He ran from his father — he was quick — and when he was finally caught, he struggled. While this was going on, his little brother, who was already in the car, was getting out and heading back to where the action was.

So here was a perfectly nice family going home after a routine outing having what amounted to a pig-calling contest followed by a calf-roping exhibition. And this was just on weekdays. On weekends, they had the complete rodeo.

The noncompliant child usually thinks an immediate "no" when someone tells him what to do, no matter how reasonable it is. We think of the knee-jerk "no" as a characteristic of the "terrible twos," but when it persists into the

The twins, JAS* and JAM*

JAS JAM

*JAS = Just A Second
*JAM = Just A Minute

elementary school years, we think of it as a real problem, in fact one of the most common problems for which parents seek help.

Noncompliance, a close cousin to defensiveness disorder, is also often a reflexive behavior. A child who has a severe problem accepting authority, who never wants to be told what to do, is often diagnosed with an official child psychiatric term: "Oppositional Defiant Disorder." This type of behavior is obviously an obstacle to teaching conflict resolution, as well as to teaching anything else.

You tell the child to do something, and the child digs in his heels. He refuses, does just the opposite, or pitches a fit and calls you "mean." Or he says, "Just a minute," and you know the minute is going to last until the next eclipse of the moon. Or maybe he just "doesn't hear you." So you repeat your directions several times, each time speaking a little louder. Your child has trained you to raise your voice, and he will only respond when you get to a certain threshold. Then he gets upset with you for yelling. Over the years, many parents have been "trained to yell."

There is a strategy for this pattern between parent and child, one that I see as calm and firm at the same time. The following steps will help your child learn to comply and accept authority and make you more powerful while yelling less.

Step One

Evaluate the frequency of your interventions and commands, and decide to let the little instances of misbehavior go unreprimanded. To test for "size" of misbehavior, ask yourself if you think you will really follow through with making them comply despite resistance and whether you want to correct the misbehavior for its own sake or only because of the defiance.

For example, if you tell a child to close his mouth when he chews, you soon learn that you have very little control over the chewing behavior. You can control whether he goes outside to ride his bike by locking the door or the bike, but chewing is so small, so automatic, and so much out of your hands and in his mouth that frequent reminders usually fail. You have to ask yourself, is it worth getting into a power struggle? Is it the open-mouth chewing that you can't stand or the defiance? Probably the defiance. Being concerned with the defiance is understandable, but do you really want to go to war over the chewing, especially as you're likely to lose?

In other words, pick battles that are important and where you can appropriately prevail. Only give commands that are necessary. Let the rest go.

Step Two

Having picked a battle, tell the child that he gets one opportunity to explain why he doesn't want to do what you told him to do. If his objection meets two criteria, you will reconsider: first, is he making a good point, and second, is he making his point in a good way, that is, respectfully. If the child's objection meets these two requirements, you may (not must) choose to change your mind. Give the child's point respectful thought, then make your decision. To those who say it's weak to change your mind, I say it's smart to change your mind if the child has made a truly good point. To refuse to consider a reasonable objection is to be hardheaded. To let your child "win" in this manner teaches her appropriate self-care and assertion.

Step Three

If you stick with your original request or state a compromise request, and your child still refuses to comply, don't argue, plead, or bargain. Instead, say the child's name calmly and firmly with these words: "I'm serious about your doing. . . ." The words "I'm serious" replace yelling, threatening, scolding, and pleading. "I'm serious" is a code you both know means that this is the bottom-line statement and there is no more negotiating.

Step Four

If the child still does not comply within seconds, he gets an automatic "time-out" to interrupt activity. This time-out, which I call a "level one" punishment, need not be more than five minutes. This time-out asserts that you have final say and that they still have to do the thing you told them to do. The five-minute count starts when they cease resisting and settle into the time-out appropriately. After the time-out, they still are required to follow through on the original request if applicable.

Step Five

If they still don't do what you told them or don't do their time-out properly, you double the time-out period. I call that a "level two" punishment.

Step Six

If they don't submit to level-two punishment, go to level three: Choose something your child cares about and which you can control and deny it for twenty-four hours. This could be an electronics blackout — no telephone, no computer games, no TV, for example.

This system seems like a long, demanding effort at first, but usually the multilevel phase will not last long. When the child sees that he will not get off the hook and that you will have the final say, he'll tire of going through the whole process and will comply earlier in the system.

When he does show improvement over previous behavior for three days or a week in a row, reward him. Improvement might mean no behavior requiring a level-one punishment or even no behavior requiring level-two punishments. The child learns through this system who is in charge and that there is a clear code, yet the system doesn't invite undue anxiety. In fact, children will feel more secure and respected when non-yelling parents are still "in charge of the family."

One word about modeling before we leave the noncompliant child. If you call a child and tell him it's time to go home and then you say a few more goodbyes and then you say you forgot something back in the house and you start up a new conversation inside and then you take a tour of the garden before you get to the car, the child may reasonably believe that "it's time to go home" means it's time to begin to consider the possibility of leaving over a fifteen-minute period. Even an adult sometimes sits alone in the car for fifteen minutes waiting for a spouse who has said it's time to go home. So keep in mind that when you tell the noncompliant child to come to the car, don't say it until you mean it. Only then are you justified in saying you are "serious."

This program of teaching compliance works if you do it consistently. Anytime you start this program and then give in (as opposed to changing your mind because of a well-thought-out, polite, and assertive objection), you undermine the power of the program.

GETTING YOUR GOAT

Ten-year-old Susan finds it provocative — "nauseating," she says — that little sister Rachel, who is always sweet, cute, and funny, gets so much attention from their parents. The girls compete constantly for their parents' attention. They compete even to see, for example, who can get dressed the fastest in the morning. The parents are pleased the girls dress so quickly. But they wonder why Susan seems to be seething inside.

Rachel has observed her power over Susan. Whether or not she wins a particular competition, she has discovered a routine where she always wins. It's what I call "getting your goat" behavior.

It goes like this: The family was going out to eat and the parents asked the girls for suggestions. Cute little Rachel named a restaurant, Applebee's, and Susan chimed in cheerfully, "Oh, that would be fine with me!" It sounded like harmony.

Harmony was shattered, however, when Rachel, cued by Susan's good cheer, hurried to say with a provocative smirk, "I didn't really mean Applebee's. I'd rather go to Steak n Shake."

Susan was furious, and it had nothing to do with her preference in restaurants. It had to do with her accurate perception that, in withdrawing her first choice of restaurants, Rachel was out to get her own way and at the same time "get Susan's goat."

You can identify this behavior because the goat-getter is not in conflict with the victim because of something the goat-getter wants and the victim opposes. That might be solvable. The object of the goat-getter's behavior is the pure pleasure of making the victim angry. It often revolves around something small so as not to attract the clear disapproval of parents. In fact, the parents often scold the victim for her expression of anger, even if they recognize the goat-getting provocation, because the overt anger is more noticeable and serious. Often the goat-getter sits in smug innocence.

Goat-getting behavior is often an entrenched pattern, and it has its own reinforcement — the realization of power over the other's emotions. The ability to make another person very unhappy with a minor effort is an enormous power. Since the object of goat-getting is to make the other person mad, it's not easily resolved by the usual conflict resolution steps.

If you have a sensitive child who is easy prey for a goat-getter, you need to know how to coach your child to take away the power of the goat-getter. I include this behavior and a remedy in this book because it is a very common dilemma and one that will frustrate you if you try to apply the conflict resolution model to it. The model applies to people who, though angry or hurt or jealous or humiliated, basically want a fair solution and goodwill.

Goat-getters — insofar as that behavior applies — do not.

I heard on the radio that this expression came from the horse trainer's practice of putting a goat in the stall with a temperamental racehorse to calm him the night before a race. To agitate such a horse, a rival would steal the goat. When the goat was gone, the horse fretted, breathed heavily, paced back and forth, and generally acted the way all of us do when someone gets our goat. I cannot personally vouch for the truth of this etymology, but I can tell you that "getting your goat" behavior is common among siblings, in peer teasing situations, and is even used by some children to achieve power and control in relating to parents. In my experience, it's usually a difficult pattern to break.

The person who engages in getting your goat can be a bully, a tease, a show-off, someone who feels inadequate or powerless, someone who is bored and wants some "action," or someone who isn't mature enough to understand the impact of his behavior.

Much of goat-getting behavior can be verbal put-downs or taunts. Name-calling may refer to physical attributes ("Shrimp" or "Hippo") or social status ("Loser" or "Nerd") or it may be a general insult like "Butt-head" or "Jerk." Goat-getters sometimes use ethnic slurs. Or they threaten a child with physical harm and then, when he cowers, insult the child's courage: "Wimp," "Chicken," or "Sissy."

Not all goat-getting is verbal. One girl complained that her brother jabbed at her face with his fists every time he walked by her but stopped his blows an inch from her face. The threatened blows kept her nervous all the time and very angry. If he had actually hit her, the parents might have intervened. In this case, when the parents heard their daughter cry out, "Stop!" they saw the brother's behavior as relatively harmless or normal sibling rivalry, and they would often leave it alone or fuss at her for overreacting. The brother's "victory" spurred him on. When the parents turned their backs, he was swinging at his sister again and, sensitive to her parents' criticism, now she couldn't even cry out. He had become even more powerful, and she was even more powerless.

Adults can also engage in goat-getting behavior, such as sarcasm, overly intense competition, eye-rolling, deliberate withdrawal, acting "above it all," insults, and other annoying acts. What distinguishes it from other negative behavior is the deliberate intent to provoke. The behavior of the goat-getter is determined by whatever he discovers is the victim's point of sensitivity.

The success of the goat-getter does not totally depend on how bad his behavior is but also on the perception and general sensitivity of the targeted person. Sometimes, the behavior starts out innocent enough as just "joking around" and gets a sensitive reaction of anger. At this point, the goat-getter may begin to enjoy his power. He is reinforced to repeat the provocation until he tires of it, a big argument breaks out, someone leaves, or someone intervenes.

It's often easy to empathize with the victim of goat-getting and appreciate his hurt, embarrassment, anger, and desire for retaliation. Remember, however, that the recipient is not without some better tools to cope, and he may even achieve, to some degree, a feeling of resolution with or without the cooperation of the goat-getter.

A Strategy

What follows is a strategy I have encouraged for years, usually with good results.

First, you need to ask yourself, "Who is this goat-getting person and what is his likely motive?" If it's a good friend with whom you normally have a good relationship and who is just playing an occasional game at your expense, you could use conflict resolution skills as you would with anyone of goodwill. Tell him that his behavior really does hurt you and ask him to agree to work towards some sort of resolution. Be open to the idea that he might be genuinely angry with you and is using his behavior to retaliate. There might actually be an issue between you that needs resolution.

If, on the other hand, the goat-getter is a passerby, a child from another grade, or someone you hardly ever see, then it's okay to let it go, shrug it off or "ignore the behavior." The occurrence is too rare to warrant a fight and, when you react, you are giving the person what he wants.

But maybe the goat-getter is your nemesis who is around you so much you can't ignore him — your sibling, the class bully, a teammate who treats you like dirt. Chances are your teacher or parent has told you to "ignore" this goat-getter, too. "Pretend you don't care. Act like you didn't hear." And chances are you already know that doesn't work very well. The goat-getter likely knows you're still vulnerable, that you still hear and care. He knows you didn't get an instant Teflon coating, so he tries even harder. It becomes a challenge to get you to respond. Ignoring usually escalates goat-getting behavior, and eventually your goat is gotten.

Instead of the scenario above, when dealing with your nemesis, it's often useful to shift your goal. The new goal is no longer to make goat-getters stop because, after all, only they have control of their behavior. Your new goal is for you to learn to sincerely not care so much — "to ignore with your feelings."

To succeed, realistically, it helps to understand what's going on with the goat-getter's motives. He usually taunts you for one of these reasons: He's showing off to friends, he's bolstering his own esteem at your expense, he's jealous, or he simply enjoys the power he has to make you mad and thinks it's fun.

This thought may help you: You, too, have some power because you understand the goat-getter's game. Your power is more internal. You tell yourself, "I know what you're doing, and it ain't gonna work," or "Sorry, buddy, not this time." Instead of overreacting internally or fighting back, you'll undercut his power by learning to "out-mature him" and laugh it off.

For example, one kid I know named Joel was very bright in math and science. He was small, wore glasses and slicked his hair back — and was labeled a nerd. A couple of his classmates competed in insulting him. Joel and I talked about the "ignore with your feelings" strategy. I suggested that instead of fighting the taunts, he play along with them, using his sense of humor. One day soon afterwards, a kid called out to Joel, "Hello, Goober."

"Hello, Raisinette," Joel replied with a grin.

The taunter's buddies chuckled. When the victim wins the admiration of the peanut gallery, the goat-getter often quits. Remember, however, your objective is not so much to change the goat-getter's behavior as to change the way you feel about it.

On another occasion, Joel was at a Halloween party dressed in a toga. A classmate said to Joel, "You're such a geek."

"No, Roman," Joel quipped. That time Joel felt a lot better than his goat-getter.

Not everyone can be as quick-witted as Joel. Still, cultivating a feeling of being more mature than the goat-getters — because you are "on to them," because you see them as silly or sometimes even pathetic — can diminish your pain and, ultimately, the conflict.

I remember Rick, a boy very sensitive about his admittedly big nose. Kids would tease him about his big nose, and his whole face would turn red; then they would tease him about his red face. Using examples, I explained to Rick this "ignore with your feelings" concept.

"So you mean I should look at them and sorta grin and say: 'Are ya having fun?'" Rick said. He caught the essence of the concept.

Sometimes just smiling at the goat-getter's taunt will quickly defuse the situation.

"Oh," said Rick. "It's like your smile is your secret weapon."

Yes, and, interestingly, sometimes it gets the goat-getter's goat that he can't get your goat.

You can begin to teach your children to handle a goat-getter by going through these explanations and examples at a time when they are receptive to input. But of course, old reactive reflexes are hard to change and take time, patience, and repetition to replace.

Every little mental trick helps. One kid got a toy goat to keep on his dresser to remind him of how to deal with goat-getters.

When the Shoe Is on the Other Foot

On the other hand, maybe goat-getting is not something you have to help your child with: Maybe your child is the goat-getter and he's getting your goat.

I knew a child named Joey. He clowned around to resist control; he hated his vigilant parents critiquing him all the time, but at the same time he provoked them constantly to invite their criticism. For example, one

Sunday when his mother was making him go to church and fussing at him to hurry up, he deliberately put on white athletic socks with dress pants just to bug her.

Defensive kids like Joey can be goat-getters, retaliating even before the anticipated critique.

One day in my office, he was deliberately yawning and flopping around just to get his father's goat so his father would tell him to straighten up. It appeared to be a way for him to crank up his righteous defensiveness, proving his parents are always on his back. In this way, children will sometimes provoke you until you behave badly so that your bad behavior justifies their anger. It becomes a cycle.

The "ignoring with your feelings" principle applies to your own dealings with your child when they are "button-pushing." I describe it as a "refuse to fight" strategy — not giving children the angry reaction that they are pushing for. Instead, you can either choose to overlook the little things as if they don't matter or, if you must intervene because of the severity of the behavior, then do so as quickly, matter-of-factly, and dispassionately as possible. Then distract the kid to other matters.

If your child is a goat-getter to a sibling or other children, then it becomes more a matter of discipline than a roadblock to teaching conflict resolution. You should try to get him to realize the potentially hurtful and serious nature of this pattern. You can develop a "behavior problem project" subject to goals, strategies to improve, and appropriate punishment.

These three behavior patterns, defensiveness, noncompliance, and "getting your goat," have foiled many a conscientious attempt to teach conflict resolution. These behaviors may be observed to a greater or lesser degree in most children at one time or another, but if your child has a serious problem with any of these patterns, you may need to deal with it in order to teach conflict resolution.

THE RELUCTANT SPOUSE

I counseled a couple recently whose child was "difficult." I explained the general approach to resolving conflict that forms this book. The mother was saying things like, "That makes sense," and "I see what you mean," and "I'll try that." At the same time, the father was saying, "That will never work because he . . ." and "He'll just say . . ." and "The trouble with that is. . . ."

Some parents are eager and upbeat and others are more resistant.

Somewhat more frequently, the mother is the more help-seeking and the father is the more committed to his own style of parenting. However, the obstacle of a spouse or parent figure who is reluctant to participate in learning, using, or teaching better conflict resolution skills is equally pertinent to the mother in spite of the awkward "he" used in this section.

Getting Your Act Together

In two-parent families, spousal cooperation is critical. Parents undoubtedly will have some subtle differences and children will appreciate that they have different personalities and styles. Parents, nevertheless, need to fundamentally agree on how and what to teach their child about conflict resolution. At times they should teach together and at times one parent should speak for both of them — "Your mom and I think . . ." — so that the child perceives them as a unified force. It's particularly important to prevent a child from "splitting parents" and developing a coalition with one parent against the other.

If a reluctant or pessimistic spouse is a significant obstacle to teaching your child, you might be able to find a way to persuade him.

If he won't read the book, wants to yell, and demands respect instead of winning it, you can still be direct and assertive about the treatment of your children. If you have strong convictions, don't let issues die prematurely lest you pay later with continuing conflict or increased internal resentment that isn't good for you or your spouse. Be more persistent. Figure out a way to condense major points of conflict resolution, and influence him to be more open-minded.

Your disagreement over how to raise the children is a good issue on which to try the conflict resolution model. The first part, The Thinking Steps, don't require that you have the other's cooperation or contribution. By doing them well yourself, you'll do better and be less inflammatory in Part Two. In The Talk/Listen Steps, don't refer to the book, saying "the book says. . . ." Use the steps, don't explain the steps. For instance, after finding a good time and place to be alone as a couple, say, "Let's make sure we both understand what the other is thinking and feeling about this." Then, try to draw him out on what he doesn't like about the book or method. Try to find out what is the underlying issue.

He may say this method is too idealistic and simplistic; it just scratches the surface. The situation with Billy is much more complicated.

On the other hand, he may say this method is too complicated and time-consuming.

Or he may say something like, "As a parent I need to have authority.

You and your method give up authority. A family is not a democracy. Kids need discipline. It's that simple. You're too soft and that's all there is to it."

Or he may say that when he's rough and yells at his son, the child does what he's told, adding, "You let him get away with murder. I get results."

Use active listening and when you both are sure you understand his objection, you can state your views appropriately, matter-of-factly, with an eye to resolution.

You may say that if the model seems to just scratch the surface, well, some of the surface behavior is the most damaging. If you take care of the surface behaviors first, then you can talk about the deeper stuff. Besides, a lot of The Thinking Steps can be pretty deep when you understand and work at them.

You can say that the method seems complicated, but it's not intended to be a short-term fix; it's a long-term solution. It's not all learned at once. You don't have to focus on the whole process all the time. You could improve problem areas first. If you spend some time now, you'll save time later. Some of the steps with big impact are rather easy to focus on and accomplish in a demonstrable way. For example, you could set up a plan around your family's bad process habits of yelling, interrupting, and seeking coalitions.

As for parental authority, suggest that a parent ought not to see it as disrespectful if a child brings up a conflict in an appropriate manner with a genuine desire for resolution. His approaching the parent means he feels safe enough to bring it up. This is not disrespect but appropriate assertiveness and autonomy. Children, like adults, are entitled to their feelings and opinions as long as they express them properly. After all, the reluctant parent doesn't want his children to be wimps.

In sum, the conflict resolution model is not about losing your authority but using your authority to get kids to think logically and behave appropriately, especially when they are angry.

Agree that your child may indeed do as he's told when his father yells, but that yelling, threatening, hitting, insulting, and other such parental behavior ultimately could make the child resentful. Resentment results in emotional distance, greater resistance later, and passive-aggressive behavior.

As for letting your child get away with murder, you'll perhaps agree that you may overcompensate for your spouse's style of parenting by being too protective and not firm enough. You wish the two of you could meet in the middle rather than overcompensate for each other.

Having said all that, or the part of it that's appropriate, ask your spouse for active listening. You don't have to label it; just say, "I'm not sure I've done well at communicating my point of view. What are the main points that have come across to you?"

Furthermore, admit what you have contributed to conflicts with your child, your own poor process errors. Then draw him out: "I just told you what I did wrong. Do you see that you do anything wrong?" Even if he doesn't respond in kind, at some level he probably recognizes your maturity and reasonable approach, especially if you say all this with a sincere, positive, and not too critical or confrontational manner.

You'll feel good, or at least better, knowing you have behaved in a mature way even if there's not as full a resolution as you'd like.

If he has taken in what you've said and you are closer to being on the same wavelength, you can move on to Part Three, The Solving Steps. Ask him to work with you to develop a plan for dealing with your child that uses some of the principles you do agree on. Then do it. The fact that you haven't agreed on every step doesn't mean you can't make some progress. Also, you can use the steps he doesn't buy into on your own, if it doesn't confuse your child or put him in the middle. For example, you could fairly easily work alone with your child on not yelling but would need to act together with your spouse on curfew rules.

What if this resolution process has almost totally failed and your spouse wants no part of it? It's still not time to give up.

In this case, I say that one is better than none. If one spouse is using the method, especially with a noncombative, noncompetitive (over who's the best parent) approach, the other one will feel less intimidated and less judged and will likely be less defensive and more cooperative. The spouse who is not participating may eventually follow the leadership of the one who is. Any change in one partner's behavior can cause a change in the other's behavior, especially if you aren't "holier than thou" or "rubbing it in."

The model allows you to behave better even if the other parent doesn't. If you inject good process into areas of conflict, it almost always is constructive or interrupts a downward spiral. Good process is contagious. Also, even if alone, you'll still have an influence on your children as they model your behavior.

And what if the other parent persists in being a bad role model? Of course, this is a matter of degree and frequency. I don't feel parents should "back each other up" if the other one has been clearly abusive.

Anytime something is done badly, it can serve as a catalyst for teaching. Preferably your spouse would recognize his own bad behavior and use it to teach. When you are alone with your child, if he says something about his father's behavior and you feel you should respond, you could say, "I realize Dad was yelling at you, and I wish he hadn't. And yet he was making a good point. You probably paid more attention to his yelling than to his point." You could also say, "If you don't like the way he yells at you, maybe you can tell him in a nice way. And you can work on not yelling yourself, since you know how bad it feels to be yelled at."

In the extreme, poor handling of anger or authority that borders on abuse and can't be resolved could be considered grounds for divorce, but try family therapy first.

A less severe impasse doesn't mean the children won't love the person with the poorer style of handling anger. Over time, children learn that parents, too, have difficulty with anger and conflict, but it's usually balanced by a loving side.

CHAPTER 4

Teaching Infants, Toddlers, and Preschoolers to Resolve Conflict

The ability to understand language seems crucial to the overall model of conflict resolution described in Chapter One, but actually the skills a person needs to handle conflict can be acquired early on and evolve as language develops.

INFANTS

Infants can show emotions through facial and vocal expression. Most of us have watched the mobile face of a tiny baby. His mouth screws up, then stretches out. His eyes roll and squinch. He gurgles, bleats, and sighs. While these earliest expressions often seem more random motion than efforts to communicate, at least one study has found that babies from one to nine months show bona fide expressions of interest, joy, surprise, anger, disgust, fear, and contempt.

Studies have shown that untrained observers can accurately identify infants' emotions from photographs, and even seven-year-olds can tell the difference among cries that mean pain, hunger, and desire for attention. Their own mothers and fathers, of course, know babies' expressions best.

Newborn babies cry when they hear other newborns cry, demonstrating a connection known as "social referencing." At about eighteen months they show empathy to peers, offering teddy bears, for example, to distressed children of their same age.

At first, newborns show a wide range of apparently random expressions. When mothers and babies are face-to-face, one study shows, the mother's expression changes on the average of eight times per minute — less than half a second after her infant's expression changes. The baby settles into those expressions which, apparently, are reinforced by the mother's response.

While some theorists think the ability to show emotion is innate and preset (even blind babies smile without ever having seen a smile), most studies show that interplay on a social level is important. There is a link between outward expression and inward emotional development. When parents respond to infants' expressions, the link is set up.

Establishing the link is natural, but making it a happy, healthy one is not necessarily easy. In the early weeks after a baby's birth, common problems compete with joy: sleepless nights, financial worries, in-law friction, visitors, jealous behavior of older siblings, uncertainty about how to raise a child, and the difficulty of comforting an infant who won't be comforted. There may be difficulty feeding, colic, or other medical concerns for the child or the mother. The mother may suffer the common complaint of postpartum blues, or even postpartum depression. The father may not like the feeling of being the last one to get the mother's attention. There may be anxiety about the resumption of sexual relations. Common anxieties blend with normal irritability, and the result may be conflict.

Research, as well as common sense, shows clearly that moods transfer to babies. It has been demonstrated that babies of depressed mothers imitate both the facial expression and the vocal expression of the mother. Share your joyful hours with your baby. Spend time with him when you are relaxed and cheerful. Coo, smile, play with him.

If the happy, relaxed hours are rare or too hard to come by, get help with household tasks and child care from friends, relatives or, if possible, hired help. Do the best job you can of resolving conflict with those around you. Seek psychiatric help for serious postpartum depression. Happy parents generally make happy babies.

These general suggestions for a happy baby are the first step in raising a child who can handle his anger well. You may think the specific matter of conflict resolution will be left till later. You are only partially correct.

Your newborn baby makes a few thin, high-pitched cries and then, after a spell of wiggling and grunting, these little cries turn into a lusty bout of yelling. This looks like anger. Anger is a signal, just as it will be throughout life, that something needs to be fixed. You recognize that expression of anger as normal, realize that she can't fix it herself, and you pick her up and rock her in your arms.

Infants are developing fast, their nervous systems are still getting organized, and their brains have great potential and plasticity. During this phase of rapid learning, you have a great opportunity. Babies will gradually internalize language and learn adaptive processes. From the moment a child cries for you to meet a need, a social interactive pattern will get started that will be hard to change later.

It goes without saying that infancy is not the time to teach directly all fifteen steps of the conflict resolution model, but it's time for you to learn them and begin now to model and reinforce them.

Although there are certain discomforts you can do little about — colic, for example — or certain illnesses that you are powerless to remedy, you as a parent obviously have the power to satisfy many needs and alleviate many discomforts of your infant.

Perhaps you pick up your baby at the first flash of an angry cry, grunt, or whimper. There's nothing wrong with that — you are modeling the expectation of harmony, making him feel secure, and giving the message that you tolerate his anger and respond to it.

Early on, children learn basic trust. They are helpless, except by communicating in a manner that gets your attention. It's okay for them to communicate needs by being demanding. It's natural for you to meet their needs. It's also important to have no long separations that are overwhelming to the child, especially from age six months to three or four years. Children need secure attachment and a predictable, loving adult in order to develop trust.

But do you meet their needs on their schedule or yours? Although it's unrealistic to expect parents to understand and meet every need or to be there all the time, parental response should be more on the baby's schedule at first in order to develop basic trust. Over time, it will evolve to a blend of their schedule of needs and yours, or the "real world's."

Soon your baby will have to learn to tolerate short periods of mild discomfort, separation, or doing without. Babies are — and need to be — frustrated in small ways to master their feelings of loss and frustration and evolve some capacity to delay gratification. Gradually, they become accustomed to short periods of such normal discomforts as hunger, wetness, and boredom. If handled well, babies also learn that routine separations aren't permanent. Through all this, your baby will encounter unmet needs that make him really angry. Or anger will surface because he isn't able to do everything he wants.

As your baby develops, your intimate knowledge of her and your common sense will help you decide whether to "give in" to an angry demand or not. For example, you will deny her the kitchen knife she wants to hold but help her get the teething ring she's crying for.

> Babies arrive with a built-in temperament. Don't take it personally. There are inborn differences in temperament and style from ho-hum or sunny to moody or wired. There are individual differences in how much emotional or physical discomfort a kid will tolerate before he responds and in the intensity of his response. One out of ten children is "difficult."

However, you can teach your baby more than you might think. You can recognize, actively encourage, and reinforce appropriate expression of anger. And you can discourage inappropriate expression.

When your baby indicates a want, decide rather quickly if you are going to meet her demand. If you are going to, then do so right away. If, on the other hand, you decide you are not going to comply with your baby's demands, don't change your mind for inappropriate expression of anger. A child's scream that is "okay" at three months is less okay at twelve and twenty-four months. Do not "give in" for hitting, biting, or temper tantrums, especially at their peak intensity. Once you've allowed a conflict to begin, try to get a more appropriate expression of anger before you give in.

Rock a screaming child, talk to him, soothe him till he stops kicking and screaming before you give him what he wants. In that way, you'll reinforce his calming-down behavior and teach him to soothe his feelings. If he then reaches, points, gestures, or begins to vocalize a need, give in with a smile of pleasure.

Increasing mobility introduces a new area of conflict: the desire for some autonomy. As parents set limits and say no to exploration, they are in more direct conflict with the child's desires.

As your children grow older, you can differentiate between those demands that represent true needs or reasonable wants and those demands they make only because they want to get their way and to be in control. Of course, desire for some control is normal and appropriate; whether it is excessive is a judgment call.

Eating, going to sleep, and toilet training are areas where children can take a stand for autonomy. You'll have a hard time controlling their bodily functions. It's usually better not to try.

For example, when a child between two and three deliberately refuses to go to the bathroom and you know he needs to, don't tell him angrily, "You are going to do it in the potty next time!" You'd be encouraging a power struggle. On the other hand, don't be too sweetly pleading or talk baby talk about how "you're such a big boy." Instead, be crisp and matter-of-fact. When your child succeeds, be mildly but not excessively pleased. Reflect his success back on him; tell him, "I think you'll be happier this way," instead of how much his potty training pleases you as a parent. The essence is to try not to give too much emotional attention, either positive or negative, to his excessive power struggling, which is an inappropriate style of conflict.

Modeling is a very important way to teach at this age. If your small child screams, kicks, or bites, and you yell or slap in response, you are setting up a pattern she will follow. If you severely or inappropriately punish her first expressions of anger you may set up the fear of expressing healthy anger or interrupt the bonding process by which you would otherwise influence your child's development. Instead, model the kind of calm expression that you would like to see from her.

Language is another avenue for teaching even a very young child. Talk about emotions before your baby can truly understand words, because hearing that talk early on is how he'll learn. "Oh, you're very angry." "Calm down. Take it easy." "That's good." "It's okay to be angry but show me nicely." The tone of voice you use communicates a lot and becomes associated with the words. An approving tone of voice also reinforces good behavior.

Recent research shows seven- to eight-month-olds being able to recognize certain words and later on recognize the more correct grammatical structure, long before they are able to give any meaningful verbal expression.

TODDLERS AND PRESCHOOLERS

Toddlers, I don't have to tell you, are often unreasonable. Toddlers overdue for a nap can be very unreasonable. Once I heard a tired two-year-old crying inconsolably in the waiting room. Looking to see what terrible thing his mother was doing or refusing to do, I saw the child pushing and pulling his mother's legs, all the while sobbing, "Do it. Do it. No! No! Do it. Do it."

The mother was lifting her legs, bending them, putting them in different positions, but nothing would make the child happy. "I don't know what you want me to do," she said helplessly as the little one howled.

She finally discovered that the child wanted her to "make a tunnel" so he could crawl under her legs.

The child's tiredness was undoubtedly a factor. A bigger factor was that he didn't have the verbal skills to describe what he wanted. If she had understood, his mother would have been willing to accommodate his wishes. In a few short months, he'll be able to say, "Make a tunnel," and peace will reign.

Resolving conflicts depends on communication. The "terrible twos" often become not so terrible as soon as the child learns to communicate verbally. Talking is a fantastic tool that grows by leaps and bounds in the preschool years. Teaching the two- to five-year-old to resolve conflict gets easier as language develops.

Preschoolers are in an intense learning period not only in terms of language acquisition but in developing emotional control, understanding relationship patterns, and, in general, becoming socialized. Children are said to develop a lot of their personality by age five. The child's fundamental reaction to anger — whether to be fearful of it or to feel "entitled" to retaliate or to be willing to resolve the problem that caused the anger — is well on its way to becoming an established reflexive style. Therefore the importance of establishing good attitudes about anger and conflict resolution in the preschool years is paramount.

Preschoolers are creative, imaginative, and original; they appreciate the humor in absurdity. They are silly. They are cute. These are qualities that facilitate our teaching. Because of children's playfulness, however, there's sometimes a tendency for adults not to take their feelings seriously and to shrug off their anger or crying. Because their feelings sometimes are fleeting and they bounce out of bad moods with placation or distraction, you might easily miss opportunities to teach them about anger. Don't discount their feelings to the point of not teaching skills to manage emotion. Instead, use their playfulness to teach.

AVENUES OF TEACHING

Play

Teaching preschoolers should take into account how central play is in their lives. Play gives them an opportunity to work out scenarios and situations in a nonthreatening way. Play also affords you a way to sneak in some lessons about emotions and relationships, especially about anger-provoking situations. Engage in imaginative games or join them in make-believe with their action figures, dolls, playhouses, and animals.

Observing preschoolers' imaginative play reveals what they have learned from us. What do they say to their dolls in a parental voice? What do they say to other drivers when they push their cars around the floor?

Children's Literature and Art

Good books, pictures, and other art forms convey universal truths as well as aesthetic appeal. Stories and art are often based on conflict and, usually, its resolution. It is good to talk with your child about the processes and values made concrete through the characters and events in children's literature and art.

Rhythm and Music

Preschoolers also appreciate rhythm and music. They easily learn words and ideas set to music or made into rhyme. Even some of the steps to managing anger can be learned in rhymes and songs, as you will see.

Styles of Teaching

Teaching goes on all the time — when your child watches you do something, when you make a casual remark, when you ask your child questions that lead him to think, and when you deliberately instruct him. The younger the child the more he learns from less formal styles of teaching (see hierarchy of teaching styles in Chapter Two).

Preschoolers are impressionable; they learn a great deal by observation. They soak in a lot of what they see and hear. For this reason, it is important that parents and other adults be well on their way to absorbing and using good conflict resolution skills themselves — hence the adult model of conflict resolution in Chapters Eight through Ten.

Your own mood, tone, and style are major influences. When you are teaching children about their anger during or after an incident of conflict, work to stay calm and firm and express your own anger in an appropriate tone. Be serious, attentive, concerned, supportive. Be physically close to your young child.

While modeling and casual comments are more effective styles of teaching the preschooler, direct instruction can be successful in small doses.

Get your child's attention first. Use short sentences and simple language. Do not make too many points at one time. Let your child absorb one point before going on to another. Tell her the same thought in several different ways to avoid misunderstanding. On the other hand, adults sometimes talk beneath a child's level. Preschoolers understand more from context than we might think, even when they don't understand the words. This, in part, is how they learn the words.

> Most preschoolers can understand and repeat the language, "new and better way," "three parts," and "think, talk/listen, solve."
>
> These phrases are no harder to learn than "Pease porridge hot" or "Won't you be my neighbor?"

As a check of comprehension, occasionally ask the child a question to see if she can rephrase in her own words what you have said.

HOW TO GET STARTED

Let your child know, in language he can understand, that you are beginning something new to manage anger, that it's something good to learn. Of course, you will not attempt to get your preschool child to distinguish and remember fifteen steps. It's realistic, however, to teach the three parts of the model: the thinking part, the talking and listening part, and the solving part.

The following examples of language and techniques for getting started on the conflict resolution model may be followed closely or, if you prefer, they may serve as a general guide to introduce the model naturally.

★ Say, "People don't like yelling, hitting and throwing things. . . . I want to help you find a new way to fix things when you're angry. I know a good new way! We can think, talk and listen, then solve. Think, talk/listen, solve. Can you say that? Think, talk/listen, solve. Think, talk/listen, solve."

★ Make a sing-song of these four key words. Rock or march to the rhythm so the child will remember the words while he learns their meaning.

★ Say, "The *old* way was yelling. The *old* way was hitting. The *old* way was throwing things. The *new and better* way is thinking, talking and listening, and solving."

★ Devise a physical pose for each of the three parts of conflict resolution and make a game of going through the phrases.

For example, establish a thinking pose as a symbol for The Thinking Steps — something like Rodin's statue *The Thinker*. In fact, it would be helpful to get a small copy of the statue to talk about. You could find a bookend model of *The Thinker* and talk about *The Thinker's* pose. "I wonder what he's thinking about? Is he thinking about something that made him mad? Is he wondering what he's going to do about it?"

The talking symbol could be the "yak-yak-yak" sign with the hand crisply opening and closing. Similarly, the pose for listening could be cupping your hand around your ear and leaning attentively forward. A hand puppet that can move its hand and open and close its mouth can also help dramatize the talk/listen stage.

The solving part might be represented by a writing gesture — but only after you have illustrated the meaning of the act by drawing up a plan with simple drawings on paper.

These gestures and the words "Think, talk/listen, solve" can be used to mark progress through the conflict resolution process long before the child knows that the fifteen steps exist.

★ At each episode of anger or other negative display, remind the child, "Oh, you're hitting (yelling, pushing, grabbing). Remember, that's the old way. What's the new and better way?" Prompt if necessary: "Think, talk/listen, solve." Then proceed with steps.

HOW TO TEACH THE STEPS

What follows are examples of words and phrases that illustrate the different steps for preschool children. This sampling is not all-inclusive; there are many good ways of saying things. These are just some real-life examples that you might feel comfortable with.

PART ONE: THE THINKING STEPS

The Thinking Steps are, among other things, a delaying strategy, an obstacle to impulsive and thoughtless action taken in anger. Beyond that, a stop-and-think moment offers an opportunity to feed one or two ideas into the child's head with the hope they take hold over time. You can't control thought; you can only offer food for thought.

Step 1. **Assess Emotions.**

In the first step, you are trying to teach your child the value of reflecting on how he or she feels and to label emotions with the proper words. Here are some things to say or do when your child seems to be feeling a negative emotion:

★ "You look like you're angry. What do you think?"

★ "First you think. Let's see. What will you think about? It's good to think about how you feel."

★ "What's the matter? Let's think about it."

★ "It sounds to me like somebody hurt you. Are your feelings hurt?"

★ When your child is obviously hurt or angry with *you,* say, "Did I hurt your feelings?"

★ "Do you feel two feelings? Are you mad *and* scared at the same time? Are you sad *and* sorry?"

★ "How are you feeling? Happy?"
"No."
"Sad?"
"No."
"Angry?" "Hurt?" "Disappointed?"

★ Disappointment is a common and complex emotion involving an expectation and a less-than-desirable outcome. Deliberately teach the harder or subtler words for emotions when no one is angry. Say, for example, "I'm disappointed there are no more cookies in the cookie jar. I wanted a cookie. I thought there was one." Your child will, in time, pick up the expression.

★ Sit together in front of a mirror or give the child an unbreakable hand mirror to play with. Let the child explore his facial expressions. Suggest, "Make an angry face," "Make a sad face," and "Make a happy face." This helps the child become familiar with his own expressions of emotion and what they convey to others.

★ "Your voice sounds like you are angry. Are you angry?"

★ "Some little girls [boys] show they are angry with their face, some little girls [boys] show they are angry with their voice, and some little girls [boys] feel angry deep down inside. How do you show you are angry?"

★ If you have a book about a person who felt angry or had hurt feelings that the child understands, refer to the book to help clarify feelings. For example, Rumpelstiltskin got so mad when the princess guessed his name that, in one version, he stamped and stamped and stamped himself right into the ground. When your child seems angry, find the picture in the book and say, "Do you feel like Rumpelstiltskin did?"

★ Make pictures on a felt board or chalkboard that show happy, sad, mad, scared, and sorry faces. Add to these as your child can identify new emotions.

NANCY®/ by Guy & Brad Gilchrist

NANCY reprinted by permission of United Feature Syndicate, Inc.

★ Cut out comic-strip faces that express definite emotions. Carefully establish correct associations with these faces.

★ Charts and "feelings" posters are often available in educational catalogues and children's sections of bookstores. Images representing emotions can be found in advertisements, in fine art, and even on tee shirts.

★ When looking at a face or image showing an emotion, say, "Can you make a face like that?" Say, "What words do we say when we feel that way? Sad? Sorry? Scared?"

★ Help your child label emotions when you are reading him stories or watching children's TV shows. Pick out books that present realistic issues appealingly. Also, talk about other people's feelings when you have observed them in real life. For example, when you have seen a child having a tantrum in the grocery store, say, "That little girl was really angry. And her mother was embarrassed because the little girl was screaming and everyone was looking at them."

Step 2. **Accept Anger, Behave Well.**
Reassure the child anytime he expresses an emotion appropriately that the emotion and its reasonable expression are good:

★ "It's okay to be angry. But don't hit."

★ "When you're angry, talk, don't yell."

★ "I don't blame you for being angry. I would be angry, too. But first you *think* so you won't do something you'll be sorry about."

★ "I understand. Being mad is all right. Now let's think what's good to do next."

Step 3. **Gauge Intensity.**
Whereas adults and older children can rank anger on a scale from 1 to 10,

preschoolers will do well to deal with a three-way choice: "Are you very, very angry? Are you angry? Or are you just a teeny bit angry?"

★ "If you're very, very angry, it's better to calm down first."

  If the child seems to be very, very angry with someone other than you — a sibling or play-mate, for example — calming techniques include:

> **The Thinking Chair**
>
> The Thinking Chair is comfortable, has pillows, and maybe a stuffed animal at hand. Sitting in The Thinking Chair is calming; it is not punish-ment for anger but, at times, a place to cool down. The angry child sits there until he feels better (and more like talking). Thus, it's okay to be angry; it's how you deal with it that counts. As an illustration, you, the parent, might sit in The Thinking Chair occasionally when you need time out to get back in a reasonable frame of mind.

1. Physical comfort: petting the child's hand, stroking his head, putting the child in your lap and rocking.

2. Distraction: listening to a song (which you sing or play), playing with a favorite toy.

3. Conscious self-calming: taking a deep breath and letting it out slowly; sitting in The Thinking Chair.

★ When the child says he's angry, rather than very, very angry, say, "You are angry, but you seem calm enough to talk about it now. Okay?" Then you move quickly to the next step.

★ When your child says he's just a teeny bit angry, say, "If you're just a teeny bit angry, maybe you can just forget about it."

★ Here's a jingle to remind children how handling of anger should fit the degree of anger:

After you have used this jingle successfully for some time, just humming the tune becomes a signal to remind the child to evaluate his feelings before over- or underreacting. When the child hums the tune to you when you overreact, you know the lesson has been learned!

Step 4. Who and What?

You may think a tantrum stems from sibling rivalry issues or a destructive act comes from being interrupted or told what to do. However, remember to get your child to label the feeling, the person, and the problem himself instead of jumping to conclusions.

Your child's answer to "What are you mad at?" may be something very specific. Note that similar complaints may arise often and be part of a larger pattern or issue that you could work on with your child as one project. Some issues that make preschoolers angry and create conflict are:

* being interrupted while having fun.

* being criticized harshly.

* being yelled at.

* having toys taken away.

* being told what to do.

* being told "No."

* being hit, pushed, etc.

* being denied what they want.

* being rejected or ignored.

* being forced to separate from someone they are attached to.

* being deliberately frightened.

Get the child to focus on the person he is mad at by asking:

* "Whom are you angry at?"

* "Are you mad at me?" If the child says, "Yes, I'm angry at you," repeat Steps One through Three by saying, "It's okay to be angry at me. You need to calm down before we can talk about it. It's not good to yell and hit [or whatever the child did]."

* "Are you mad at Jason?" . . . "Are you mad at Stephen?" . . . "Are you mad at Tigger [the cat]?" The last suggestion may make the child laugh and take the tension out of the discussion.

* "Are you mad at two people?"

* "You woke the baby again when I asked you to be quiet. It seems you keep waking the baby on purpose. Do you know why you did this? . . . Are you angry with me? . . . Or are you angry with the baby?"

Draw the child out on what he is angry about by asking:

* "Why are you mad at Shelley?"

* "What did Peter do to you?"

* "What did Kim say to you that you didn't like?"

* "What were you thinking about when you started to get mad?"

* "Sometimes kids don't do what their parents want because the kids are angry. Maybe . . . is that what happened?"

* "Do you get angry when I tell you to do something?"

* "Do you get angry when I tell you to stop doing something fun?"

Step 5. **Perspective Check.**
An inappropriate thought process may correspond with overreaction or underreaction. Try to discover and gently correct misunderstanding. Preschoolers need to be deliberately taught to acknowledge their own contribution to the problem and consider the other person's point of view. A new perspective on the cause of the conflict sometimes changes a child's attitude from hostile to more cooperative and willing to resolve the problem.

If a preschooler overreacts to a perceived wrong done to him, try these comments:

* "Let's think some more. . . ."

* "Was that a teeny bad thing Jack did to you? A bad thing? Or was it a very, very bad thing?"

* If the child says, "teeny," say, "If Jack did just a teeny thing, do you know why you are acting very, very angry?"

* Encourage your preschooler to choose a phrase that helps him put small problems into perspective. Suggest to your child that he tell himself "no big deal," "relax," "cool it," or "chill" as a reminder to stop and think before reacting to provocation. Invite him to make up his own phrase like the "No biggy piggy!" invented by the child introduced in Chapter One.

On the other hand, if a child seems passive and lets people bully him, putting things into perspective may mean ratcheting his reaction up a notch, telling him it is okay to be angry. You can say something like:

* "If someone took my favorite toy away from me, I'd be angry. Then I would tell him I want it back."

* "If someone hit me that hard on purpose, I'd be hurt and scared and ANGRY!"

Help your child see that he may have contributed to the problem:

* "Were you taking more than your share?"

* "Did you do something bad to Robin first?"

* And model admitting fault, when you yourself have misjudged or jumped to the wrong conclusion or overreacted, so that the child may see these errors and hear their correction: "I made a pretty big mistake: I think you should be angry at me."

Learning to see things from another person's point of view leads to empathy:

* "I think Elizabeth pushed you away because she was afraid you were going to take her paints. Or she was afraid you were going to jiggle her arm while she was painting. She didn't want you to stand so close. It made her nervous."

* "Let's think about why Jack did that to you. Was he trying to hurt you? Or did he want your toy because it's such a nice toy?"

* "Aaron can't run as fast as you can so he doesn't enjoy playing running games with you. You always win and he always loses. That makes him not want to play with you."

* "I think it was an accident and Jason said he was sorry."

* "Remember, Sandy is only two years old. She doesn't really understand that it's your toy."

PART TWO: THE TALK/LISTEN STEPS

Now is the age to let your child know it's her turn to talk about problems and anger and that you will not punish her for it provided her expression is appropriate. In fact, you will be pleased and encourage her to verbalize her anger.

Step 6. **Time and Place.**
Suggest that some times and places are more appropriate than others:

* ★ "Now is a good time to talk to Jack about it. Let's go to a quiet place."

* ★ "Let's go over there so the other children won't bother us."

* ★ "How about waiting till Jack finishes his juice?"

* ★ "Look, Jack is talking to Mrs. Roberts. It's better to wait until they are finished."

* ★ "Jack is sleepy now. He's fussy when he's sleepy. We can wait until after he's had a nap."

* ★ "Daddy is watching the news on TV. He doesn't want to talk now. It is better to talk to him after the news is finished."

Step 7. **Avoid Coalitions.**
Point out who is appropriate to resolve conflict with, based on Step Four, and guide the child to keep the discussion between himself and that person. You become the referee of the conflict resolution process, helping both sides to do a better job.

* ★ "Did Kimberly take your toys? No, Jack did. So it's good to talk to Jack. Kimberly, you go play in the other room. This is Eric's and Jack's talking and listening time."

* ★ Do not let the preschooler enlist you to her side as the only way to resolve the problem, especially when you were not involved. When a child says to an adult, "Allison took my toy. She grabbed it like this . . .", after listening, say, "It's good to talk to Allison. I'll help you talk to her. Since I was not there, I didn't see it all and it's better if I don't take sides. This will be good for you and Allison to solve. I'll help both of you do a better job of talking it out."

Step 8. **Express Appropriately.**
Remind your child of The Thinking Steps (especially Step Four), urging him to express how he feels and why. This is the step where you teach skills such as appropriate tone, being clear and assertive, and not yelling, threatening or bullying:

★ "Slow down. . . . Use your regular voice. . . . Use a calm voice."

★ "Your voice is too high [fast, whiny, loud]. It upsets me [Dad, Thad, Susan, Mrs. Brown]." "Are you angry or hurt? . . . All right. Tell Karen you are angry. . . . That's good, Patrick. Now tell Karen why you are angry. . . . Patrick, stand back a little bit. You are talking right in her face; that frightens her. Tell her how you feel and tell her in a regular voice. . . . That's good, Patrick. Now she knows how you feel."

Also, guide your child to express the problem as something specific and concrete that has the potential for resolution:

★ "Todd, saying 'You're mean' is too big a thing to fix. Say, 'I don't want you to . . . ' and tell me what you want me to change."

★ "Mandy, saying 'I hate you' doesn't help. Tell me what I did that made you mad."

★ (Multiple choice) "Which one of these do you mean? You don't think I listen to you. You think I say 'No' too much. You think I pay more attention to Larry than to you."

Step 9. **Listen Actively.**
The preschooler may be coached through the process of active listening, that is, listening then rephrasing what he heard until the other person agrees he understood.

★ "Melanie, did you understand what Erica said? Do you understand how she feels? . . . Good. Now tell her what she said, just to be sure. What did Erica say? . . . Okay. Is that right, Erica? Did Melanie get it right?"

★ Model active listening yourself: "Josh, let me see if I understand what you said. You are angry because you are busy with your farm animals and you don't want to go to bed in the middle of playing with them. Is that right?"

"I'm glad I got that right. Now let me tell you what I'm thinking. I'm thinking you may be busy playing with the toys until very, very late and then you will be so sleepy tomorrow morning when it's time for preschool. What will I do then? I don't like to have a problem getting you to bed and a problem getting you out of bed. . . .

"How do you think I feel about your playing with your toys instead of going to bed? Can you tell me how I feel?" This question is good to ask, even though the child may not be able to give you a satisfactory answer. Listen carefully to what your children say about your behavior and take it seriously.

Step 10. **Admit Fault.**

It's hard to get a child to admit fault openly without seeming to blame the child, but it is an important step. It's a great gift to teach a child not to be defensive or shift blame but to accept responsibility for his contribution to the problem. Guide the child to talk about his role, however small, in the problem:

★ "It's good to learn to tell what you did wrong, too."

★ "Joe, I see Tracy is sitting in your place. I can see that makes you mad. But she is mad, too. What did you do to make her mad? Did you do something, too? Did you try to push her out of the chair? If you are sorry you pushed her, it would be good to tell her so and next time try to ask for your chair nicely."

★ "I understand why you're mad but I hope you're feeling sorry that you pushed her. If you are, it would be good to tell her."

★ "Do you always take the front seat? Do you ever let Tracy have the front seat? Sometimes one person hogs the front seat. Do you think maybe that makes Tracy mad? It's good to tell her you know you take the front seat too much."

PART THREE: THE SOLVING STEPS

Your child has come to you these few years of his life for you to fix things and make them better. Now it's time for him to begin — in small ways and with your guidance — to learn a way to contribute to the solution.

Step 11. **Brainstorm Solutions.**

Begin with open-ended questions, but be prepared to make most of the suggestions for your preschooler. This is a teaching process!

While this step is intended to solve solvable problems, it's also a good way to help a preschooler learn to accept the unsolvable. For example, if your preschooler cries inconsolably because it's raining or all the leaf piles he liked to jump in were carried away by the trashman or because the cookies are all gone, ask pleasantly, "What can we do to fix that? Can you think of something?" The child's inability to think of a solution may help the child see there's no use crying over it or at least to separate the solvable from the unsolvable. If, in the case of the cookies, your child says, "Make some," that's a possibility you could consider. In fact, making cookies together when your child came up with this solution teaches that you take his suggestions seriously as well as take problem solving seriously. Let's hope you have time for this lesson!

Here are two open-ended questions:

★ "What's a better way? Can you think of something fair?"

★ "Wesley, you want to play GeoSafari on and on and I want you to stop for dinner. I don't want to call and call and call. How can we all have dinner together and still give you time to play?"

Accept any suggestion the child makes as one possibility. It is good to reinforce a child's thoughtful participation. You don't have to say, "That's a good idea." Just acknowledge, "That's an idea." Take turns making suggestions. The possibilities are many. Here are some samples:

★ "What would be a better way? Can we set a timer and you can play till the bell goes off?"

★ "How about taking turns? Let Melanie sit in the front seat today, you sit in the front seat tomorrow. Then Melanie sits in the front seat the next day."

★ "Since it's so hard for you to stop the game, how about if we don't turn it on till after supper and then you can play till bedtime."

★ Draw pictures on a chalkboard or paper to show the ideas that are being considered. For example, for a plan allowing a certain amount of time, draw a clock.

Step 12. **Pros and Cons.**
Discuss the merits of several of the better ideas, and occasionally, the silly, impractical ones the child offered just to show you do not dismiss his efforts. Try to get the child to laugh at the silly suggestions and to seriously see the value of the better suggestions. Instead of focusing on whose idea is going to "win," key in on choosing the plan that is likely to work best.

★ "Is . . . a good idea? Could you do that?"

★ "You don't want to? Why not?"

★ "Why is it too hard? How could we make it easier?"

★ "What is good and what is bad about that idea? Let's see."

Step 13. **Decide and Plan.**
Try to guide your child to make an acceptable decision. With the younger child, parents often either make the decision or "let the child decide" from several acceptable alternatives:

★ "Which one is best?"

★ "Which one do you want to do?"

★ "Which one do you think you will do almost every time?"

★ "Sorry, but I don't think I can do that because. . . ."

★ "I think I can do that. Is that the one you want? Okay. We'll try it."

Then lead the child to implement the decision:

★ "Let's find a way to make sure the plan works."

★ "Let's make a chart to show how we do . . . every day."

★ "Let's put a sticker on the chart every day you share . . . with Patrick. You can choose the sticker."

Preschoolers can equate days on a calendar with days in their lives. Every morning, you draw a picture of some activity that identifies that day. Then put a check or a star on that day if the plan was followed. Be regular. Similarly, divide the day square on the calendar into breakfast, lunch, and dinner or before school, after school, and bedtime to facilitate plans that require several-times-a-day application.

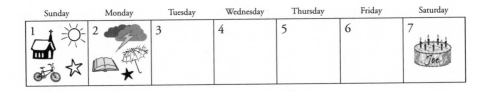

Use an egg-timer. Almost everyone can do an agreed-upon activity (like pick up toys) for the few minutes that an egg-timer runs. One family I know has somewhat resolved the problem of clutter on the floor with this plan: One parent turns over an egg-timer and everyone in the family picks up his own things for the three minutes while the sand runs in the timer. It's like a game. When the child sees the others scurrying to pick up things, he happily joins in.

Step 14. **Do It.**
Reminders and reinforcement will be necessary:

★ "Don't forget our plan."

★ "Remember why we made our plan? So you and Melanie don't fight over the front seat." (If your child follows through with the plan without a reminder, be positive:) "I'm glad you remembered our plan."

Step 15. **Review/Revise.**
Critical evaluation is an important but difficult skill. Teach the child to look at data:

* "Let's look at our calendar and see how many days you and Jason put the toys back without fighting. That's a lot of stickers! You and Jason are doing very well."

Sometimes the best-laid plans get off track:

* "We have to figure out why our plan isn't working and come up with a new one."

* "I only see two stickers this week. That's not a lot. Are you and Jason still fighting over the toys? Remember this morning you were yelling at Jason. That upset me and I had to go sit in The Thinking Chair! I don't think this is working. We will have to think of another plan."

At the height of anger, preschoolers may push away from a parent; still, physical closeness is a major source of comfort and separation is painful. It can be a sign of resolution when they will seek out your lap and wriggle under your arm after working out a conflict. Successful execution of a plan, as determined by data, is often accompanied by a feeling of resolution and forgiveness. Point out the expectation of better feelings to your child:

* "Since you and your brother worked this problem out, I hope you are feeling better about each other now."

* "I hope you're not mad at me now that we have talked it out."

PUTTING THE STEPS TOGETHER: A SAMPLE CONFLICT RESOLUTION FROM BEGINNING TO END

Car Pool Chaos

Karen is the young mother of four-year-old Will. She is talking to a friend on the telephone while Will entertains himself with a wooden train set. He has several sets of tracks, bridges, and tunnels, and several trains. He is enjoying a rather intricate scenario wherein several trains come together and one has to back onto a side track to let the other one pass. Suddenly, Karen sees that she has let time get away and she is almost late to pick up Will's eight-year-old sister Jenny from her music lesson and take her to tutoring. She runs into Will's room where he is engrossed in his railroad fantasy.

KAREN: Hurry up! We have to pick up Jenny, and we're late.

Will doesn't reply or move. He gingerly pulls one train off onto a side track by a water tank and puts a little wooden man on the scene to direct the maneuver.

KAREN: I mean it, Will. Now!

WILL: No! I'm busy.

KAREN: It doesn't matter if you are busy. We have to go.

Karen tugs at Will and he jerks away, screaming.

KAREN: (loudly) Don't give me a hard time. Here are your shoes. Here is your coat. Put them on.

Will slaps the shoes away. Karen takes his arm and pulls him up. He struggles, hitting at her with his other fist and crying. Finally he kicks his railroad bridge and the water tower down and scatters the pieces.

KAREN: Now see what you've done.

Karen forces the shoes and coat on Will and carries him kicking to the car. When they get to the music class, Jenny gets into the car. Will is still pouty. He won't move his legs so she can sit in the back seat because he says he is taking a nap. She calls him a brat. He calls her a baby. Karen lets Jenny sit in the front seat, which she usually doesn't do because she thinks the back seat is safer and besides she likes to have the front seat free for her pocketbook, umbrella, and some clothes she is taking to the cleaners.

Will puts his feet up against the back of Jenny's seat and pushes hard. Jenny complains, "Quit that!" and Karen complains, "Stop that, both of you." She has a headache. Then, when she goes through the drive-in window of the cleaners and asks Jenny to hand her the cleaning from the floor of the front seat, Jenny says, "All right," in a highly annoyed way as she flings the cleaning at her. Then they go to Jenny's tutoring and Jenny refuses to take her notebook in, saying she doesn't need it even though Karen has heard the teacher tell Jenny always to bring the notebook.

Karen finally gets Jenny and Will back home, and her husband Jeff comes home.

KAREN: You take the kids for a while; I'm going out to get some Chinese food; I don't feel like cooking.

JEFF: (wincing) I wanted to jog.

KAREN: (sighs) You never want to keep the children; I'm here all day. I just want to get out by myself for a while.

This was just one afternoon, Karen and Jeff recalled, but the pattern of tantrums and lack of cooperation, children bickering, Karen losing patience and not being in a good mood when Jeff came home was repeated all too often. Finally, Karen had decided she just didn't like being a mother and something had to be done. She and Jeff agreed to try this model for conflict resolution and to teach it to the children. They decided to take one specific problem at a time, and Karen chose to deal with Will first.

The following account of a conflict resolution between Karen and Will may sound like a simple, natural conversation with some awareness of a teaching method, but more is going on than you might think. To illustrate this, I have presented the dialogue on the right-hand side of the page and labeled it with the related steps of conflict resolution on the left. Short of mental telepathy, The Thinking Steps (One through Five) have to be taught out loud. So it is hard for the reader to distinguish steps Karen is taking as her own part in the resolution process from steps she is teaching Will to think or say. Therefore, when Karen is teaching Will, I have added "teaching" to the label. I think it would be better for you to read the whole dialogue through once without paying attention to the step labels. Then reread the dialogue, this time noticing the step labels.

The next time Karen had trouble getting Will to come when it was time to pick up Jenny, they had another fight much like the one just described. But this time, while they are driving to music, Karen thought about the conflict resolution model.

Step 3. **Gauge Intensity.**	After Will was calm, Karen decided it was
Step 6. **Time and Place.**	a good time to attempt a resolution
	and teach Will in the process.
	KAREN: You know I don't like it

Step 2. **Accept Anger, Behave Well.** (teaching)

when we have these big fights like we did getting into the car. I bet you don't either. Let's think and then talk and try to come up with a plan so we don't have that kind of problem anymore.

Step 4. **Who and What?**

WILL: I hate picking up Jenny.

Step 1. **Assess Emotions.** (teaching)

KAREN: Let's try to figure this out. You looked mad. Is that how you felt?

Step 3. **Gauge Intensity.**

WILL: Real mad.

Step 3. **Gauge Intensity.**
Step 4. **Who and What?**

KAREN: I was pretty angry at you, too, because I was in a hurry and you wouldn't cooperate. . . . It's okay that you were angry and it was okay that I was angry, but we need to find a better way to deal with things. We were both angry, but neither of us got what we wanted because we were still late and your train set was messed up. Does that make sense to you — that it's okay to be angry but let's try to handle being angry better and solve the problem that made us angry?

Step 2. **Accept Anger, Behave Well.** (teaching)

WILL: (not wanting to be reminded of the incident) Okay, okay!

Step 2.
Who and What? (teaching)

KAREN: (calmly persisting) You said you didn't want to go pick up Jenny. Were you mad at Jenny? (Will is silent.) Or are you mad at me?

Step 4. **Who and What?**

WILL: Mmmm. Sorta mad at you.

Step 4. **Who and What?** &
Step 8. **Express Appropriately.** (teaching)

KAREN: Okay, let's talk about you being mad at me. Can you tell me the main reason you were mad at me because I really want to know?

Step 4. **Who and What?**	WILL: I'm mad because you made me
Step 8. **Express Appropriately.**	quit playing.

KAREN: I know I messed up your play.

Step 9. **Listen Actively &** You were right in the middle of doing

Step 10. **Admit Fault.** something fun. Maybe we need to have a better plan when we have to go somewhere.

Step 8. **Express Appropriately.** WILL: Yeah. You're always saying "Hurry! Hurry!" (He waves his arms as he imitates her.) You didn't give me any time, Mom.

KAREN: (taken aback by his candid

Step 10. **Admit Fault.** imitation of her) Well, I can see that I yelled and that wasn't a good way to handle it. It

Step 5. **Perspective Check.** didn't help things. . . . I was afraid that if I were late to pick up Jenny she would be worried. So it seemed like a big deal to me

Step 5. **Perspective** . . . . How big a deal do you think it was that

Check. (teaching) you had to stop playing your game? Was it a big deal?

WILL: (hedging) Sort of.

KAREN: The main thing that makes me angry and frustrated is that you didn't

Step 4. **Who and What?** mind me. Moms are supposed to make decisions about when to come and when to go and shouldn't have to fight to get children to do things. You are a good kid a lot of the time and mind me pretty well except when you are busy playing . . . and I can see that yelling and rushing you might not be the best way to get you to

Step 10. **Admit Fault.** cooperate. That's what I did wrong. . . .

(teaching) Can you see that you did something that might not be the best way?

Step 10. **Admit Fault.** WILL: (More friendly tone) Yeah.

Step 10. **Admit Fault.** (teaching)	KAREN: What, for example?
Step 10. **Admit Fault.**	WILL: (questioning) I shouldn't have kicked my railroad bridge down because now I have to build it up again.
Step 2. **Accept Anger, Behave Well.** (teaching)	KAREN: Yeah, that's one thing. It shows how you can mess up when you are angry and act without thinking. Anything else?
Step 10. **Admit Fault.**	WILL: I hit you?
	KAREN: Yeah. What do you think of that?
	Will is silent, looking slightly embarrassed and guilty.
Step 8. **Express Appropriately.** (teaching) *Step 11.* **Brainstorm Solutions.** (teaching)	KAREN: Well, you're right, talking is way better than hitting. Let's make a plan for the times when I have to make you stop playing to do something else. . . . Do you have any ideas? Let's think of several ideas.
Step 11. **Brainstorm Solutions.**	WILL: Don't rush me when it's time to go. Give me some time.
Step 9. **Listen Actively.**	KAREN: That's a good idea. I could tell you a few minutes ahead of time that we will have to leave. I'll try to remember that. Any more ideas?
Step 11. **Brainstorm Solutions.**	WILL: Get someone else to pick up Jenny.
	KAREN: That's an idea. Another idea is we could keep a game or a really good toy in the car and you could look forward to playing in the car so the ride would be more fun.
	WILL: Yeah, we could get a transformer robot.

KAREN: Or you could keep books in the car and look at them while we drive.

WILL: Or we could let Jenny wait sometimes. She could just do more music until we get there.

Step 12. **Pros and Cons.**

KAREN: Well, we've thought of several ideas. Some of them are better than others. Let's see which ones might work and which ones might not. First, let's talk about letting someone else pick up Jenny. I don't have anyone else to pick her up. Gramma doesn't live here. Daddy is at work. I did try to get a car pool to help but no one lived near us. Besides, even if we carpooled, sometimes it would be my turn and then I'd *really* have to be on time. Other mothers don't like the driver to be late. Do you see why that idea won't work?

WILL: I see.

Step 5. **Perspective Check.**
(teaching empathy)

KAREN: I also have a problem with letting her wait because she gets worried — you would too if I were late for you. Besides, we'd have to pick her up later anyway and you'd probably still be playing with your toys. So I don't think later is any better than earlier. What do you think of our idea about keeping special toys in the car for you to play with?

Step 12. **Pros and Cons.**

WILL: Would you get me a transformer robot?

Step 13. **Decide and Plan.**

KAREN: Well, okay, and it would stay in the car so it would be special and I would put some books in the car too, just in case you liked them better sometime. If we did that, your part would be to come right away when I call.

WILL: Okay.

KAREN: That reminds me of something else you said. You said I rushed you too much. I'll give you five minutes before we have to leave so that you can finish up your playing and come without arguing.

WILL: Okay.

KAREN: Let's try these things tomorrow: toys in the car and a five-minute warning.

Step 14. **Do It.**

Karen bought the transformer robot, even though it was not one of her favorite toys, and also a few little surprises and a few inexpensive grocery store books and put them in a sack in the car. The next day they picked up Jenny, Karen made sure she called Will early.

KAREN: Five minutes till we leave, Will. I have a bag of new toys in the car for you to play with like we planned. Please be ready.

She waited a few minutes.

KAREN: One minute left. Are you ready to go?

Then she got her coat and pocketbook and called again. Will came cheerfully. Karen hugged him.

Step 15. **Review/Revise.**

KAREN: This sure is a better way, isn't it?

When Jenny got into the car this time, Will didn't bother her and things went fairly well. Jenny had some habitual grumblings. Karen thought about what Jenny's problems were and how she would involve Jenny in the model and get her to solve problems constructively, too.

The feeling that she had some power now to solve problems put her in a better mood. Everyone was happier when Jeff came home. Later, she and Jeff worked out a plan for him to relieve her of childcare for an hour each evening three days a week so she could work out at the club, if she would hold the fort on the three days he jogged so he could make use of the daylight hours.

In this case, solving the conflict with the preschooler first facilitated resolving other situations involving the whole family. Often, learning the model with a preschooler and then moving on to older children and then to adults is the best way to learn.

CHAPTER 5

Teaching Elementary-School-Age Children to Resolve Conflict

When Livia got mad, her parents took cover. They were afraid she would explode. Even arguing and yelling did not relieve the eight-year-old's anger. What's more, when her parents tried to get her to express her feelings in a more civilized way, they were often alarmed by the physical signs of rage. Livia got so mad she trembled and shook and made fists.

Livia's parents came up with the idea of offering Livia an escape valve — a safe and acceptable avenue for letting out her anger. They gave her a box of art supplies and told her to make a picture of whomever she was most angry with. They assured her that she could safely put all of her feelings into that picture. Livia took the supplies and attacked the task with astonishing energy.

She drew a picture of her mother, bloodied the nose with red paint and gouged holes in the paper with her fingernails. She drew Band-aids on the wounds, and, when it was done, she presented the picture to her parents. They were impressed. "Wow," they said, "you had a lot of anger to express, didn't you?"

They took the picture and talked about it calmly, allowing Livia to say the words "angry" and "hate." Finally, Livia's parents honored her efforts

> **There Was a Little Girl**
>
> There was a little girl,
> she had a little curl
> Right in the middle
> of her forehead.
> When she was good,
> she was very, very good,
> And when she was *mad*,
> she was horrid.
>
> *(with apologies to*
> *Henry Wadsworth Longfellow)*

by framing the picture and putting it on the wall.

By accepting Livia's anger instead of punishing her for it, Livia's parents showed her that anger was okay, a signal that there was a problem to resolve. They knew from the intensity of Livia's emotions that they needed to teach her quickly how to manage her emotions, to behave appropriately, and to frame her concerns in resolvable terms.

Fortunately, Livia was at that wonderful age when curiosity is a motivator, logic and language have become usable tools, learning has not yet been labeled "work," and talking to parents is still reasonably cool. Elementary-school-age children are perhaps at the optimal period for learning conflict resolution skills.

They are moving from a play orientation to a work-and-play orientation, which gives parents two avenues to approach teaching. Parents can be playful and use humor, games, stories, and other parent/child activities as casual teaching opportunities. At the same time, they can tap into the child's desire to learn and achieve. Children this age are aware of the importance of accomplishment, and they are learning to enjoy productivity.

Children in elementary school are much more sophisticated in their ability to think than they were as preschoolers. They conceptualize and formulate abstract thoughts. They see cause and effect and have increasingly logical thought processes. Their ability to process language makes it easier to explain things to them and to draw them out. Their newly acquired reading skills mean you can transmit more information, give written reminders, and show their progress on charts. Children this age also have a greater capacity to delay gratification than they had as preschoolers, and they no longer need to express every impulse they feel.

On top of these winning qualities, elementary-school-age children are not in as much conflict with adults as adolescents. They are reasonably close to their parents and usually like to please them. While they are influenced more and more by teachers, coaches, and other role models, and they may be experiencing some disillusionment with their parents' behavior, they still look to parents for guidance.

Outside of the family, they are becoming more involved with their peer group. Where they fit in and what their peers think about them are big issues. Play is getting more social, often involving games, sports, and clubs. An emphasis on who wins or who gets status is sometimes intense. As their social exchanges increase and the stakes go up, their need to control anger, express themselves appropriately, experience empathy for other people, and get what is fair for themselves becomes paramount. The window of opportunity between their acquisition of the necessary skills and their waning willingness to learn from you makes this a very auspicious age for teaching your child to resolve conflict.

STYLES OF TEACHING

All four styles of teaching are valuable in the elementary school years. Modeling and casual comment remain primary styles for elementary school children as they were for preschoolers. In addition, their growing facility with language allows greater use of drawing out and direct instruction.

Modeling

A child who observes general harmony as a norm will usually have a desire to work things out peacefully in his own life. It's good for the elementary-school-age child to see you resolve a conflict reasonably with the other parent, their siblings, and others. Don't involve a child in a highly emotional spat that you're not sure you'll handle well. Do let him see you work out minor disagreements about chores, scheduling, sharing information, etc.

Modeling is also a tool to use deliberately in teaching specific techniques of conflict resolution. For example, Step Ten of the conflict resolution model is admit fault. A child does not usually do this on her own. She may not even know what it would sound like. So the adult "goes first." He says what he has contributed to the impasse so the child hears what that sounds like and feels the result: the relaxing of hostility. Then the child is better able to tell what she did to make the problem worse.

Casual Comments

A one-liner about the behavior of a neighbor, a relative, or a stranger at the mall can be thought-provoking. Be on the lookout for everyday incidents that illustrate good and bad process in resolving conflicts. Explain why you did something a certain way for a positive reason; point out that you're sorry when you make an error. Teaching comments might include saying your "thinking steps" out loud.

You can teach by casually commenting on any story whether a TV sitcom, a movie, or a book. Teaching through books is especially suited to this age group because elementary school children can understand a lot, but they still like to be read to. Older ones who prefer to read for themselves aren't out of reach; you can bring home good books and comment on them after your child has read them without threatening his autonomy.

A lot of books for children (and adults), as well as TV shows and films, feature intense action and a villain who is overcome in the end by power or trickery. Or the conflict may pit the hero against the elements of nature. Sometimes the situation is solved by luck or a fairy godmother. Not too many books are based on a conflict that the characters skillfully resolve, but there are some. And these are ones you can recommend to your child.

You can, however, point out in many other stories that the problem or impasse was caused by a poor conflict resolution process. After you have studied the fifteen-step conflict resolution model, you can notice and point out process errors or ask the child to point them out. You can even ask a child where he thinks the turning point in the story occurs and how the hero turned the conflict toward resolution.

A favorite children's book that illustrates conflict and its resolution is *Harvey's Hideout* by Russell Hoban (Parents Magazine Press, 1969). It starts out like this:

> It was a quiet summer afternoon, and Harvey Muskrat was building a raft in the backyard. He was hammering hard when his big sister Mildred stuck her head out of the window.
>
> *"Harvey, you stop that hammering!"* said Mildred.
>
> *"I can't,"* said Harvey. *"I'm building a raft."*
>
> *"Build it someplace else,"* said Mildred. *"I'm writing a poem."*
>
> *"I can't,"* said Harvey. *"This is where the hammer and nails and all my planks and logs are. Why don't you go someplace else to write your poem?"*
>
> *"It's my house as much as it is yours,"* said Mildred.
>
> *"And it's my backyard as much as it is yours,"* said Harvey.
>
> *"You are being selfish and inconsiderate,"* said Mildred, *"and I'm telling."*
>
> *"Go ahead and tell,"* said Harvey, and he went on hammering until his mother came out on the back porch.
>
> *"Harvey,"* said Mother, *"that is a terrible racket to make so close to the house. You really ought to do your hammering somewhere else."*
>
> *"So ha ha ha,"* said Mildred, and she stuck out her tongue at Harvey.

Sound familiar? In this case, the muskrat mother and father eventually intervened and did what mothers and fathers usually do. They got some peace only by separating the children. Finally Harvey said something to Mildred that got through to her. So they talk/listened, brainstormed, and worked out a plan so they could play together in peace.

Harvey's Hideout has some teaching value without a word from you. You could maximize that value by making a casual point that when the muskrat children started talking about behavior that bothered them — telling who and what they were angry about — instead of name calling, they were beginning to resolve their problem.

There are not many books as clearly focused on conflict resolution as *Harvey's Hideout*. Many children's books, however, present parts of the process clearly, such as empathy, a change of perspective, or creative problem solving.

Drawing Out by Asking Questions

At this age, you can draw children out with several specific purposes in mind. First, you can ask questions; ask what they think is good to do at this point. If your question gets a good response and all you do is approve, the child feels it's his idea and is likely to buy into it. Repeating his phrase can help him feel his ideas are more important and reinforce his memory of them.

Another purpose of drawing out is to get the child to teach you something about his thinking that you didn't know or to tell you something about the problem you didn't know.

Also, as the child responds to you, he's "thinking out loud," and you can reinforce or guide his thinking. Especially for The Thinking Steps, drawing him out is the main way you know if you're succeeding in getting him to learn new, better ways of thinking.

Direct Teaching

Elementary school children are used to the style of teaching called direct instruction. They see it in school. Your child, however, may decide it's not your place to teach in this way and it's not his place to listen! There are, however, many ways to motivate him. One of them is for the child to realize he'd be better off knowing this information; another is curiosity about what you're going to say.

Some parents say they just don't know how to get started presenting conflict resolution skills to their children. The following "getting-started language" can get you both going.

HOW TO GET STARTED

At this age, you can tell your child directly that you want to develop a better way to handle anger, a better way to solve arguments, a better way to act when you're mad, but drawing them out is often a better approach. It's a good idea for you to give him a chance to express a desire for "a better way."

For this reason, I've divided the following samples of getting-started language into "openers" and "follow-ups" because, at this age, an opener from you just might elicit a reply that shows your child is ready to take some initiative. Wouldn't that be wonderful! Just remember to leave a long pause after each opener so he can mull over what you've said and decide to fill in the silence you've left him.

Openers

* ⋆ "I'm tired of yelling, aren't you?" (Wait.)

* ⋆ "You know what the trouble with this kind of arguing is? It hardly ever fixes anything." (Wait.)

* ⋆ "When you're mad, you don't say much, but I know you're thinking plenty. I'm thinking plenty, too." (Wait.)

* ⋆ "Does this argument sound familiar? I think we've had this same argument before. I wonder why we keep having it." (Wait.)

* ⋆ "Sometimes you're grumpy. When I'm grumpy it means that I have a problem. And when I have a problem, it's not going away until I fix it." (Wait.)

* ⋆ "Do you know some other families that seem to get along better than we do? I wonder how they do it." (Wait.)

* ⋆ "I feel it's time for a change. Let's change the way we fight." (Wait.)

* ⋆ "I love you so much but I sometimes end up saying mean things to you. And I know I'm hurt when you say mean things to me. Let's find a more loving way to talk about what upsets us." (Wait.)

Follow-up

★ "So I've been thinking that, if we do a good job of solving the problem that started this argument, it won't be as likely to happen again."

★ "I've heard about a way to work on things so we won't feel so angry so often."

★ "Games like soccer, baseball, chess, and Monopoly have rules so that everyone plays fair. Let's make some rules for living [playing, working] together so that everyone plays fair."

★ "Every big thing that sounds hard is easier if you break it up into steps. Then we can work on one step at a time."

Now you can move on to the concept of steps, taking the three parts of the model first. If you have already done this with your child at an earlier age, just ask her to remember the three big steps you take when you get mad.

> ### When I Was Going to a Fray
>
> When I was going to a fray,
> I met a man with a better way.
> The better way had three parts.
> Every part had five steps.
> Every step had four styles.
> Styles, steps, parts, way:
> How many were going to the fray?
> Answer: One. You. The others were going in another, better direction.
>
> *(With apologies to Mother Goose)*

★ "This is very important: When you get mad or upset, stop. There are three important things to do. First you think. Then you talk to the person you're mad at and listen to him, too. Then you plan a way to settle the problem. Think. Talk and listen. Solve. That's it."

★ "The thinking part is very, very important. We need to think hard first, so we won't blow it."

★ "The talk/listen part is also very, very important. You tell the other person what's bugging you. Nicely. Not in too mad a voice. Then the other person tells you what's bugging him. And you listen. Then you tell each other what you think he said just to make sure you got it straight."

★ "The solving part can be a fun part. You agree to a plan to see that this doesn't happen again. You find a way to quit bugging each other. Then you do it."

★ "Think, Talk/Listen, Solve. We both need to think before we talk. We need to talk and listen before we think of a way to solve the problem."

When the concepts of the three parts are clear, it's time to introduce the fifteen steps. If learning fifteen steps sounds hard to you, let me assure you that the fifteen steps actually make the three parts doable. It's as if someone asked you to prepare a salad, main course, and dessert. You could do it, but you would know better how to start and what to do if you were also given a menu, a list of fifteen ingredients and the recipes.

Here are some samples of language to introduce the steps.

★ "The thinking part, the talk/listen part, and the solving part each have five steps. That's fifteen all together."

★ "Let's learn these fifteen steps little by little. We can see which ones you do well already and which ones need work."

★ "These steps come more easily as you practice them."

At a grade school talent show, amid dozens of singing, dancing, and comedy acts, one performer stood out. He was a second grader, dressed as George Washington, who named all forty-two presidents of the United States without a hitch.

So when parents exclaim, "How can a child memorize fifteen steps!" I answer, "Probably a lot more easily than you can."

It often boils down to a child's motivation to learn — how interesting the material is and if there's a challenge or a reward.

Elementary school is an age when actually presenting the fifteen steps to conflict resolution makes sense. You may want to relabel the steps in language your child understands better. Explain the steps and ask your child for shorthand labels. Use what your child offers, unless they are clearly useless misrepresentations, because using his phrases will make him more likely to buy into the process and will help him remember better than your phrases will.

Here's what eight-year-old Todd came up with to replace the adult step labels.

ADULT STEPS	TODD'S STEPS
1. Assess emotion.	1. Hmmm. Then say your feelings.
2. Accept anger, behave well.	2. It's okay to be mad, but behave.
3. Gauge intensity.	3. One to ten.
4. Who and what?	4. Who, what?
5. Perspective check.	5. Is it a big deal? And what about the other guy?
6. Time and place.	6. When and where?
7. Avoid coalitions.	7. Don't choose up sides.
8. Express appropriately.	8. Tell 'em in a good way.
9. Listen actively.	9. Listen and tell it back.
10. Admit fault.	10. Here's what I did wrong.
11. Brainstorm solutions.	11. Brainstorm.
12. Pros and cons.	12. Good ideas, bad ideas.
13. Decide and plan.	13. Decide and plan.
14. Do it.	14. Do it.
15. Review/revise.	15. Check up and change.

For Step One, what Todd actually suggested was "Hmmm" while striking a thinker's pose. He offered "Say your feelings" only when pressed, but I'm pretty sure he sticks with "Hmmm" when he's talking to himself. Try to push for labels that make sense to you both, but remember these are just mnemonic devices. The real meaning behind the labels will require examples, repetition, and talking your child through real situations.

HOW TO TEACH THE STEPS

In the pages that follow, I've added some things you can say to help the child learn each step. The first line represents modeling. The next few language samples are intended to draw your child out. The last thing for each step, as you can see, is to help you formally teach it.

PART ONE: THE THINKING STEPS

The Thinking Steps for the elementary-school-age child will sound a lot like talking — you talking. You'll be teaching your child new ways to think, and hoping she replaces her own less appropriate childish thinking with more mature ideas. Some day your words will become her automatic Thinking Steps.

Step 1. **Assess Emotions.**

A lot of children have only one word for negative feelings. One says, "I'm upset," another is always "mad." Enlarge your child's concepts of emotion and its vocabulary. In expressing your own negative feelings, distinguish between mad, disappointed, frustrated, jealous, stressed, hurt, embarrassed, threatened, and all the rest. Encourage your child to do the same.

When Livia's anger mounts, her family still refers to the picture she drew to illustrate her anger. Occasionally, they see her glance at the picture in trying moments. "Remember that?" the glance seems to say. "That's how I feel now" or "That's how I am beginning to feel." A lot of families develop symbols for emotions or behavior they have discussed. Invoking the symbol substitutes for the remembered discussion and often relieves tension.

* "What Kim said really hurt my feelings and I'm mad at her for that."

* (About a story on TV) "See how she didn't tell anyone she was upset and then she finally exploded. Obviously she was angry all along. Do you think it would have turned out better if she had understood how she felt and talked about it early on?"

* "You notice Dad was angry with our neighbor about his dog. He was able to tell it in words."

* "I can tell that you're angry at your teacher for sending you to the office today. I'm guessing you're also embarrassed and hurt inside because you thought that teacher liked you a lot. But maybe I should stop guessing and let you tell me. How did you really feel?"

* "You look like you're in a bad mood that's hard for me to understand. Do you think you're feeling several bad feelings at once?"

* "You seem kind of anxious and angry about going to your Scout meeting tonight. Are you?"

* "When you feel like crying or yelling or saying, 'Grrr,' that's a signal something's wrong. You're probably mostly angry."

* "There are a whole lot of ways you can feel — angry, sad, disappointed, jealous, left out. All those different ways to feel bad are just a way to

know you've got a problem you need to fix."

★ "The first step of our new way to handle arguments is to stop and think about your feelings for a few seconds and see if you can name how you feel."

Step 2. Accept Anger, Behave Well.

This is the step where you teach the child not to act on the first reflexive thought that comes into his head. No hitting, yelling, breaking things, insulting, or name-calling. One family chose the acronym TBA (Think Before Acting) as a first thought for their son Gene to replace the knee-jerk thoughts of the past. Gene's family quietly reminds him to "TBA" when they see anger mounting. A secret code like this one is less intrusive than a warning or a reprimand.

★ "I'm trying to keep a good attitude. Even though I'm angry at the neighbors, I know I need to think through the problem about the dog and behave well. I could make things worse if I don't."

★ "I noticed Sam stepped out of the room because he was so-o-o mad. I bet he remembered to handle his anger well."

★ "What sort of thoughts come into your head when you first get mad? What sort of thoughts did you think first when Jamie drew on your picture?"

★ "What do you think is a good way to teach about feeling anger?"

★ "What sort of thoughts do you think are good to think when you get angry?"

★ "Do you think it's okay to be angry? What do you think Mom and I think when you're angry?"

★ "It's okay to be mad. Anybody can get mad when something goes wrong. The important thing is to stop and think what's the best thing to do about it."

★ "Hitting, yelling, and saying mean things are not allowed. And they just make you and everybody else madder. Thinking first, talking and listening well, and then solving really works better."

★ "I expect you to be mad. I would be mad, too. But then I expect us to think of good ways to change things so we won't be mad anymore."

★ "The second step is to say to yourself, 'It's okay to be angry.' Then you
   need to follow these fifteen steps instead of doing bad things."

Step 3. **Gauge Intensity.**

Gina, an eight-year-old girl with whom I discussed this step, said she
never made it to a 10 on the anger scale. Even so, she recalled recently being
angry at a six-year-old neighbor for not inviting her to her birthday party.

"I was a 5 or 6 being angry. I was a 3 or 4 being jealous of the people
who were invited. I was a 6 at having my feelings hurt."

The scale concept gave Gina no trouble at all. It was also easy to teach
her that she should let a provocation go at a 1 or 2, talk things out at a 3 to
7, and cool off at 8 through 10. These concepts gave her a measurable
framework for thinking about anger.

The gauging intensity step also supposes that your child can learn,
with your help, ways to calm himself down if he's too angry to talk constructively. Notice what seems to calm your child, whether it is having you
read to him, exercising, listening to music, or having his back rubbed.
Then use these techniques to soothe him when he's angry. Also, ask the
child to figure out what activity works to reduce his anger and choose a
phrase to remind him to do it. Or suggest he think of a place where he
always feels good — the beach, the woods, a special nook in the house —
and then, when he's angry, close his eyes and pretend he's there. He could
even listen to a relaxation tape of a rippling brook or woodland birds available in music departments.

★ "I'm about a 5 now thinking about how Jan told me she had a ticket to
   the concert for me and then she took Marge instead. That means it's
   worth talking to her about, and I'm not too angry to do a good job. So
   the next time I see her . . ."

★ "Look at that little girl screaming at her mother. I'd say she's at least an
   8. Too mad to talk. Let's see what her mother does to calm her."

★ "Can you think of any good reasons for figuring out how angry you
   are?"

★ "If you're really, really angry, what do you think would be a good thing to do?"

★ "If you're just a teeny bit angry, what would be reasonable for you to do?"

★ "The third step is to say to yourself how mad you are and to decide if you're ready to do the fifteen steps now, or if you should forget about it, or wait till you aren't so mad."

★ "If 1 is a teeny bit mad and 10 is very, very mad, how mad are you? If your child can rank his anger, then say: "If you think you're 1 or 2, try to forget about it."

★ "If you think you're a 8, 9, or 10, you are too mad to talk, so you need to do something that cools you down. Like play Nintendo or kick the soccer ball around or just get outside."

★ "If you think you're a 3 to 7, that's a good time to talk about what's making you mad."

★ "If you're at a 1 or 2 and you were much higher earlier, it's still good to talk."

Step 4. **Who and What?**

Who your child is mad at or what he's upset about is sometimes obvious. But sometimes children, like adults, target the wrong who-and-what. Teaching this step may require catching your child in a mistake. Then you can demonstrate that clarifying who-and-what is helpful and feels good.

Here are some common issues that make elementary-school-age children mad. Some of these issues are process errors that underlie a wide variety of content issues.

Common mad-makers for the elementary-school-age child:

★ being interrupted when they're interested in something else
★ someone taking their stuff
★ being teased
★ being criticized
★ being bossed
★ being told no or to do something they don't want to do
★ being left or abandoned (separation fears)

* not getting attention or feeling neglected
* being embarrassed by someone else
* losing a competition
* being treated unfairly
* being yelled at, hit, or scared repeatedly

Here's some language you could use to teach this step:

* "You know I wasn't really mad at you. I'm just frustrated because Dad is coming home late and I especially wanted him home early tonight."

* "I don't think Jimmy is mad about that toy at all. He didn't want to play with it until Aunt Erica came. I think he's mad because he wants Aunt Erica's attention and she's playing with the baby. He probably sees that the baby gets people's attention first. That makes him feel left out."

* "Sometimes we get in a really bad mood and we don't know why." (Wait.)

* "Sometimes it's confusing to think about what made you angry because it might seem to be a little thing, but you're really angry anyhow. Do you know what I mean?"

* "Do you know when this angry feeling started? Maybe we can go back and figure out what it's about."

* "Sometimes you feel mad at everybody, but usually one thing or one person made you mad. Can you remember what made you mad?"

* "The fourth step is to be sure who you're mad at and to tell yourself what that person did that really made you mad."

* "Many people, even adults, take their anger out on the wrong person. It's really not fair and it doesn't lead to solving the problem."

* "Sometimes it's hard to figure out what it really is that's making you mad. We'll work on it so you can get better at it."

Step 5. **Perspective Check.**
Putting a problem into perspective means asking two questions:
1) Is your emotion out of proportion to the provocation? If so, why?

2) Is there "another way" to look at the provocation, especially by looking at the other person's point of view?

Perspective takes experience and can be hastened by your pointing out how other people look at similar situations and how other people feel. It was for this step that a seven-year-old chose the phrase "No biggy piggy" to remind himself as soon as he got mad that the things that bothered him were usually no big deal.

The same family that uses the initials TBA (Think Before Acting) as a reminder has another abbreviation for Step Five: NOTGY (Nobody's Out To Get You). Gene, the child, is trying to replace his reflexive thought that someone's out to get him with the new, positive, more realistic appraisal that, in fact, no one is out to get him. Then he has to think that the person who has made him mad has another reason for acting as he did and it's up to Gene to figure out what it is.

Gina, the little girl who was angry, jealous, and hurt over not being invited to a birthday party, was asked to think of some reasons that she wasn't invited other than the ones that made her mad — the six-year-old didn't like her or wanted to be mean. "Maybe she just forgot," Gina suggested. Her mother reminded her also that the neighbor's mother may have set a limit on the number of children to be invited and she may have said, "Only children in your class" or "only six-year-olds," or "you have to invite everyone in your car pool." Gina, inspired by her mother's reasoning, added, "Or maybe they were just going to play kindergarten games, and I'm too old." This was a perspective check.

Here are some ways to talk about perspective:

★ "You know when I thought it over, it wasn't that big a deal."

★ "I thought about it and decided maybe he was just joking, so I'll ask him what he meant before I tell him I'm upset."

★ "The short boy in the story thought the tall boy was making fun of him. He got angry and started planning to get back at him before he really knew what the tall boy meant. The whole story would have been different if he had asked the tall boy to explain."

★ "How bad is what Joe did to you?"

★ "When you feel yourself getting mad even though you know what made you mad was only a small thing, try to say something to remind your-self that it's no big deal. You could say, 'It's no big deal' or 'Relax,' or 'chill' or 'no sweat' or 'small potatoes' or 'whatever.' What expression would you like to learn to say when someone bugs you?"

THE FAMILY CIRCUS

"Mommy! Jeffy's pointing the
empty paper towel roll
at me again!"

THE FAMILY CIRCUS reprinted with permission from Cowles Syndicate, Inc.

★ "Why do you think he did it?"

★ "Can you think of another reason he might have done it?"

★ "Would other people get as mad about that remark as you do? Can you help me understand why this makes you so mad? Is there something else to it I'm missing?"

★ "What do you think he's thinking about it right now?"

★ "The fifth step is to decide to look at the situation a different way. Ask yourself what most people would feel. Think about the other guy's point of view. What was he thinking when he did this to you? Was he just trying to make you mad? Or did he think he had a good reason?"

To the child who underreacts or doesn't stick up for himself, however, you may have to encourage greater assertiveness, as in the following example:

★ "If I were you, I'd be even madder than you are about Jason taking your baseball glove without asking and then losing it. I'd not be afraid to tell him you're angry. Then you could work out a way for him to replace the glove."

PART TWO: THE TALK/LISTEN STEPS

How often do you demand that your school-age child listen to you? Do you always listen to what he has to say? And do you speak appropriately to each other? Teaching The Talk/Listen Steps involves giving reasonable time to each of you and equal value to talking appropriately and listening well.

Step 6. Time and Place.

Almost every child tries to talk to you somewhere, some time when you least want it — when you're on the telephone, through the bathroom door, or when you have company. Tell her, when you are not angry, which are your worst times and places for talking seriously and which are your best. Then ask her to tell you the times she doesn't want to have a talk. Remind her of this exchange when she tries to engage you at the wrong time or place and try to respect her wishes, too. Encourage her to notice when and where her other parent, her teachers, and her siblings seem most approachable. Here are some things to say to teach this step:

* "The baby is tired now. He'll get mad at anything we do when he's sleepy so I'm going to wait until after his nap."

* "Your dad and I will have a better time to discuss this after you go to bed."

* "Did you notice how that mother was trying to work that out with her kid in the grocery store? They would have done better to settle it in private."

* "You did a smart thing to get Karen to talk to you under the tree instead of in the group. That way it was just between you and Karen."

* "What's the best time to talk to Mrs. Walker? When she's talking to the class? When the other children are working quietly and she is at her desk? Which one seems better?"

* "It seems to me that you need a reasonable amount of time to discuss this. How much time do you think it would take?"

* "We should probably talk about this privately. Where do you think we can do it best?"

* "Sometimes if you try to talk to someone about a problem when he is mad or busy, you just make the problem worse."

* "You can say, 'Mrs. Walker, I need to talk to you about something. When would be a good time?'"

* "Riding home on the bus, you could sit down beside Sue or ask her to sit beside you. She has plenty of time then."

* "The sixth step is to pick a good time and a good place to talk to someone."

Step 7. **Avoid Coalitions.**
"You're mean and Jamie thinks so, too."
"Give me that truck or I'm telling."
"Dad, Mom won't let me play with the game."
"Hit him, Philip!"

Children (and adults) are quick to seek allies. Getting other people to take your side seems to be a natural skill, but it's one that almost always escalates feelings and lessens the likelihood of genuine resolution. Avoiding coalitions allows fair discussion so that both sides feel better in the end. (Of course, parents being in a good coalition with each other to help their children is appropriate.)

* "I know you have some ideas, but the disagreement is between your sister and me. So you don't have to worry about it. It will be better if we handle this on our own."

* "Did you notice in the movie how Jake got madder when Pete got the whole group to agree with him? Jake felt it wasn't fair for them to gang up on him."

* "Whoops! When you say, 'Isn't that right, Dad?' you're trying to get him on your side."

* "We're not choosing up sides here!"

* "Looks count just like words. I see you guys cooking up something together just by looking at your eyes."

* "How do you feel when someone you're arguing with gets someone else on his side?"

* "I notice you sometimes ask someone else what they think about your

disagreement. Do you think that will help us get this settled?"

★ "If you have something to say to Miss Thompson, how come you're taking Lisa with you?"

★ "I feel like it's a good idea to keep the argument between you and your brother. Your dad and I will help you do a better job in talking but we won't take sides. We'll let you do the talking as long as you're not being hurtful or mean."

★ "The seventh step is don't try to get people to take sides. When you have a problem with someone, talk to him alone and don't spread it all around."

Step 8. Express Appropriately.

The way you tell the other person what the problem is and how you feel about it determines how well that person will react. Expressing appropriately means without yelling, whining, name-calling, making faces, etc. "Appropriately" also means stating a single problem simply and briefly. When you go on and on about a problem or try to discuss several problems at once, you lose focus and the other person feels attacked rather than told. "Appropriately" also includes telling the problem in resolvable terms. "I'm furious because you don't like me" is not about specific behavior and is hard to resolve. But "I'm hurt because you won't play with me" is more concrete and is more likely to lead to a solution.

★ (in calm, low voice) "I come home tired because I get up early and work all day and then when I come home, you children are playing or watching TV. You haven't done your chores. I mainly get angry because you don't seem to do very much to help out."

★ "Joe did a good job telling why he was angry and it didn't take long to bring the main idea out."

★ "Miriam explained it to me without yelling or making bad faces and she stuck to the subject, too."

★ "I'm afraid I still disagree with you, but I appreciate your telling me so nicely and honestly."

★ "When you're telling someone you're angry, how do you think it's best to say it to them?"

★ "How do you feel when I make a mistake and yell at you? Do you think my yelling helps the argument?"

★ "Tell Sean you're angry and then tell him what he did that made you mad. Don't yell though."

★ "Don't call names or threaten. Just state the facts and how you feel."

★ "I think it's important, when you are telling someone you're angry, to be able to tell them the main thing. Save the little, less important things for later."

★ "Step Eight is to say what you are mad about. Think it out and then say it simply, clearly, and in a good voice."

Step 9. Listen Actively.

Listen actively means "really" listen and don't interrupt or counterattack. Just tell the other person what you heard him say. This doesn't mean parroting; it means telling what you understood in your own words. Both sides listen actively until they are satisfied they have understood each other's facts and feelings.

★ "I hear what you said. Now let me see if I have this right. . . ."

★ "I can tell Tina is a good listener because she does a good job of saying what she heard."

★ "Don't you think it would be a good idea to really, really focus on being a good listener when we have a disagreement?"

★ "It would help me know that you understand if you will tell me what I said in your own words." (Wait.)

★ "It's really cool to become a 'listening expert' so you can repeat what the other person says. It makes the other person feel good that you listened that well."

★ "It seems to me that when two people disagree, it's just as important to be a good listener as a good explainer or a good talker. What do you think?"

★ "Now, Joe, it's your turn to listen so you can understand Timmy's point of view. Timmy, it's your turn to tell Joe how you see this problem."

★ "Step Nine is to listen carefully, then in your own words tell the other person what you think he said. Then it's your turn to talk and he listens."

Step 10. **Admit Fault.**

Admitting fault may feel like unnatural and novel behavior to an elementary-school-age child. What comes more naturally is: "It's not my fault," or "Well, he did it."

Modeling is particularly useful for this step. When you admit a process error, the child feels the tension diminish and understands the power of the step. And in direct instruction, when you are teaching your child to admit fault, you will in all probability have to "go first" to show that admitting fault doesn't hurt. It's not "giving in"; it's being honest.

★ "I know I sighed when you started talking and I guess that made you feel I was mad or didn't care or something."

★ "I know I'm not a perfect parent and what I'm doing wrong this time is making too much fuss over your noise. I think it's because this problem has come up so many times. But I shouldn't overreact to this one time because I can tell you weren't trying to irritate me; you were just playing."

★ "I was impressed with that man on TV when he said he shouldn't have spoken to his workers that way. It's hard to say that you're wrong."

★ "When you are angry, it's easy to say, 'It's all your fault,' but it's almost never all one person's fault. Usually both people have done something that made things worse."

★ "I know it's hard but it helps move things along if you could say what you are doing wrong, too."

★ "Step Ten is to say what you did wrong that made this situation worse. So think a minute and see if you know something you could have done better."

PART THREE: THE SOLVING STEPS

In The Solving Steps, children have a chance to think about their own strengths and weaknesses and to solve their own problems taking these into account. Since there's more than one way to solve a problem, the process encourages creativity, thinking ahead to possible outcomes, and using good judgment.

Step 11. **Brainstorm Solutions.**

Brainstorming solutions means generating several possible solutions without worrying too much about whether any of them will work. It is a creative process, not an analytical one. In a brainstorming session, no one critiques his own or others' ideas or worries about which one will be chosen. That way, off-the-wall ideas are encouraged as well as "standard" solutions. This step is usually fun because it is creative and nonjudgmental.

Children don't always get the right spirit. As soon as one person suggests an idea, the other jumps on it and says what's wrong with it or complains about how that idea will impact him. If you get into a fresh argument over every idea, that's not good brainstorming.

Sometimes using humor or a lighthearted suggestion will ease tension and allow true brainstorming. For example, once I was working with twins who would argue frequently about who got to play with the cat. By the time they got to the brainstorming phase, they were still a little competitive, but enjoyed the brainstorming nevertheless.

One said, "I could play with the cat in the morning, and you could play with her in the afternoon."

The other said, "I could play with her one day and you could play with her the next."

They suggested flipping a coin, drawing straws, pulling for the highest card, or guessing numbers. One of the parents suggested getting rid of the cat. One girl suggested getting another cat and having two.

The other parent finally said, "I think we ought to let the cat decide." The twins thought that was so funny, they forgot about their own competition and stopped worrying about who was "winning" the brainstorming step.

★ "Doing the same chore gets tiresome. We could make a plan to change. We could switch chores every week. Or every month. Or we could each have a chore for a while and when someone has a birthday, we could change chores and the one who has the birthday could choose his chore to keep until the next person has a birthday."

* "Notice how Ben had several ideas about fixing this problem. He asked his friends if they had ideas, too. Usually, a lot of ideas is better than just one idea."

* "Do you think it's a better idea to come up with lots of possible solutions to this problem or to pick one solution quickly and try to get other people to agree to it?"

* "It could be sort of fun to come up with lots of creative ideas for solving the problem without worrying too much yet about what's right and what's wrong with each one. Coming up with a lot of creative ideas is called brainstorming."

* "Let's see. What are some ways we could solve this?"

* "Step Eleven is to think of different ways to solve the problem. Don't worry about whether yours is the best idea or if somebody else thinks it's silly. Just say what you think. Then think of something else."

Step 12. **Pros and Cons.**

Chances are, at your child's age, she'll only come up with a few ideas when you brainstorm, so perhaps you'll be able to discuss them all. If not, choose the best. Be sure to give your child's ideas due respect. Try to find advantages and disadvantages for each of hers and each of yours so you can teach the process as well as solve the problem. The aim is to find out if each idea is likely to work and if you and your child will really do it.

* "The trouble with choosing your new chore on your birthday to keep until someone else has a birthday is that Jan's birthday is only two days before Ken's so Jan would only get her choice of chores for two days. Ken would have his for four months until Susie's birthday. That doesn't seem fair."

* "I noticed how each of the Huxtable [Cosby] kids got to say what they thought were the good and bad points of their mom's ideas. It was pretty easy after that to see what was best."

* "It seems to me we probably have enough ideas. Let's go back and choose several ideas that seem the best."

★ "I'll tell you which of these ideas I think will work and you tell which ones you think will work. And then we will talk about just these."

★ "Let's look at each idea and decide if we can do it and then if it will work."

★ "Step Twelve is to read the list and for each idea, you say what's good about it and what's bad about it. Would you be willing to do it? Will it work or not? Here's the list. Let's start."

Step 13. **Decide and Plan.**

You've talked about all the ideas, and now it's time to pick one. You are teaching your child the decision-making process. Try to guide him to a reasonable consensus with you while giving him room to express himself freely. Point out which ideas have more advantages and fewer disadvantages, explaining, if necessary, why you must give some points more weight than others. If you can't agree, in the end, it's appropriate for you to use your parental authority. Don't accept an idea that you know won't work.

Also, don't forget to build some reinforcement into your plan, for example, the point system described in Chapter Two.

★ "It's hard to guess the future, but we think we've picked the best plan we had to choose from, one that gives us both something we want and we can both stick to."

★ "Dick and I talked about all the ways we could take care of this problem. It was a good talk. But we never decided what we would do. So nobody will do anything and all the good ideas were wasted. One of us should have said, 'Okay, what do you want to do?' and then agreed to do it."

★ "Now that you've heard what we all think about each idea, which ideas still seem good?"

★ "Can we find a way to work around the disadvantages?"

★ "Let's think this through. What do we do first? How often do we do it?"

★ "What is your job? What is my [her] job?"

★ "How will we know if we did it right?"

★ "What do you think will make us follow through? Do you have any ideas about keeping track of how we're doing?"

★ "You tell which of these ideas you think is best and I'll tell you what I think and we'll choose one."

★ "We're still having a disagreement about which plan is best. So, since I'm your parent, I'll have to make that final decision from the ideas we have chosen as best. I'm thinking about your feelings and thoughts as I choose."

★ "Okay, you two guys can't seem to agree on one of these two better plans. Can you think of a plan that's fair and that is somewhere in the middle? Neither of you will get exactly what you want but both of you will get something you want. What's that going to be?"

★ "Step Thirteen is to choose the idea both of you think will work best. Then work out a plan to make sure it will work. Tell who will do what and how often and how we'll keep track."

Step 14. **Do It.**
You have to be committed to do your part just as your child must do his part, in order to make the plan work. If your child forgets and slips, it's okay to remind him of what you all agreed to do. It's okay if he reminds you, too, as long as he does it respectfully.

★ "I don't feel like doing the dishes now, but I promised Karen I wouldn't leave them sitting out. She promised me something I wanted, so I want to do my part. So here goes."

★ "I remember that Sue and Ben told each other they were going to take turns with chores and, by golly, that's what they're doing."

★ "Now remember that all that talk was just wasted if we don't do this the way we said. Are you all with me on this?"

★ "How's the plan going?"

★ "It's okay to remind each other if one of us forgets the plan."

★ "Step Fourteen is to really do the plan we chose. Every morning when we wake up, think about it, so we will remember it during the day."

Step 15. Review/Revise.

If a problem reappears, discuss with your child where the plan went awry. You now have the experience to adjust the plan and recommit to it. If, on the other hand, the plan is working well and the problem has been solved satisfactorily, be sure to let your child know you notice and appreciate his efforts.

★ "Actually, this misunderstanding about the concert made Jan and me make plans for several things we can do together. I think we're having more fun now than if the problem had never come up."

★ "Your mom has been good about doing her part of the plan, but you and I need to work harder. What could we do to make it easier to do what we promised?"

★ "What's your impression of how we've done?"

★ "What parts of the plan are working well? What do we need to change because it's not working?"

★ "Why do you think that part is not working?"

★ "Let's count these checks on the chart. Do we have more today than yesterday? Is this week better than last week?"

★ "Do you think it's working? What seems to be too hard to do?"

★ "If we gave you ten minutes instead of five minutes would you do it, or do you just not want to do it at all?"

★ "Step Fifteen is to go over the plan and see if we're doing it like we said we would and decide if it's working. If it's not, we need to talk it through again and make some changes."

PUTTING THE STEPS TOGETHER: A SAMPLE CONFLICT RESOLUTION FROM BEGINNING TO END

Morning Madness

If I had an easy answer to eliminating conflict over the morning routine, I'd be a candidate for the Nobel Peace Prize. Kids, like grown-ups, are often in an irritable, grumpy mood in the morning. There's conflict over how they are awakened, how soon they will get out of bed after they are awakened, and when they will show up ready for breakfast and school. There are complaints that they dawdle and they're slow getting ready for the bus. There's the morning litany of "You can't wear that," "Put on your coat," "You forgot to make your bed," and "How can you say you brushed your teeth when the toothbrush isn't even wet?"

> It's unlikely that you will solve "morning madness" in the morning. People aren't usually in the greatest mood to be reflective or to talk reasonably about what's going on. And besides, there's no time!

And there's the heartfelt "Awwww, Mom!"

The kid who doesn't want to get up displays a reactive, impulsive irritability, and the parent who is waking him up is in a frustrated hurry and sometimes even takes it personally. Anger begets anger.

Here's a step-by-step example, all the way through, of a family's resolution of morning madness:

Ken Matthews had taken over the job of waking Kenny, his nine-year-old, because Kenny was hard to get up and Ken was irritated by his wife Frances's sing-song and ineffectual "Ke-e-e-nn-e-e, time to get u-u-u-p."

On one particular morning, Ken had shaken Kenny's feet through the covers, telling him firmly to get up. When the boy didn't stir, Ken remembered the morning before, one of many when the car pool had honked and was left waiting while Kenny gathered his school stuff. This morning's slow response and the memory of yesterday's fiasco really made Ken mad. He ripped the covers off Kenny, grabbed the boy by the ankles, and pulled him off the bed yelling, "You're not going to be late again today!"

Kenny hit the floor mad. But when the car pool arrived, he was ready. Frances, however, was disturbed by this morning conflict, no matter how it ended, particularly when Ken admitted that he got so mad that he sometimes even felt like hitting Kenny. The couple decided to use the conflict resolution model to work on this issue. They quickly reviewed the fifteen steps in the kitchen before supper. They decided Ken would lead the process.

It's important to notice that the first five steps of the conflict resolution model are Thinking Steps. The parent who initiates the conflict resolution model by talking to the child is supposed to have already gone through The Thinking Steps, but the child has not.

In this case, Ken had easily identified his anger (Step One: Assess

Emotion). He accepted his feelings as reasonable (Step Two: Accept Anger, Behave Well) but realized that yelling was disturbing to the rest of the family and it had not solved the repeated problem. In fact, it had made it worse. Ken was also alarmed at his urges to pick Kenny up and throw him into the bathroom. He didn't think he would actually do that, but he saw that his behavior was unacceptable and he'd have to find a better way.

His anger, which typically started at about a 4, was now hitting a 7 even before he told Kenny to get up (Step Three: Gauge Intensity). His anger this evening, just thinking about the problem, was only about a 2, but he could picture if Kenny gave him any backtalk it would be a 7 in seconds.

He calmed himself by saying that after this talk, things would be better. He considered what he was angry about (Step Four: Who And What) and decided that part of it was the fact that Kenny embarrassed him by keeping the car pool waiting and also made them late leaving when it was their day to drive car pool. He was equally frustrated by his helplessness in controlling Kenny and angry that he didn't obey. A strong parent shouldn't have this problem, he thought.

Ken took the time to reflect and do Step Five: Perspective Check. He thought that, after all, this morning problem was a common problem and some of his friends had mentioned having the same issues with their children. He reminded himself that Kenny was usually a "good kid" and that he honestly didn't think Kenny was being all that deliberately defiant. But at the same time this issue was serious because it inconvenienced others. And it was not good for Kenny to start off his day in a rush or in a fight. He also empathized with Kenny: It was hard for him to get up himself in the morning, and were it not for his vigorous shower and a good dose of caffeine it would take him a while to "ungrump" himself.

Ken had gone through all of The Thinking Steps, and he was ready to talk. He realized that the initial talking for him was largely a repetition of The Thinking Steps only done as a teaching dialogue. He knew that he would be teaching Kenny what kinds of things were good to think and what ways would be good to talk at the same time. He sighed. That was a big order. But, as Frances had pointed out, he did this sort of thing as a manager at work all the time.

After dinner, Ken asked Kenny to stay at the table a while so they could talk:

Step 6. **Time and Place.**

KEN: How much homework do you have?

KENNY: Not much.

KEN: Then we have some time to talk before dessert, don't we?

KENNY: Yeah.

Step 8. **Express Appropriately.**

KEN: I hope you had a good day because I still remember how frustrated I was with you this morning. How many mornings this week did we get off to a bad start?

KENNY: All of them were bad. I hate mornings.

Step 6. **Time and Place.**

Step 7. **Avoid Coalitions.**

KEN: It would really be nice if we had a way to deal with it and I bet you'd like it better, too. This might be a good time to go in the den and talk about this. (to Kenny's older sister) Carolyn, Kenny and I are going to talk in here. Please take your homework into your room.

Step 8. **Express Appropriately.**

KEN: It would probably help to figure out what we're all thinking when we have these morning battles. How do you feel first thing in the morning?

KENNY: I'm sleepy and want you to leave me alone.

KEN: And how do you feel when we make you get up? What words would you use to say how you feel when we have these fights?

KENNY: Tired and sleepy. And then I get mad when you yell at me. Dad, why are we talking about this? I'll get up okay tomorrow, I promise.

Step 4. **Who and What?**

KEN: I know you want to do the right thing, Kenny. But like we said, this happens almost every day and if we get a good plan, maybe it will go a lot better for a long time. And besides I need to change some, too. And you know, you might have some good ideas I'd like to hear.

KENNY: (reluctantly) Okay.

KEN: You said you're mad at me because you don't want to get up? And because I get upset with you?

KENNY: Yeah, sorta both.

KEN: So who are you mad at? Are you really mad at me?

KENNY: Yes. Because you don't let me get up by myself.

Step 2. **Accept Anger, Behave Well.** (teaching)

KEN: It's okay not to want to get up and it's okay to be angry at the person who tells you to get up. But since it's not my fault you have to get up, it's not fair to yell at me. So it's okay to be angry but not to yell at me. Do you see the difference?

KENNY: But *you* sound so mean.

Step 9. **Listen Actively.**

KEN: So let me see if I have that. I'm mad because you don't get up in time and you're mad at me because of how I talk to you. Is that it?

KENNY: Yeah. I also said I'd like to get myself up.

Step 3. **Gauge Intensity.** (teaching)

KEN: If we think about being angry on a scale of 1 to 10 and 1 is not really angry at all and 10 is fighting mad and 5 is about medium, how mad are you about being waked in the morning?

KENNY: Oh, I don't know. It changes.

KEN: Well, I'm about a 2 if I go to wake you up and you just groan. But if you yell at me for doing it, I get to be a 7 real quick. How about you?

KENNY: Maybe a 5.

KEN: If a person is just a little mad, say a 1 or 2, I think it's okay to just forget it. If you're an 8, 9, or 10, you're too mad to talk and you need to calm down. But if you are somewhere from 3 to 7, you're mad enough you need to talk but not too mad to talk reasonably. Since we both get to a 5 or 7, that means it's important enough to try to solve. Right now I'm not mad at all. But are you getting a little mad now?

KENNY: A little. You're making me nervous.

Step 5. **Perspective Check.**
(teaching)

KEN: Let's see if I can talk so you stop being nervous. First, let me say I've thought about this. I realized I was, as I said, angry to about a 7. I've tried to look at this from your point of view. I realize being waked is aggravating and being pulled from bed would make me mad, too. Do you think you could try to see my point of view and think about how I feel when you yell at me for doing what I have to do?

KENNY: Okay, I'll try.

Step 8. **Express Appropriately.**

KEN: I'm mostly upset that you don't get up when I tell you it's time, you don't come downstairs ready to go on time, and we don't meet the car pool on time. Those are the facts of the matter.

Also, when you snap at me when I tell you it's time to get up, I feel like you are unfair to me. Because I'm trying to take care of you, to help you do well in school and not get off to a bad start.

Now when your mom was waking you up. . . .

Step 4. **Who and What?**

(Ken then realized he's also angry at Frances because she insisted he be the one to get Kenny up so he had to be the heavy in the morning. Then, she judged his parenting negatively. This issue with Frances got his adrenaline up now with Kenny. But he realized he should "file" these feelings about Frances and discuss them later with her.)

Step 9. **Listen Actively.**
(teaching)

KEN: I really do want you to understand this but I also want to hear the story from your side. Can you tell me in your own words what I said I am angry at?

KENNY: Yes. Me being late and me being angry.

Step 2. **Accept Anger, Behave Well.** (teaching)

KEN: You being late, that's right. But no, I'm not angry at you for being mad; I'm angry at you for yelling at me when I'm only doing what I have to do. Angry is okay, yelling is not. So, just to be sure you understand, what am I mad about in the mornings?

KENNY: Being late and yelling.

KEN: Yes. Now you tell me how you feel in the morning.

KENNY: It's so cold when you pull the covers off. It's so hard to get up. If you would just let me do it slowly. And don't yell at me.

KEN: So the problem with getting up is it's cold and it's hard to get up suddenly. Is that right?

KENNY: Yes. But you didn't say I got mad at you for yelling at me.

KEN: You're right. The other part of the problem is the way I get you up. You say I yell at you. Okay, I think we understand each other.

Step 10. **Admit Fault.** (teaching)

Also, I admit I try to get you up by making you uncomfortable, like jerking off the covers and pulling you. I also yell at you if you yell at me or if you are too slow. And that doesn't help, I see, because yelling doesn't work. It just makes you madder.

If I yell at you and that makes you even angrier then I clearly shouldn't yell. (Wait.)

See, that's what I do poorly. I yell. I'm telling you what I do wrong. Now it would be good for you to tell what you are doing wrong. That's one way of solving this problem: we both say what we do wrong.

KENNY: I just hate to get up.

Step 2. **Accept Feeling, Behave Well.** (teaching)

KEN: A lot of people hate to get up. That's a feeling. It's okay to have feelings. It's what you do that counts. Tell me what you do that's wrong.

Step 10. **Admit Fault.**

KENNY: Well, I'm slow. I make other people late to work and everything. But you make me get up sooner than I have to. . . .

KEN: Remember for this step, we're telling what we do wrong ourselves. You don't get to say "but" and blame someone else at this step.

Okay, you've said you are slow and you make people late. I'm glad you realize that.

Step 11. **Brainstorm Solutions.**

So what can we both do to solve this? What can I do about my yelling and what can you do about being slow and yelling at me?

KENNY: Try harder?

KEN: Let me tell you what the next step is. Brainstorming. That means thinking of many different ways that might solve this problem. Many different ways to make waking up, getting up, and getting ready easier. We both say all the ways we can think of, but nobody says whether it's a good idea or not right now. That's so we can just say things and not worry if they are silly.

Like maybe an alarm clock with a snooze button. The one you have goes off and you turn it off and then you go back to sleep. You could get a snooze and get up at the second alarm.

KENNY: At least get a nicer sounding alarm clock. The one I have ruins my day.

KEN: Okay, that's an idea. Let's write that down.

KENNY: Maybe a clock radio like you

and Mom have so I could get music.

KEN: You could go to bed earlier so you won't be so sleepy in the morning.

KENNY: But Dad! I already go to bed at nine. And I just lie there because I'm not sleepy.

KEN: Hold it. When we're brainstorming we just say the ideas, we don't criticize them.

KENNY: Okay, how about if you wake me up some nice way like rub my back or bring me a warm wet washcloth for my face.

KEN: (rolls his eyes) Oh, brother.

KENNY: Hey! You're not supposed to criticize my ideas.

KEN: Sorry. (chuckling) You're right.
Okay, the alarm is scheduled to go off at 6:50. How about if I come in at 7:00 and, if you're up and dressing, then you get pop-up waffles and syrup; if not, it's cereal as usual.

KENNY: And if I'm up and dressed by 7:05, you will say nothing about hurrying or getting ready.

KEN: Or you could just set the alarm earlier. Let's add that to the list.

KENNY: Since I'm cold in the morning we could get a little electric heater for me to dress by.

KEN: Or if you are seven minutes late getting up, you get up seven minutes earlier the next day.

Okay. I have jotted down these things about waking up and getting up. I have nine things.

Now let's brainstorm some ways to get you ready on time after you get up. Here's one:

You could have a schedule and certain things must be done by certain times. Like have your clothes on by 7:15. And be downstairs by 7:25. And you could have a reward for doing that.

KENNY: If I'm all ready to go and finished breakfast by 7:45 for a whole week, I get to go to a movie with a friend that weekend.

KEN: We could set a timer for your shower, make it five minutes and the bell would go off. That would help. And how about laying out your clothes the night before?

KENNY: That's enough.

KEN: We have a long list. What ones seem the most reasonable here?

Look at the list and we'll check the best ones.

Step 12. **Pros and Cons.**

KEN: Okay. We take each one and we give the pros and cons. Do you know what that means?

KENNY: Mmm. Sorta.

KEN: The good things are pros and the bad things are cons. Like this: the clock radio. The best thing is that you are in charge, and the music is nicer than a buzz. The worst thing might be if it were so pleasant you didn't get up. You don't have to get up to turn a radio off. Do you think the radio would work? If it doesn't we just wasted the money.

KENNY: What about the back rub? The good thing is that it feels good and I can stay in bed while you're doing it.

KEN: The bad thing is that it takes a few minutes from both of us and the whole idea is to be quicker. It's one more thing to do.

KENNY: What about the heater?

KEN: The heater? It sounds good, might make getting up and dressing easier. The con is the expense and you might not want to leave the heater to come down.

KENNY: The movie if I do a whole week is good.

KEN: Yeah, I like that. Is there any downside? Yes, Mom or I would have to take you and some weekends we might have to miss. Some weekends there's nothing good for kids at the theaters. Pretty soon you would have seen them all.

KENNY: How about if I'm up, you say nothing about hurrying?

KEN: Fine with me.

KENNY: Lay my clothes out the night before. That's okay. But I doubt it will help.

KEN: It's a good idea, but that's up to you to figure out how to be dressed on time. If you want to do it that way, fine. If not, fine. Whatever works.

KENNY: A shower timer? Okay.

KEN: Set alarm earlier?

KENNY: No. That just makes it worse.

KEN: Okay. Let's look at the pros and cons now. We seem to have agreed that most of this works, except getting up earlier and I'm cool on the back rub.

Step 13. **Decide and Plan.**

KENNY: Okay, let's do all the other things.

KEN: So, I can agree not to wake you up, not to mention hurrying to you, not to yell of course. You get yourself up with the alarm. We could combine all this stuff to make it easier — a clock radio, a timer for the shower, a schedule and if you aren't late once all week and we don't have to hurry you, we take you and a friend to the movies.

KENNY: No heater?

KEN: It seems a bit much.

KENNY: If I'm ready on time two weeks in a row, can I get the heater?

KEN: Oh, you are a tough negotiator here. Okay. It will be worth it. But if you are late once, it goes into the closet. And you have to get up earlier the next morn ing by however many minutes you are late.

KENNY: Yikes. I'm never going to remember all that.

KEN: We need to do a schedule. The car pool leaves at 7:45 so we'll start back from that. How much time do you need for

> breakfast? Ten minutes? And five minutes
> to brush your teeth afterwards . . .

Father and son worked out a rough chart and adjusted it the next day as they saw how it worked. They actually had to set the clock for ten minutes earlier than before to get in teethbrushing and bed-making as well as getting ready and eating breakfast. This was Step Fourteen: Do It.

After two weeks, the routine was better but Kenny had been late once each week so there had been no movie. It was time for Step Fifteen: Review/Revise. Ken and Kenny, this time with Kenny's mother, talked it over one night after dinner. They decided to take Kenny and a friend to the movies that weekend because being ready four days out of five was a dramatic improvement. Then they decided the movie reward would be once a month if Kenny had been late only three days in the month. That would mean another slight improvement and a longer wait for Kenny but it allowed for some slips. Kenny wanted to know what would happen to his heater.

"It's almost spring," Frances said. "By the time you go two perfect weeks, you'll be wanting your own fan."

And so it went. In about six weeks, the problem was solved most of the time.

"Let's go over this again the week before school begins in the fall, so we'll get off to a good start," Ken said, and they all agreed.

Finally, Ken remembered his anger at Frances, but it had faded. He thought how cool it was that he and Kenny had worked out the morning routine. He felt good about being an effective, involved parent. He was glad Frances had trusted him to work it out and hadn't coached from the sidelines.

In this way, solving a problem in one significant area reduces stress across the board. And when one person improves his behavior it helps some, but when both sides improve, the effect more than doubles. Resolutions build on each other just as conflicts do.

The resolution process may seem very time-consuming, but every time you use it you are assuring less time spent in fruitless arguments in weeks and years to come. Each time you go through the process successfully, the next resolution is easier. Finally the process is internalized and becomes a part of your reflexive thinking and behavior.

CHAPTER 6

Teaching Preteens to Resolve Conflict

Becky took her eleven-year-old daughter Trisha to Florida to visit longtime friends of the family. Their first evening together, Becky was filling their hostess in on recent family events. Suddenly the hostess began to laugh. Puzzled because she had said nothing funny, Becky asked, "What are you laughing at?"

"Every time you say something, Trisha contradicts you!"

Becky knew she had not felt quite relaxed yet, as if she were driving in heavy stop-and-go traffic, but she hadn't realized what the problem was. As soon as it was pointed out to her, Becky realized that Trisha had corrected every statement, disagreed with every opinion, and disputed every fact she'd uttered. This daughter who had been, since birth, generally eager to please had recently become tirelessly argumentative.

Trisha was behaving like many preteens. In addition to being more argumentative than before, children approaching adolescence generally are . . .

* eager to make their own decisions.

* less likely than before to defer to your opinion.

* more defensive when criticized or told what to do.

* enjoying a significantly more sophisticated sense of humor.

* more concerned about popularity, boy-girl issues, cliques, and various peer and social issues as opposed to academic and family concerns.

★ likely to be embarrassed when you're around their friends, not wanting other kids to feel they're too close or too attached to their parents.

★ likely to be more preoccupied with appearance and often feeling unattractive.

★ more emotionally up and down during puberty.

★ likely to behave sometimes like teens and sometimes like younger children. They may careen back and forth from being surprisingly grownup to amazingly "childish."

The general volatility of a preadolescent's emotional state, especially during puberty, and an increasing desire for autonomy make for more conflict with parents over a lot of traditional issues. Parents are often looking ahead to the scarier teen years and the looming problems with dating, drugs, alcohol, and driving. Parents might be trying to get in as many "lessons" as they can while they think the kids are more amenable.

STYLES OF TEACHING

Modeling

It's important to handle your own conflicts well so the preteen can see disagreement without loss of respect or inappropriate behavior and, hopefully, can observe successful resolutions.

When in conflict with your preteen, don't let him provoke you to your own worst style — whether that is being haughty, sarcastic, disrespectful, or out of control. Unwittingly, preteens may provoke you to behave badly so they can blame you for your bad behavior — and thereby excuse theirs. They often know how to hit your hot buttons. Anticipate this and resolve to keep your cool and return calmly to the real issues of the conflict.

Casual Comments

Teaching by making casual comments during a real conflict with your child is a good middle-ground strategy between modeling and direct instruction. As you go along, you can point out your own efforts, for example, to see his point of view, or to avoid coalitions. This kind of strategy keeps you straight and reminds you of what you should be doing as well as instructs your child. Such verbal reminders emphasize an awareness of process and the concepts of the steps.

You're probably no longer reading to your child or having a large role in choosing his reading material, but you are, the polls say, still watching a lot of TV together. As you watch a TV show or movie together, you'll notice examples of conflict where something was either handled well or not. Casually mention the way the characters dealt with conflict, just don't ruin the show by overdoing it.

Drawing Out by Asking Questions

Using a real or fictional conflict, try drawing your preteen out about what the participants in the conflict could have done differently. Ask questions, but try not to ask in a patronizing way that suggests you already know the best answer. Be genuinely curious and interested in how she sees what is happening. Take a cue from her responses, even confrontational remarks, to further draw her out.

Direct Teaching

When giving direct instruction, try not to "lecture." Give short comments with space in between instead of long discourses. A pause after you say something gives the child time to take your comments in. If you pause long enough, the child may say something in reply that clues you into his feelings and how well your lesson is going. (But don't expect him to say anything like "I see what you mean." Preteens often don't give you the satisfaction of letting you know they learned something from you — not until they are at least forty.) If you don't pause, you're likely to overdo the lesson before you even know if your child is receptive.

Try concentrating on one of the most critical steps of the conflict resolution model or the one the preteen does least well because a full-scale teaching or critique session may not go over well during a real problem or during a good show.

HOW TO GET STARTED

Getting the preadolescent to buy into learning to resolve conflict is often a challenge. Here are some examples of things you can say to start the process:

★ "I personally feel we have way too many arguments about this issue. Do you agree?"

★ "I wish we didn't fight or argue about these things so much. Even though I know that it's normal in many ways, it still puts us all in bad moods and gets in the way of our relaxing around each other."

★ "When we fight this way, it often doesn't accomplish anything. I'd like to try to work on doing a better job of dealing with these things that make us mad at each other. Hopefully, you agree."

★ "Would you like to see us get along better as a family? To do that, we would all have to agree that we each had to make some changes and work on it."

★ "I don't think it's so unusual that we argue about homework (bedtime, grades, money, clothes, friends). Lots of families do. What bothers me is that our arguments don't seem to go anywhere. They don't help us get anything settled so we end up arguing about the same stuff over and over."

★ "I know you might think it seems a little hokey to sit down and have a serious talk about this, but if we could talk this thing through reasonably and come up with some plan, I am sure we would be glad that we did it. Especially if we followed through with what we came up with."

★ "I've found a book that outlines a pretty good way to stop arguing and start solving. I think this method would work for us if we tried hard to really do it."

It's much more likely at this age that your child will resist these overtures of yours. Instead of deferring to your suggestions, you may get a response something like these:

★ "What does a guy who is writing a book know about us anyhow?"

★ "Yeah, right. This is just another way to get me to do what you want."

★ "Are you kidding? We never get anywhere when we talk."

★ "You won't ever listen to me so it's useless."

★ "I hate these kinds of talks; they just make me madder."

★ "Why don't we just forget it?"

★ "Have you been reading that psychology stuff again?"

When kids say these types of things, it's a good opportunity to draw them out further by asking them what they mean, asking them to elaborate, asking them to give examples, asking them if there's anything else about talking things out that bothers them. In other words, take the resistant remarks at face value. Don't retort or snap back, but encourage your youngster to talk his resistance out. Being allowed to do so sometimes brings kids around.

Next you might want to accept and agree that things have not always gone so well in the past and that you know that part of the reason there hasn't been a settlement or resolution is due to parents, not just kids. Find something they say that you might agree with, then add:

* ★ "This is really important for how we get along," or

* ★ "This is something that will be good for all of us," or

* ★ "This is something that as parents we have a right to say and to expect you to work on."

One of the elements of dealing with resistance is being sensitive to it and aware of when it is developing. Rather than letting resistance provoke you into getting defensive yourself, follow the sequence of staying calm and drawing them out with genuine curiosity. If your child makes valid points, go ahead and admit the validity, address the points, and deal with them. If the child's resistance is pure avoidance of the issues, then point out the resistance and discuss resistance or defensiveness as a direct issue in a straightforward manner, making that one of the main problems that gets in the way of resolving many others. (See Reflexive Defensiveness in Chapter Three.)

When you get resistance to resolving a conflict or learning how to resolve a conflict, you might offer the child a little time to think the issue over. But be clear that you will be discussing the issue later. Suggest a reasonable time and stick to it.

HOW TO TEACH THE STEPS

Here are some language samples — things to say to teach each step of the conflict resolution model. Some of them are natural-sounding and represent modeling and casual teaching; some of them are formal teaching for when your preteen has clearly agreed to learn and use this method.

PART ONE: THE THINKING STEPS

What goes on in your preteen's head? A lot of childish stuff and surprisingly adult ideas all mixed up. Which one will pop up at any given time is anyone's guess. But they are now almost consciously replacing childish ideas with more mature ones. Take advantage of this impressionable age to offer a variety of mature ways to think about anger and conflict that can make a positive difference in their relationships for a lifetime.

Step 1. **Assess Emotions.**

Preadolescents often don't want to do this touchy-feely stuff, especially boys, and "we need to talk about our feelings" may sound like a joke about therapy. When many kids of this age are anxious, they don't want to say they're anxious, so they are angry. They don't want to admit, even to themselves, that their feelings are hurt. They want to seem more mature than that. So you have to lead them to identifying their feelings "just between you and me" and soon "just in your head."

★ "It seems like something's wrong. I'd guess you are annoyed."

★ "I sometimes see that when people are angry — or when I am angry — it's not just anger all by itself. A lot of times there are other emotions going along with it. It helps to know what those are."

★ "Sometimes people's feelings are hurt but they don't act hurt; they act angry as a way of protecting themselves."

★ "The goal of the first step is to make you be more careful to understand exactly what you feel so you will know what to say."

★ "The more you can pin down how you feel, the easier it is to solve the problem."

For the preteen who seems too passive, lets herself be taken advantage of, or who smolders or gets depressed:

★ "Maybe being angry scares you and that is part of the reason you hate to have conflicts."

★ "Sometimes being angry might make you feel immediately guilty because you think being angry is bad. Sometimes it's natural to be angry and it's okay to say so."

Step 2. **Accept Anger, Behave Well.**

Telling someone to be "nice" with their anger might not sit well with some preteens; it might not seem strong enough. So don't say, it's nice or it's polite, say it's more mature to handle anger well. "Losing it" is immature; handling anger better is more brainy. You want to "outmature" rather than outpower the other person. The most immature way to solve a problem is to intimidate.

* "When you are angry it is easy to have a first reflex of wanting to get back at somebody. But you can train yourself to think quickly — right after you become angry — that there is nothing wrong with feeling angry but you must not lash out at anyone. Then you have time to think of better ways to deal with the problem."

* "We are concerned about your losing control and you should be, too. You can choose how you handle anger more than you think you can."

* "Learning how to handle anger so that it leads to something good is one of the most important things you can learn."

* "People vary a lot in how intensely or suddenly they feel anger. Learning to control how you behave in anger is one of the main keys to a happy life."

* "It's good to think to yourself that it's okay to be angry, but it's how you behave that really counts."

To the preteen who is passive or doesn't stick up for himself:

* "When someone has tricked you or been unfair to you, it's natural to be angry, and it's good to speak up, especially if you do it in a good way."

CURTIS reprinted with special permission of King Features Syndicate

Step 3. **Gauge Intensity.**

Puberty is a time when kids often exaggerate their feelings. They may even say, "I want to kill her." At the same time, there's more cognitive ability, so you can teach them to better use their logic to manage emotion. Using a number scale helps your child delay impulsivity and react better to anger.

* "On a scale of 1 to 10, just how angry would you say you are?"

* "When you're angry it's important to know just how angry you are because that helps you make a better decision about how to handle it."

* "If you are just a little bit angry, say a 1 or a 2 on a scale of 1 to 10, then it's okay to just forget about it and let it go by. Because people who bring up every little thing often create more conflicts than they settle. I know you hate it when we nag about every little thing."

* "The best time to talk about a problem that bugs you is when you've been a 3 or more on the scale but are now below a 7. You're concerned enough to settle it, but not so mad you'll say or do something to make it worse."

* "If you are really high on the anger scale, like an 8, 9, or 10, then you're likely to do things that mess up the chance of the conflict getting settled. We think it's better for you to say that you are too mad to talk right then. . . . Then it's okay to leave and cool down and come back later and talk it out."

* "Calm down to the point where you can communicate well — that would be less than 8 on the scale — lower would be even better."

* "Figuring out how angry you are can help you talk to the other person about the importance of your feelings. Sometimes other people don't know how much something matters to you. I know I sometimes don't know how much something matters to you."

Step 4. **Who and What?**

Help your preteen focus on the person he's actually angry at, the one who is in fact responsible for the situation. Also, encourage the child to identify the specific complaint and the larger issue or pattern that it may represent. Common issues underlying many different conflicts at this age include:

* being interrupted while busy.

* people not respecting their time, their stuff, or their opinion.

* an adult committing their time without asking if they are busy or making them do something right now that doesn't have to be done right now.

* being criticized or demeaned.

* being embarrassed in front of their friends.

* being punished "unfairly" or punished at all — they think being punished is being treated "like a child."

* interference with their relationships with peers (e.g., "You can't have so and so over because he's not the kind of person I want you associating with.")

* your being angry at them and yelling, grabbing, or doing anything physical to them.

* being talked down to.

WHO?

Here are some things to say to help your preteen focus on the appropriate person with whom to resolve a problem:

* "It's important to know exactly who it is that is causing you to be angry."

* "Are you mad at me personally or at the situation?"

* "Sometimes you might be mad at both of us as parents or sometimes it might be just one of us."

* "It could also be that you are angry about something that happened with someone else."

* "Sometimes kids are upset about something at school, and they come home and take it out on their parents because it's safer to show anger with your parents. After all, we are used to seeing it."

WHAT?

* "It's very important to figure out exactly what it is that made you angry. I know that's not always easy."

★ "Sometimes somebody or something outside you makes you angry. But sometimes it's the thought you had when something outside happened that really made you angry. What was the first thing you thought of after . . . ?"

★ "Sometimes somebody does something that makes you think, 'This always happens to me.' Or, 'You always do that.' You're recognizing a pattern. You're more mad about the pattern than about that one little thing that happened. It's important to recognize patterns. The neat thing is, if you can resolve the issue behind a pattern, then you can fix it for the future and not just for then."

★ "If you are talking to the right person about the right problem, you have a good chance of settling it."

Step 5. **Perspective Check.**

At this age, the preteen may have a knee-jerk thought, a first response that comes from childish thinking, such as, "She won't let me do anything by myself," "He thinks he's better than me," or "Just leave me alone." Preteens, if anything, are in a time of change; such automatic response thoughts are no longer appropriate, if they ever were. Similarly, you, the parent, may have thoughts that are no longer valid like, "He doesn't know how to do that. He'll get in trouble," or "Because I told you so. . . ." Both parent and preteen need to look at how the child has grown up and ask, "Is it really so bad?" or "Maybe it's time I looked at things in a different way." Perspective check means not only seeing things in a different light but seeing things through another person's eyes, a learned skill that takes experience and practice. Here are some points you can gently make:

★ "A lot of times when you're angry you can overreact and have a hard time seeing what other people see about that situation."

★ "Sometimes you can be so caught up in your own thoughts and feelings that it is hard to step back and look at the situation some other way."

★ "If you can figure out what triggered you to be angry and stop and say, 'Wait, is there another way to look at this,' you might find other accurate ways to see it that will help you stay cool enough to deal with it better."

★ "It's good to step into the other person's shoes and wonder what they're thinking and feeling about the situation."

★ "Try to understand why another person did something. Try to think of good reasons as well as bad reasons."

★ "Talk to one of your friends about this. Don't tell them how mad you are; tell them just the facts of the problem. Then ask, 'How would you see this and how would you feel?' or 'How would you take that?' Often, the friend will interpret the situation in a way that never occurred to you. Try it."

CURTIS/ by Ray Billingsley

CURTIS reprinted with special permission of King Features Syndicate

If your child is overly passive, is fearful of displeasing people, or doesn't stand up for himself:

★ "At times, when you're angry, you may underreact because you're afraid bringing a conflict up will cause a bigger problem. It's okay to be pretty angry at this. This would upset anybody."

★ "If I were in your shoes, I'd be angrier than you seem, and I'd want to push this to a resolution."

★ "I'll bet you were upset when that person behind you in the line got waited on before you did. It's okay to say, 'Excuse me, I think I was next in line.'"

PART TWO: THE TALK/LISTEN STEPS

Ever notice how your preteen's conversation is more detailed and open with peers or with their favorite aunt than it is with you? What is it that the peers and the aunt have that you don't have? They don't have as much at stake as you do, so your preteen's thoughts, even recitation of scrapes they've been in, childish opinions, and less-than-noble motivations don't panic or offend them. They listen with less judgment than you might. You can't reproduce that nonchalance because you care so much, but you can try to concentrate on process and downplay content when teaching conflict resolution. Go through the motions of the steps with them and feel good if the process has been better, not judging the content too much. When you get the hang of greater objectivity and are generally more accepting, you'll not seem so threatening to the preteen, who in turn may feel freer to open up. Then you can master resolving content, too.

Step 6. **Time and Place.**

"Do we have to?" your child may reply when you say he needs to sit down and talk about a conflict.

Your answer should be: "Yes. Otherwise we'll just argue like this over and over." Let him know it's not a matter of "if" you talk constructively but "when and where." Try to get the child to prioritize an issue and agree to spend time on it and, at least some of the time, let him choose the time and place.

If an issue comes up incidentally and the child seems receptive, use that opportunity to teach, but when you have him and then lose him, it's probably good to let it go. Don't provoke greater defensiveness by overdoing it.

★ "Let's find a good time and place to talk about this conflict. We will probably need X amount of time in my opinion. What do you think?"

★ "It is good that we not be interrupted and that we not have extra people there. When would that be?"

★ "Let's agree on this time and place and we'll both be there."

★ "When you are trying to settle your argument with Susan about who to invite to the party, try to do it after school instead of between classes or at lunch when everyone's around."

Step 7. **Avoid Coalitions.**

"You keep out of this!" is a line frequently spoken, frequently yelled, by a parent or teacher at a child who butts into a "discussion" between her and another child.

"I was only trying to help," the interloper whimpers, while the kid on the hot seat looks on in dismay or triumph depending on whether he thinks the one who was reprimanded was an ally bearing excuses on his behalf or an enemy heaping on another accusation to the problem.

Separating the people whose business it is from those who are not involved is often the appropriate prerogative of a parent or teacher. "You keep out of this!" should be an unwritten family rule rather than a battle cry. Here are better ways to set this rule from the beginning:

* ★ "I notice when we get into arguments that it's easy for us to want somebody else to take our side. That's natural, but we need to settle problems among just those people whose business it is."

* ★ "I notice that other people seem to be ganging up on me [you, her] and it would work better if we tried not to bring in people to agree with us because that usually just makes everybody involved more stubborn and angry."

* ★ "And what did she say to you when you told her you were unhappy about her behavior? . . . Oh. You're saying you didn't tell her? Well, go back and tell her in a clear and calm way and see what she says. Maybe you'll be able to work it out."

A preteen often thinks that parental coaching is demeaning and definitely not cool. So don't try to teach him when he has a friend present or the child may try to prove to his friend that he is not much influenced by you. That is another form of "coalitioning" (to coin a verb).

When you and your child have a private dispute, settle it between you. However, sometimes your business with your child is also the business of the other parent. In these cases the two of you should act as a unit, resolving conflict with your child together. Explain this to your child when the situation calls for it:

* ★ "Of course, Mom and I need to be a good team and agree on most things to be good, consistent parents."

Step 8. **Express Appropriately.**

Preteens generally are maturing toward a greater desire for autonomy and privacy so "expressing" personal thoughts to others, especially parents, in a straightforward manner may be difficult. They may not want to talk about their feelings. That's fine. Teach them to state the problem briefly and in resolvable terms with a minimum of "feeling" statements. Then whomever they say they are angry at, whether it's you or someone else, be adult enough to take it and don't punish them for expressing themselves as long as they do it appropriately.

★ "When we tell each other that we are angry about something, let's try not to raise our voices or yell. When we yell, we get even more angry at being yelled at than we were about the original problem."

★ "Let's try not to be too wimpy about it. It probably should take a paragraph or two being very clear about what is the real thing, the main thing, we are angry about."

★ "Try to stick to the issue and not blame too much or criticize too much . . . just say what it is you yourself are feeling."

★ "Here's an example of what you could say to me, 'I feel mad at you because you promised you would take me to the mall, then you got busy and said you didn't have the time. I think you do that promising and not following through with your promise a lot.' Or 'I get angry with you at times like this because I don't think you are willing to ever change your mind, even if I am making a good point.'"

Step 9. **Listen Actively.**

When your children were little and you gave them directions, you probably said to them, "Now tell me what I said." You were checking on their attention, comprehension, and memory. So the technique is familiar to them, only now they get to do it back to you. Step Nine involves telling, listening, and telling back, and both sides get a turn.

Every preteen knows someone among her peers who is a "good listener." People seek this person out to talk about their problems. A good listener doesn't just listen but accepts what you say, doesn't try to solve the problem, but asks clarifying questions and encourages you to go on. Point out to your child that in her peer group people value good listeners. Encourage her to be one.

★ "When people are telling us what they are angry about, they want to be carefully listened to. One of the ways that you prove you have listened is to say the same thing back to them, but in your own words. This way they can understand that you were paying attention and that you understood what they said."

★ Try to model active listening and then teach it by saying, "Some ideas of how to start are:
'Well, let's see if I got that right. . . . '
'To summarize, you said. . . . '
'I want to show you that I was being a good listener. You said. . . . '
'Can I make sure that I understood that correctly? You said. . . . '
'What I think you just said is. . . . '
I know this sounds a little too much like robots talking but that doesn't mean you're not sincere. It really works and then after a while you stop sounding like a robot."

Step 10. **Admit Fault.**
Preteens often have a hard time acknowledging their part in a conflict. If they do admit it, they want to add "but. . . ." An admission of fault with no "but" can change the mood of the other person from anger or skepticism to openness and trust in an instant. It doesn't make the "admitter" lose power but lets him gain cooperation. Show the preteen that it may help him get more of what he wants rather than less. It's a way to "outmature" the other person instead of overpower him.

★ "It really helps if you ask yourself what you're doing wrong and then, when you figure it out, have the maturity to tell the other person."

★ "It's sort of like apologizing but mainly just letting the other person know that you know it's not all their fault — you have your part, too."

★ "Every argument has two sides, and usually both people are doing a little something annoying or unfair. It's good to figure out what you are doing wrong and admit to it."

★ "You might start by saying . . .

  'I know I have some faults in all this and they are. . . . '

  'I know I am not perfect. I have to admit I. . . . '

  'Don't get me wrong, I know I have said some things that it's natural for
      you to get mad at. For example, it wasn't so good when I said. . . . '

  'I honestly don't think it is mostly my fault or even mainly my fault but
      here are the faults I think I do have. . . . '

  'I can see I contributed to this problem in this way. . . . '

  'I wish I hadn't done [said] . . . because that was not quite fair.'"

PART THREE: THE SOLVING STEPS

It's respectful of preteens' increasing autonomy to allow them to participate in The Solving Steps. In this strategy, you don't lose your parental
authority because you never go along with a proposal that you honestly
don't agree with just to please your child. You don't lose your enforcement
role since a lot of plans have reasonable consequences built in and you, the
parents, are the ones who judge success. At the same time, you teach your
child to problem solve, plan, and follow through on commitments.

Step 11. **Brainstorm Solutions.**
Now's the fun part. Brainstorming can be a game, and your preteen may
take to it readily. If not, the field is open to you. Propose some good ideas
you'd like to see put into action, some flawed ones your kid might be
inspired to improve on, and even some far-out ones. You're trying to solve
a problem here, and you're also trying to teach the creative process of getting multiple options out on the table.

★ "Now it's time to let our minds run free and think of anything we can
  to solve this problem."

★ "It's okay to be a little silly or to come up with ideas that don't sound
  like they were good ones to begin with."

★ "Let's think of as many possible solutions as we can and not worry about
  whose idea it is."

★ "When one of us says something you think is a bad idea; don't say anything now. Don't argue, just think of good ideas yourself."

Step 12. **Pros and Cons.**

If your preteen is like a lot of kids her age, she'll love finding something wrong with your ideas! The lesson here may be to be objective, to determine what is good about each idea, no matter whose it is, and what is impractical or falls short of the goal. This kind of critical thinking will serve her well in many areas of life.

★ "We really ought to pick the solution that is going to come closest to working. I think the best way to figure that out is to think of the good and bad parts of those suggestions and ideas."

★ "Okay, here's the first idea. Let's first say what's good about it."

★ "What are the bad things about that idea? Are the disadvantages something we can fix?"

★ "Will this idea really have a good chance of working or not? If not, why not?"

Step 13. **Decide and Plan.**

At this point, you have to agree on the basic idea and work out a detailed plan to carry it through. It should include criteria to judge if it is going well and ideas for reinforcement, such as the point system described in Chapter Two, if they seem necessary.

Here are sample ways to talk about choosing one of the brainstormed options and developing a plan to implement it:

★ "When it comes to deciding which one, I hope we can all agree."

★ "The best idea may not be a perfect one, but one we can all accept and follow through on."

★ "Let's look over our pros and cons for the ideas most likely to work. Which idea has the most important advantages?"

★ "Then how can we overcome the disadvantages and make this idea work?"

★ "If we don't agree on one solution for some reason, then, as parents, we have to make the final decision."

★ "After we decide what we're going to do, it's a good idea to come up with a plan to make sure we do it."

★ "Who is going to do what part of this plan?"

★ "How will we keep track of our success?"

★ "Will we have a reinforcement for doing well? Not doing well?"

★ "Wouldn't it be good to write this down? Could we have a chart on the refrigerator? Okay, how about inside the upstairs closet door?"

★ "And what time limit are we going to give ourselves to do all those things?"

★ "If for some reason our plan is not working, it is smart to come back and talk about it again and have maybe some extra ideas that we didn't have before on what will and will not work. So let's set a review date as part of our plan."

Step 14. **Do It.**

This step is where many parents begin to solve a problem — by telling the child to "do it." Now you're resolving problems in a different way. You've got your child's input into a plan, and she's agreed to try to implement it. You can appeal to her pride and maturity in following through on the commitment.

★ "It's easy to make a plan and then forget about it in a couple of days. It's especially important to keep reminding ourselves about our part and take pride in getting it done."

★ "Once we spend all this time thinking about this and talking about this, we sure better do it or else we're all going to get frustrated."

★ "It's okay for you to remind me of what we agreed to do. Would you mind if I reminded you?"

Step 15. **Review/Revise.**

If the plan makes a significant improvement in the conflict, it's important to acknowledge the power of the whole conflict resolution process and celebrate its success in order to reinforce its use. If the plan has not made a significant improvement in the conflict and your child's feelings, he needs to know why. Was it his lack of commitment, the other person's, or an impractical part of the plan? He shouldn't shrug his shoulders and let it go. Not only does solving the current conflict depend on reviewing and revising the plan, but your child's confidence and continued use of the conflict resolution model depend on it.

★ "So generally, how do you think this plan has worked out?"

★ "These are the improvements I have seen. . . ."

★ "Here's what I think didn't work very well. . . ."

★ "Why didn't we see progress here? What went wrong?"

★ "What parts of the plan worked? What didn't?"

★ "What could we do to make it work better? Let's revise our plan and write it in."

PUTTING THE STEPS TOGETHER: A SAMPLE CONFLICT RESOLUTION FROM BEGINNING TO END
Homework Hell

Eric had been an average, relatively easygoing child until he turned twelve and "got a mind of his own." He became increasingly resistant to his parents' advice, guidance, and, especially, criticism. His parents, Patricia and Ed, realized their approach of reminders, insistence, and punishment wasn't working. Eric was becoming disrespectful and they were nagging all the time without success. They were good candidates for the conflict resolution model. They tried it a few times on minor, easy-to-solve disagreements to gain experience with the model before they used it to tackle the big problem, "Homework Hell."

Eric frequently didn't do his homework. He procrastinated, dawdled, and finally turned his work in late. Teachers had noted this problem on his report cards. Patricia and Ed kept track of Eric's major assignments and tried to get him to start work on time and keep at it till he was finished. He got very angry about their urging and, in fact, seemed to dawdle worse after they tried to get him going. He was vague or even lied about what was due and when. Sometimes he pouted and slammed doors, but most of the time he just didn't do his homework. The more they tried to change his behavior the worse it got.

"Homework Hell" is one of the most common conflicts involving parents and preadolescent children. Fortunately, it is often improved through good conflict resolution. The following scenes show how Eric's family used the conflict resolution steps to solve the problem.

Eric's family did not always go exactly in step-by-step order. Instead, they were familiar enough with the steps to flow into a natural adaptation of the model, formally or informally covering all the steps. As noted before, some of The Thinking Steps, which are usually meant to be done internally before talking, may initially have to be taught in discussion. So The Thinking Steps and The Talking Steps blur. Patricia, who had studied the method the most thoroughly, talked through the steps that she hoped all of them would some day do spontaneously as thinking steps.

In the following conflict resolution, the steps are identified on the left as they occur in the dialogue on the right. Here's how it went:

Eric flips the TV channel and flops on the sofa. From the next room he hears:

PATRICIA: E-E-Eric.

ERIC: (angrily): What?!

PATRICIA: Have you done your homework?

Silence, except sound of fist in pillow.

PATRICIA: Your father said you couldn't watch TV until you have done your homework. Have you done your homework?

ERIC: I'm gonna do it.

ED: Do your homework first.

ERIC: But if I do it now, I'll miss my favorite show. I can do my homework later.

ED: But you never do. You say that, but you never do. Get up to your room NOW.

ERIC stomps to his room, slamming his door behind him. After a long silence, they hear bouncing over and over as if Eric is throwing a ball against the wall repetitively.

PATRICIA: E-E-Eric, it doesn't sound as if you are doing your homework.

Noise stops. Long silence. A half hour later his father goes to Eric's door, opens it without knocking, and finds Eric on his bed reading *Return From Planet X*.

ED: You're not even doing your homework! By God, if you don't. . . . (He grabs the book away.)

Eric ducks under his father's arm and runs into the laundry room screaming. His father is in hot pursuit. Eric slams the door shut to keep his father out.

ED: You come out of there. You can't just run off. We've got to settle this.

ERIC: I'm a 10, can't you see? 10, 10, 10!

Step 3. **Gauge Intensity.**

ED: Well, I'm a 10, too, and being a 10 doesn't give you a right to behave like this.

PATRICIA: He's right, Ed. You're both too angry. Let's have a talk tomorrow after school. We'll come up with a better way to handle this.

Ed backs off.

Step 6. **Time and Place.**

PATRICIA: (through door to Eric): We'll talk about it tomorrow. (To Ed) All three of us can talk tomorrow?

ED: Yeah.

The next day after school, Eric is shooting baskets in the yard. Patricia sees him and immediately wants to call to him about his homework. But she doesn't. She waits until time for Ed to come home about six o'clock. Then immediately she calls for Eric.

PATRICIA: E-E-Eric!

Eric tries to get in five more three-pointers to see his average out of twenty.

PATRICIA: E-E-Eric!

Eric dribbles into the kitchen, shaking the whole house.

PATRICIA: We agreed to talk about this homework situation today. Is this a good time?

ED: (Sighs.) Could you let me change my clothes first and unwind a little?

PATRICIA: Okay. If you are going to need some time first, then let's get supper out of the way. Then we'll talk. Is that okay with you, Eric?

ERIC: Hey, you are the ones who want me to do my homework right after supper.

Patricia acknowledges Eric's joke with a smile.

After supper, Eric and Ed sit down to watch a ball game on TV.

PATRICIA: Hey, guys, we all know we should talk about the homework problem. Didn't we all agree this is a reasonable time?

ED: Okay. It's as good a time as any. Eric?

Eric grumbles but he turns off the TV and tosses the remote control onto the sofa as a sign of acquiescence.

Step 2. **Accept Anger, Behave Well.**

PATRICIA: A lot of families have conflict over homework. It's normal to feel angry about it. But we're having way too many arguments over it and we're not getting anywhere. Please let's try to solve the problem. Let's really try to keep our talk constructive and figure something out for everyone's sake.

ED: Okay. Honey, why don't you go first?

Step 1. **Assess Emotions &**
Step 8. **Express Appropriately.**

PATRICIA: (to Eric) I feel on edge as soon as you get home from school because I'm worried about your homework and what I should say and do. It's taking up too much of my time and draining my energy. Ed?

ED: (to Eric) I'm just angry because you won't do what you're told. I'm frustrated because it happens over and over.

PATRICIA: Eric, how do you honestly feel about all this?

ERIC: Honestly? I really do feel like you're on my case all the time. I'll get my homework done eventually. My grades aren't that bad anyhow.

Step 1. **Assess Emotions.**
(teaching)

PATRICIA: Okay. But can you give some words to your feelings when we talk about your homework?

ERIC: I just get upset.

PATRICIA: Upset can mean a lot of

different feelings. Are you feeling hurt?
Or are you mainly angry?

ERIC: Yeah.

PATRICIA: Which?

ERIC: Angry.

Step 4. **Who and What?**   PATRICIA: When do you feel angry:
(teaching)   when we first speak to you about
                                      homework or when we punish you or yell
                                      at you later? Or are you just mad you have
                                      to do homework at all?

Step 4. **Who and What?**   ERIC: It's not the homework. I'm gonna
                                      do the homework. It's you. I'm getting
                                      mad right now because you're bugging me
                                      with questions.

                                      PATRICIA: Does any particular thing we
                                      say about homework make you angry?

                                      ERIC: It used to be maybe just when you
                                      yell, but now anything you say makes me
                                      mad. Even right now.

Step 3. **Gauge Intensity.**   PATRICIA: How angry are you right
                                      now?

                                      ERIC: A 5, heading up.

Step 2. **Accept Anger,**   PATRICIA: That's fine. It's normal to be
Behave Well.   mad at your parents from time to time.
                                      What triggers the angry feeling? Is there
Step 4. **Who and What?**   one word that gets to you? Do you start
(teaching)   out feeling okay and then some one thing
                                      makes you feel mad?

Step 4. **Who and What?**   ERIC: I get mad right from the beginning
                                      — when I hear you saying, "E-E-Eric," I
                                      get mad.

PATRICIA: But that is just your name.

Step 8. Express Appropriately.   ERIC: It's the way you say it. I can't stand your voice. Doesn't her voice annoy you, Dad?

Step 7. Avoid Coalitions. *(teaching)*   ED: Whoa! You're trying to get me to criticize Mom.

ERIC: Whoops.

Step 9. Listen Actively.   PATRICIA: So it's my tone of voice?

ERIC: Yeah. Also, you always say: 'You know your father said. . . . '

PATRICIA: Go on.

Step 8. Express Appropriately.   ERIC: You say, 'You know your father said to do your homework before you can watch TV' or 'You know your father said . . . whatever.' It's like you are his messenger or something.

Patricia thinks this over. Eric is right. She hadn't known that this was an annoyance before.

Step 4. Who and What?   ERIC: I feel mostly mad . . . (hesitates) at you, Dad.

Step 8. Express Appropriately.   ED: I'm glad you're telling me calmly. What are you mad about?

ERIC: You always boss me. And it doesn't matter what I do, you never seem to like it anyway.

Step 9. Listen Actively.   ED: Okay. You're mad at me because you think I boss you around all the time and you think I'm never satisfied with what you do.

PATRICIA: And you are mad at me because I bring you messages from him and you are sensitized to my voice calling you. Is that it?

ERIC: Yeah. There's more, but that's mainly it.

Eric is noticeably pleased that his concerns have been acknowledged and understood.

ED: Is there anything else on the subject of the homework itself?

Step 8. **Express Appropriately.** ERIC: Yeah, you don't trust me to get it done by myself.

Ed wants badly to say, "The record shows you can't be trusted. The teachers say you don't do your homework on time." But he holds his tongue. Instead he says:

ED: Well, let's resolve it. Let's see. What's first? Brainstorming?

PATRICIA: No. We forgot the last talk/ listen step: Admit Fault.

Step 5. **Perspective Check.** They are silent for a minute gathering their thoughts and courage. The adults know they have to go first because it's very difficult. Finally . . .

Step 10. **Admit Fault.** ED: I know that if my boss came into my office to see if I was doing my work, I would feel irritated, too. . . . I admit I overreact and I know yelling doesn't help and escalates the conflict.

Ed looks at Patricia to show her it is her turn.

PATRICIA: I didn't know my voice was so irritating. I also didn't realize that I often say, "Dad says." I guess it's a way of making him responsible when I didn't want you to be mad at me.

Patricia and Ed look at each other, acknowledging that this admission is a step toward intimacy between them. Then they look at Eric, but he says nothing, so Ed prompts him:

Step 10. **Admit Fault.**
(teaching)

ED: Do you think there's a little overreacting on your part, too?

Step 10. **Admit Fault.**

ERIC: I don't know. Anyway, I do put things off; I'm not as organized as I should be. I also know that I am defensive about this thing. I guess I overreact to your telling me to do my homework. I guess

Step 5. **Perspective Check.**

you don't know what to do because, if you say something, I get mad, and, if you don't say anything, I don't do my homework.

Patricia and Ed are both amazed that Eric does understand their position after all. Heartened by this discovery, they admit further:

PATRICIA: Our intentions are good but our technique is bad.

Step 10. **Admit Fault.**

ED: I guess I haven't really worked on staying calm. I'll try to do better. So what can we do to solve it?

Patricia gets out a pad of paper to write down their ideas. Many families do not want to formalize brainstorming by writing down the ideas, which may be few and simple. But occasionally writing them down, especially in the first attempts at using the model, may help keep the process clearer.

PATRICIA: Okay. Now that we know what the issues are, let's brainstorm solutions. Here, I'll write them down. Eric, do you have any ideas?

ERIC: You could leave my homework to me and let me sink or swim. If I don't do it and get a bad grade, that's my problem.

Step 11. **Brainstorm Solutions.** ED: We could leave all your homework to you and let you sink or swim until your next report card and then if it's good enough, okay, if it's not . . . back to the old drawing board.

PATRICIA: You could bring all your homework assignments to us when the teachers give them and we could sit with you every night and watch you do them.

ERIC: You could hire a tutor to do that.

ED: Each night you could bring us the assignment and the homework and we could send you back until we think it's done right.

PATRICIA: We could send you to a special school that has two-hour study halls for homework after school.

ED: We could send you to a summer program where they teach you how to get organized and have study skills courses.

PATRICIA: We could send you for testing to see if you have attention deficit disorder or some kind of learning disability.

ED: We could negotiate a homework contract with certain criteria you agree to meet and certain consequences if you don't meet them.

ERIC: Like what kind of criteria? What kind of consequences?

ED: Like where you do the homework, is your music on or off, what is a reasonable start time, how many reminders to start before you have violated the agreement. Consequences would be good or bad, depending on what you do. There would be good consequences for sticking to the plan: if you stick to it one entire week, you get to have a spend-the-night on the week end. That kind of thing.

Step 12. **Pros and Cons.**

PATRICIA: Is that it? Looks like a pretty good list. Are there any more or are we ready to do the pros and cons? Can we eliminate some ideas right off?

ERIC: Yes, the one where you sit with me is out. The con is I'd be mad the whole time and couldn't work. Besides that would tie you guys down majorly.

1. Sink or swim

2. Sink or swim until next report card

3. Tell us your assignments and we sit with you

4. Hire a tutor

5. We check homework

6. Special school with study halls

7. Summer program for study skills

8. ADD testing

9. Homework contract with consequences

ED: I agree that's out from all our points of view.

PATRICIA: Okay, the first one is: Leave all the homework to you and let you sink or swim.

ED: The pro is, it's the least hassle for us. The con is that it's unrealistic to let something so important go on indefinitely without being sure of progress.

ERIC: That's the beauty of the next one. It just lets it go for one report period. That's three months. Plus it's the least hassle for you. Pro!

PATRICIA: I agree with those pros and cons for the first two. What about the next one, you bring your assignments to us each night to be checked.

ED: Not too bad. We're still tied down to it every night. Eric?

ERIC: It still means you have to go over it and that makes me mad.

PATRICIA: Okay, the cons are, it still makes Eric mad and ties us down somewhat. The pro is, it gets the job done. What about the next one: send you to a special school that monitors homework time?

ED: This isn't free, is it? Costs are a con. Besides, if we could agree to a time for homework here at home, we wouldn't need it, would we?

ERIC: Yeah, and it would be in the afternoon during basketball practice or baseball. Besides, I wouldn't want anyone to know I went. Only dorks go to homework programs.

PATRICIA: Okay, that one is too dorky. What about sending you to a summer program for organizational skills?

ED: But we need to make a change now. Summer's too late.

ERIC: My con is I don't want to do it. Summer is for vacation and camp.

PATRICIA: Okay. How about psychological testing?

ED: I don't mind testing if nothing works, but we haven't really tried. Let's hold that.

ERIC: Suits me.

PATRICIA: Okay, the last one, the homework contract: You propose what you will do and we propose what we must have and we negotiate something with consequences.

ERIC: It sounds like a whole lot of trouble. That's a con.

ED: It is a whole lot of trouble, but we've been having a whole lot of trouble arguing already so we wouldn't be losing anything. It does put a lot of the burden of management on us. That's a con. Are you up to that, Patricia?

PATRICIA: Sticking to it will be difficult, but if we both agree to help each other do it, I'm all for it. That's all. Let's see the reactions. We got all cons and no pros for some of these suggestions. We got clear pros for leaving Eric alone until next report card and for the homework contract, but we got a lot of cons for the contract, too, because it takes so much management.

Step 13. **Decide and Plan.**

ERIC: That's a no-brainer. You leave me alone until next report card and see how it works. If it doesn't work, we can do the contract.

ED: Sounds reasonable, although I worry we will have lost three months if it doesn't work.

PATRICIA: How will we define "if it doesn't work?"

ERIC: Good question. What is it you guys expect of me anyway? All A's? Some teachers never give A's. Mrs. Kidwell never gives A's.

PATRICIA: Some subjects are definitely harder than others. But we're not talking about all A's, are we?

ERIC: All B's? I've got that already. Well, almost. How about a B average?

ED: I'm more concerned that you get better organized, getting all your work in, not procrastinating, really caring about being responsible, and things like that than the grades themselves.

PATRICIA: I agree. I can accept B's or even an occasional C in a hard class, but not because of late or incomplete work. That's the whole point of this, to get the work done. How about three A's and the rest B's and no teacher comments about late or incomplete work.

ED: Okay, Eric?

ERIC: Okay.

ED: And we have to remind each other, nicely, not to bug Eric. Nothing said about homework until report card time. When the report card comes, we look it over, including teacher remarks . . . and see where we go from there.

Step 14. **Do It.**

Patricia had the hardest time keeping this bargain. She got very nervous when Eric was home goofing off during the time he was supposed to be studying. She had to start doing cleaning and laundry in another part of the house whenever she heard Eric talking on the phone. She got a lot of closets cleaned out during that three months. She went to him to talk to him instead of calling him so that her famous "E-E-Eric," to which he was sensitized, would not make him feel resistant. And she never said, "Your father says. . . ."

The last change was made easier because Eric's father said little. Ed did surprisingly well, seemingly paying no attention to Eric's evening activities except once, when he yelled at Eric for watching *The Simpsons* when he wanted to watch the basketball game.

ED: You're supposed to be doing your homework anyway.

ERIC: Hey, Dad, remember the no-bugging-about-homework agreement.

Eric felt a sort of power on this occasion

and it reminded him he had to keep his end of the bargain. Feeling in control of one's destiny is part of the magic of a negotiated agreement.

When Eric's next report card came, the family reviewed the success of their plan. First, Eric's grades were two A's and two B's and one C — not quite the target grades — and there were no comments concerning unfinished work.

ED: How do you think it went?

Step 15. **Review/Revise.**

ERIC: My grades turned out better than before, good but not great. I can see I'm not very organized and need strategies.

PATRICIA: That course in study skills is still a possibility.

ERIC: I'd like to try to figure out something on my own for one more quarter, and then we can talk about a class.

Eric's parents saw the value of his figuring out something on his own and agreed to another report period under the old agreement. They were actually pleased with the results: the grades had gone up — not a lot, but some — and they weren't arguing over homework. A clear improvement for all concerned.

The measure of success was only partly in the improved report card. Even better, Eric and his family felt good about the whole process, the subject of homework did not have the same sting, and they seemed to have forgiven each other for their earlier bad behavior. This feeling of forgiveness is a higher goal of settling a dispute, bringing harmony to families.

CHAPTER 7

Teaching Teenagers to Resolve Conflict

I remember an experience with a teenager and his family that illustrates particularly well the despair that can come from a breakdown in communication between parents and children.

A couple called me in a crisis asking me to please give them some advice. Their sixteen-year-old son, Adam, was living in another state with relatives. Until his teen years, he had been a "perfect" kid, very involved in church and sports, a straight-A student. He was easy to get along with until about age fourteen, when he started dating the "wrong" girl. Suddenly, his style of dressing changed along with his demeanor with adults. At one point he ran away for several days and, when he came home, he and his parents had a big blow-up that got nowhere. The solution they agreed on was for him to go live with relatives out of state and "start over."

After several months, the relatives found a note from Adam saying he was going to run away again, this time to New York, and never see his family again. The relatives called the parents. What should they do?

The situation sounded quite serious and I advised the parents to get in the car and drive to the town where Adam was. I recommended that on the way they think through their feelings and prepare themselves to use the following process:

Find Adam and tell him you love him and care about him. Then draw him out about what was going on. Listen, and then draw him out some more. While you are drawing him out, I suggested, be careful not to lecture,

interrupt, or even raise your eyebrows. Have an attitude of genuine curiosity about what is bothering him. You will hear some things that are hard not
to react to, I warned, but don't.

Next, draw him out about what he thinks ought to be done to solve
the problems. Further draw him out about these ideas without a lot of
judgment.

Finally, try your best to arrive at a plan you all can accept. If, in the end,
you and he are not entirely in agreement, feel comfortable as a parent to
take charge and outline a plan, perhaps using some of his ideas, that you
think will address the major points of the conflict.

You can see that this crisis management plan roughly corresponds to
the three parts of the conflict resolution model: Think, Talk/Listen, Solve.

So this couple drove four hundred miles together. On the way, they
went over the plan, agreeing to sit next to each other when they talked to
Adam and pinch each other as a reminder if one of them was messing up
the process. They met their son, rented a motel room for privacy, followed
the process, and they all talked on and off for thirteen hours. The teenager
told them things they didn't want to hear, but they listened respectfully. He
said, for example, that he'd felt somewhat abandoned when they sent him
off to relatives even though he had sort of suggested it. As for what he saw
as a solution, he wanted to come home, to go to a different school, to get
therapy, and to get a new start.

When Adam's parents first called me, I guessed that the family had lost
the ability to communicate. Adam wouldn't talk or became defensive, and
communication had deteriorated on both sides. And I'm convinced the
impasse would have happened again if these parents had overreacted and
expressed how strongly they felt from the beginning of the conversation
with Adam. The whole thing could have blown up in their faces. Adam
could have fled to New York where he was ill-equipped to live and who
knows what would have happened. As it was, Adam came around and is
now a college graduate, happy, married with a couple of kids.

Conflict during the teen years can be especially critical. Mishandling
conflict can lead to downward spirals in communication, and good communication is one of our best avenues for offsetting adolescent inexperi-
ence and risk-taking. A teen can drive a vehicle, acquire money through
legitimate or less desirable means, or be self-destructive. He may seek
solace in bad company, abuse drugs, or engage in inappropriate sexual

activity. The stakes are higher when the child is older, and intervention is often more difficult.

But the teen years generally may not be as bad as popular lore suggests. Answers to the Offer Self-Image Questionnaire for Adolescents, given to thirty thousand teens since 1962, showed that most did not perceive major problems with their parents, and their feelings toward parents were more positive than is often portrayed. Moreover, teens were generally confident and optimistic that their skills were adequate to cope with life.

The same data, however, shows a significant number of teens, one out of five, who did not feel secure about their coping abilities, felt "empty emotionally" at times or thought that "life is an endless succession of problems without solutions," or were "confused a lot" about life.

One group that may feel particular stress during the teen years are those who experience a significantly early or a significantly late puberty. They are out of sync with their peer group and often feel inadequate or "different." Fitting in is especially important at this age and rejection and acceptance issues are paramount.

Teens' Behavior Risky

In August 1998, the Centers for Disease Control and Prevention released the findings of the Youth Risk Behavior Surveillance, which surveyed more than sixteen thousand U.S. high school students. Here are a few findings:

• Fifty percent said they had had at least one drink in the last thirty days; 33 percent had had five or more.

• Seventeen percent said they had driven after drinking in the last thirty days, and 36 percent had been driven by a person who had been drinking.

• Eighteen percent said they had carried a weapon such as a gun, knife, or club in the last thirty days while 37 percent reported being in a physical fight.

• One in five teens reported seriously considering suicide in the last twelve months; 15 percent came up with a specific plan.

• Forty-eight percent said they had had sex; 16 percent had had four or more partners. About 43 percent of the sexually active teens reported not using a condom the last time they had sex.

(Information reported in "HealthWatch" of the August 14, 1998, Atlanta Journal/Constitution)

While many normal teens discuss emotional problems with a parent, troubled adolescents are much less likely to do so. With many adolescents, it will be up to the parents to observe and bring up the problem and then to guide their child toward a resolution.

Teens and parents often have different perspectives. Adolescents often feel invulnerable, bold, and daring while parents feel they don't always have mature judgment. While parents have worries about safety and character issues, adolescents sometimes think the parents just want power and don't want to give up control. "You can't wait to catch me breaking a rule," one teen screamed bitterly at her mother. What the teen thought of as a cat-and-mouse game her mother relished was the source of almost unbearable anxiety for the mother.

Adolescents frequently make reference to what their friends are allowed to do — rent R-rated movies, stay out till 1:00 A.M., go to co-ed slumber parties — while adults make reference to their own adolescence — "In my day, we stayed home and played checkers on a homemade board. . . ." Parents also spout media reports of drug use and violence among teens. These often exaggerated references stretch the already large perspective gap between teens and parents.

Parents may also feel personal rejection when teens mock them, avoid them, or prefer the company of peers to theirs. Teens no longer put parents at the top of their list.

Teens tend to be egocentric and sensitive to being evaluated by their parents, teachers, and peers. They feel that their thoughts and feelings are unique to them and nobody, least of all parents, understands them.

These differences in perspective often make it hard to win over an adolescent to a new way of resolving conflict.

A positive side of teaching adolescents, however, is the fact that they have a greater ability to think abstractly and a broader social experience. This gives them a better perspective on conflicts. Also, they are looking ahead to college or work, and that makes them easier to motivate in some ways.

It may be a comfort to parents to know that many teens who seem to reject or ignore parental teaching a few years later prove they have listened better than parents ever imagined. They sometimes adopt chapter and verse what their parents taught. A few have even been overheard repeating the lessons to younger siblings!

STYLES OF TEACHING

Modeling

Teens continue to absorb the behavior of their parents even though they are beginning to observe that not all families have the same norms for behavior. Your example of appropriate behavior and conflict resolution skills sets harmony as the norm. If your teen sees you behave badly, it's good to acknowledge your mistake to them and openly commit yourself to improving.

If you master the conflict resolution model and use it with your spouse or friends, your teen and his siblings, you will be giving him a lesson in how it's done. This increases your credibility greatly and enhances your chances of getting his attention for more formal teaching styles.

The "Do as I say, don't do as I do" school of teaching rarely works.

Casual Comments

The wide range of activities of the average teen reveals to him various interpretations of behavior and points of view other than his own. Travel and study of other cultures show him his own local viewpoint may be different from others in the world. Literature, good films — I think of *Rain Man* and *As Good As It Gets* — and TV shows vastly expand a teen's experience with changes of heart and the array of feelings hidden under behavior. He learns empathy from Sunday school lessons and by getting into the heads of characters, even villains, in high school plays. And then there's real life. Teens become increasingly aware of what's going on next door and on the national scene in the behavior of sports heroes and other public figures.

In addition to what they learn on their own, for better or for worse, anything you say related to these sources of experience imparts your values; anything you say about characters' motives or skill in resolving conflict is teaching. There are, of course, just as many examples of poor skills as good ones; be sure to comment on those, too.

Drawing Out by Asking Questions

Asking questions to draw a teenager out serves two purposes: one is to learn something new about your teen. The other is to get him to come up with an insight about an issue on his own. Any constructive point you can get the teen to discover for himself is one he is more likely to follow than a point you make to him. On the other hand, don't think you know all the "right" answers. Ask questions with genuine curiosity and you may be surprised at what insights you can get about your teen, his motivation, and his world.

Drawing a teen out by using open-ended questions should work well at this age. You should "guess" answers only if you think that makes it easier for a hesitant teen, for example, "maybe you're embarrassed that . . . ," "it seems to me you could be thinking. . . ."

If you do get an answer, pursue the direction of the conversation as far as you can: "And then what?" "So what do you conclude about that?" "How do you think you could change that?"

If you don't get an answer, the wheels may be turning in a learning mode anyway. It may be time for you to slide into a more formal mode: "Well, it seems to me that. . . ."

Direct Teaching

Because of school, your teen is used to direct instruction. He understands it, and it works at this age better than ever before. However, he recognizes the mode as authoritarian, and he may have had enough of that. Use formal explanation sparingly and at the right time and place.

HOW TO GET STARTED

The hardest part of teaching the model to your teen may be getting started. You can approach it as a good thing to know for life, as a solution to a particular personal or family problem, or as a requirement for some privilege the teen wants — whatever works. Many teens would profit from reading the book as a starting point. Here's some language that may work for you:

* "I think we all could use some help with treating each other better even when we're mad. Wouldn't you like to have less yelling [sarcasm, insulting, intimidation, humiliating, closing each other out . . .]?"

* "We seem to bring up a lot of things we don't agree on, but when we stop talking, nothing is settled and the questions aren't answered. I think we need a format that will guide us from stating our problem to making a decision and then following through on it. Don't you think we would feel more in control if fewer things were left hanging and more things were clearly dealt with?"

* "I've read a book about resolving conflict that doesn't just tell you how to negotiate but how to deal with anger and other emotions better. How does that sound to you?"

* "If you ask business managers what qualities determine which employees move up in the organization, they'll usually say people skills. One of the most critical of these skills is conflict resolution. I've

been reading about a conflict resolution model that looks as if it would work at home as well as in school and relationships and eventually at your job."

★ "This model I've been reading about has three parts. The Thinking Steps get a better attitude going for resolving an issue. The Talk/Listen Steps are about speaking to each other efficiently and respectfully and really listening to each other. The Solving Steps help you work out the issue and make a plan so the issue doesn't come back again."

★ "Jennifer, I hear you crying and yelling at Jeff on the phone several times a night and it breaks my heart. For one thing, I am sorry your relationship with Jeff is so painful. But more important, I see you have no way to solve this; you are fighting over the same things every night. I think it's critically important, not only for this relationship but for any relationship you have in the future, that you have a way to work things out. Believe it or not, you don't have to accept this pattern; there are better ways. In fact, I know of one conflict resolution model that a lot of people have found dramatically changes their ability to get along with each other. Would you be willing to spend some time talking about this?"

If your teen says angrily, "No, stay out of this," you still have several options.

You could use a purely incidental approach, dropping one-liners about the most problematic steps at appropriate times or whole paragraphs in quiet moments. Don't overdo it. If you get attention for a few minutes, quit while you're ahead.

Another way to go is to leave this book on her bed with a note saying, "I recommend this book for anyone in a relationship." Then don't ask, just hope for the best.

Or you can use your parental authority and require that your daughter schedule a certain block of time for several weeks to spend on this subject, perhaps as a condition of using the telephone. Saying, "the long, loud, emotional arguments are disturbing the household and setting a bad example for the others. You must either stop using the phone altogether or learn to use the phone time better according to the conflict resolution model."

HOW TO TEACH THE STEPS

PART ONE: THE THINKING STEPS

The Thinking Steps are meant to be done internally, as the name implies. However, if you are teaching this to your teen for the first time, you will have to suggest thoughts to him, urging him to recognize the kinds of thoughts he now thinks and make a deliberate effort to replace these thoughts with new ones more conducive to resolution. Eventually, the teen who has experienced success with this model will choose to do The Thinking Steps, or at least the ones he needs the most, on his own.

Step 1. **ASSESS EMOTIONS.**

One adolescent with a history of poor conduct was arrested for bringing a knife to school. In court, part of his sentence was a tour of the jail. On the morning of the tour, he became extremely hostile toward his parents, blaming them for everything. He looked very angry, but it was clear to his parents what was driving him was anxiety. He's a kid who cannot tolerate anxiety for even a moment because he perceives it as wimpy. So his anger was a sort of macho cover-up. It would be helpful for this teen to recognize that his anger was masking anxiety, hurt, or other emotions he doesn't tolerate as well as he does anger.

In a similar self-deception, the underreactive teen may say she feels depressed when she has repressed significant and anxiety-provoking anger. Recognizing anger would be healthier.

Try drawing out your teen and invite her to explore her feelings and learn to label them more accurately:

* "Jennifer, when you're upset with Jeff, do you think before you talk? It's good to spend more time examining your feelings than most people do. Impulsive arguing without understanding yourself can lead to a downward spiral in your relationship."

* "Jennifer, when I hear you yelling at Jeff, I would guess that you have several kinds of feelings. Maybe you're mostly angry, but maybe your feelings are also hurt. I'd guess you could be afraid he'll break up with you for good or scared you're going to lose him. Maybe you're jealous

of other girls or the time he spends with guys. Fear, hurt, and jealousy as well as anger may come into play when Jeff says or does something hurtful. But judging from your words and tone, he likely thinks that you were only angry. How do you think you come across?"

★ "People often have coexisting emotions that complicate one another. All of these feelings deserve your recognition. For example, maybe you're hurt by someone or afraid but you show only your anger and not your hurt or fear. It's easier for people to empathize with your hurt or fear, but they feel attacked by your anger, so it's good to be aware of those other emotions."

★ "I'm sorry you were treated badly by your boss. You seem down about it, as if you've given up and maybe you even feel helpless. If I were you, I'd probably feel angry. Remember anger is a signal you need to resolve a problem."

Step 2. Accept Anger, Behave Well.

Urge your teen to accept his anger and other feelings as normal, possibly justifiable, and separate from his behavior. Start by letting him know you basically accept his feelings, although you know he can learn to modify feelings by better thinking or by better problem solving. Once he acknowledges anger and/or other feelings, don't overreact, no matter how unjustified you may think his feelings are. Reinforce his appropriate expression of emotion. Then move on quickly to stating specifically what anger-based behavior is not acceptable, from violence to sarcasm to whatever violates your family's values. He should pause and think before acting in anger. With a better attitude, he might actually get his conflict resolved!

★ "Anger is okay; it's how you behave that counts. Anger is a signal that a problem needs to be resolved."

★ "Jennifer, what do you think immediately after Jeff says or does something you don't like? Often people think retaliatory thoughts or blaming thoughts or defensive thoughts. Those are understandable, but a better thought you can say to yourself is: 'It's okay to be angry; that's a part of being a normal human being, but it's important to handle my feelings properly.' That doesn't mean just give in and not stand up for yourself, but try to be smart and think good attitude thoughts so you don't make both of you madder than you already are. At the same time you are taking care of yourself, you're moving towards resolution."

★ "When you're angry, here's what's not good and you should promise yourself not to do: hitting, yelling, throwing things, destruction, threats, insults, slamming doors, leaving the house in a car and squealing the tires."

★ "When you react too quickly in anger, you often get in trouble. Try to train yourself, when you feel the first surge of anger and hear yourself think retaliatory thoughts, to say to yourself, 'Stop, think, be smart, change this bad attitude.' Give yourself some thinking time."

Step 3. **Gauge Intensity.**
Teach your teen to use a scale of 1 to 10 to rate the intensity of his emotion. Just taking the time to gauge intensity may help anger diminish. Very low levels of anger can usually be ignored, while very high levels of anger must be reduced before resolution is likely.

BEETLE BAILEY

BEETLE BAILEY reprinted with special permission of King Features Syndicate

At this age, your son or daughter can use the scale in some more complex and interesting ways as well. Encourage him to compare the numbers on the current occasion to similar occasions in the past. He can also track the progression of anger through an episode in order to recognize patterns: what triggers anger, what calms it, and how much control of his emotions he has.

★ "Jennifer, it appears there are times you are so angry with Jeff that it would better to stand back and gauge your anger before you talk anymore.

On a scale from 1 to 10, if your feelings are way up at an 8 or 9, you'd be wise to wait and take some time out to think and calm down. Let him know that you'll talk to him soon, but tell him you're afraid you'll not do a good job if you pursue the matter now. On the other hand, if your anger is a 2 or less, forget about it before you turn it into a big thing. And if, while you're talking, your anger shoots up too high again, take a break for a while and cool off."

★ "People's anger level fluctuates significantly over the course of a conflict and is different from one time to another. If you notice how the intensity of your feelings changes, you may notice what makes you flare up — certain remarks or situations or even some of your own thoughts. You may notice what words, situations, or thoughts make you calm down, too. It's good to practice those."

Step 4. Who and What?
WHO?

Knowing who you're mad at may sound easy to a teen. Who does he feel mad at? Unfortunately, who he feels mad at may not be the appropriate person to be mad at. Teens often use parents, teachers, or somebody else as scapegoats when something goes wrong, especially when the teen is trying not to blame himself. And sometimes they're just mad at everyone because they don't know who to blame. Teach your child to work on limiting her feelings to the person or people whose behavior has actually angered her.

★ "Don't blame the whole faculty for one teacher's behavior. Don't blame the whole team for one player's dirty play. Don't blame a race for the behavior of a few or a whole group of kids for two members' remarks. Don't blame a scapegoat for something that went wrong."

★ "Your anger can be at more than one person, but only if more than one person did something to anger you."

★ "Figuring out who exactly you're angry at helps you figure out what you're angry about. And figuring out what may help you decide whom to resolve it with."

WHAT?

Does your teen wear extreme make-up, pierce her body, or threaten to get a tattoo? Does he sleep till afternoon on Saturdays, put off his homework till midnight, play indecent music, hang out with scruffy friends, or go with a sleazy girl? Is her room a mess, her chores undone? Does he guard his privacy so much you think he must be on drugs? To teenagers, staying out late, dressing like their peers, putting off chores, etc., feels good; pleasing their parents is not as strong a driving force as it once was, and their standards are often driven by their peer group. For these reasons, underlying much of teen/parent conflict is the question of whose business it is to make decisions about a teen's behavior. The desire for autonomy intensifies many issues.

So when you are teaching your teen to clarify who and what angers them, remember that there may be an immediate problem to resolve but their desire for autonomy may be the main underlying issue.

Some typical teen/parent issues are: curfew, telephone usage, choice of friends, dress and self-presentation, school work, household chores, spending money, use of a car, dating rules, privacy, safety issues, drinking and drug use. Issues they have with other people include: being excluded from a group, dating and sports rivalries, school rules, and damaging gossip.

This conflict resolution process gives the teen opportunity for input and decision-making as well as responsibility to follow through. It may in itself give the teen a sense of autonomy that eases conflict.

* "Is it the time I told you to be home or the fact that I told you at all that makes you mad? Or is it the way I told you?"

* "Jennifer, I don't need to know the details of why you're upset with Jeff. That's your business. I just hope you'll think clearly about what behavior of his angers you or hurts you most and what's the issue behind his behavior. There could be a specific behavior like his not asking you to go somewhere with him this weekend or saying he was going camping with friends or something like that. Then, on top of the apparent problem there could be a process issue. For example, if every time you bring up what you are unhappy about, he blames you for something else instead of answering you, that's a process problem. If you spend some

thinking time getting clear about what the main issues are, it will help you resolve them."

★ "If you can figure out what she did that bothers you, you can ask her to change it or you can change your behavior towards her. The key is to figure out what behavior or attitude triggers your anger."

★ "State what you're upset about in resolvable terms. Don't just say, 'You make me so-o-o mad,' or 'You act like such a jerk.' Can you think of something the other person could do differently that would make you feel better? Tell him something you or he could work on."

Step 5. **Perspective Check.**

Is your teen overreacting? Underreacting? Teach her to keep anger in proportion to provocation, recognize her own contribution to the conflict, and try to see the other person's point of view. Don't say, "That's nothing to get mad about." Minimizing the hurt or belittling your teen's feelings will only worsen your relationship. Instead, ask her to compare the provocation to others, to compare her reaction with those of her friends, and to consider if her reaction is appropriate.

★ "Think a minute and tell me how bad is this thing Raymond said? How come it's worth a 7 on the anger scale?"

★ "This must be the last straw. Maybe you didn't react to Carol's needling before and now you've saved up all your anger for this one time. See if you can pretend it's the first time and go from there."

★ "I can understand why you're upset. But didn't you do the same thing to Jason last week? Maybe he figures if you did it, he can do it."

★ "Jennifer, a few more things about perspective before you talk to Jeff: It would be useful to look at the situation from his point of view. Does he know how big a deal it is to you? Why does he think what he has done is okay? Or is he trying to do this just to hurt you? Is what he did really such a bad thing? At least consider that what you see may not be the most accurate picture. You could also ask your friends if they would feel as strongly as you do if they were in your shoes."

★ "What do you think her [my] motives were?"

★ "Pretend you are Jane. Tell me what you imagine she's thinking."

PART TWO: THE TALK/LISTEN STEPS

The name "talk/listen steps" means to give equal time to listening as to talking. We all know people (sometimes ourselves!) who politely let the other person talk but only half-listen because they are marshaling their arguments for a return volley. The exchange of ideas fails if no one is really listening.

I'd like to teach all teenagers that listening is a valuable art so rarely done well that it is highly prized. The teen who masters it will be highly sought after. I remember a cartoon in the *New Yorker* magazine long ago that showed an older man sitting on a sofa beside a young woman he had just met at a cocktail party. He talked a while and she listened attentively. He talked some more while she made constant eye contact and gave him her full attention. When he was finished he patted her on the shoulder, saying, "You are a highly intelligent woman, my dear." The joke, of course, was that she hadn't said a word; she had only listened.

Introduce the idea to your teen that listening is not second to talking in the communication process. Start by listening well to her yourself.

Step 6. **Time and Place.**
You've probably had wonderful conversations with your teen that drew you closer than before. You've probably also started a conversation with your teen only to have him cut you off with an annoyed remark. The difference may have been your choice of time and place, setting and mood. The family mentioned at the beginning of this chapter, who rented the motel room in order to have a private place for a long talk, went to a lot of trouble to get their teen into the right place at a critical time, and it paid off. They couldn't have had that conversation in the grandparents' house or over the phone or between dinner and bed. In the same way, you may have no luck bringing up something when your teen is on the computer or wanting to call his girlfriend.

Teach your teen to give resolution a chance by choosing the right time and place to bring up a problem:

★ "I waited till Mom and Sally were out to bring this up, since they are not involved and so you don't have to worry about what they think."

★ "I picked this place and time to discuss our disagreement because it's quiet here so we could talk, and the waitresses won't be trying to hustle us out."

★ "When should you bring this up? Before the game when Rick may be nervous? Or after the game when he will be either excited or down about the outcome? Or maybe tomorrow after breakfast?"

★ "Jennifer, I think it would work better to pick a quiet time with Jeff to talk over your problems. And besides, you should do it where no one else can hear. Your late night arguments can be heard all over the house, and they upset us all. Some people need to give themselves enough time, but in your case I suggest you set a limit on your time. Apparently, you all can argue indefinitely getting nowhere. Give yourself a shorter amount of time to cover the problem and a reasonable amount of time to settle it. And I'll bet you'll be more focused and more likely to end on a good note than if you argued all night."

Step 7. **Avoid Coalitions.**

ZITS reprinted with special permission of King Features Syndicate

Sometimes I'm coaching two people to resolve a conflict between them, and one of them keeps talking to me instead of to the person he has the conflict with. Usually he's trying to win me over with his arguments. If I allow myself to become consistently a part of his coalition, the other person feels I'm not on his side. I have to be careful as a therapist to be aware of this trap. And so will you when you are teaching your teen to avoid coalitions or when you are "refereeing" the process with your teen and another person. Having a "second," whether a parent, teacher, or friend, brings comfort to one person and tends to alienate the other person. To truly resolve a conflict, however, teach your child by example and word to have the courage to go it alone. Remember conflict resolution is almost never done well as a team sport.

★ "I'm going to ignore that remark because I don't want to take sides in your argument."

★ "See this Beetle Bailey cartoon. Beetle says, 'And Killer agrees with me. Tell him, Killer.' I can guess that will turn out badly."

★ "Jennifer, it seems all the things you think Jeff said or did are making you mad. If you know all those things mainly because your friends saw and told you, consider telling your friends not to report on Jeff to you. Ask them to let you and Jeff work it out by yourselves."

★ "When you raised your eyebrows at Sue just then, it was a little secret communication between you two. You probably thought it was okay because you didn't use words. But any communication that two of you know about and the other one doesn't is an attempt to choose up sides. If you don't believe Katie is telling the truth or if you are shocked by what she said, tell Katie directly so everyone knows where you stand. Sharing your thoughts privately with Sue, even if it's just eyebrows, is forming a coalition, and it makes it harder to resolve your conflict with Katie."

Step 8. **Express Appropriately.**
I remember a teacher in high school who used to whine about the class's behavior and yelled and threatened, but no one ever paid any attention to what she said. Another teacher always used a low, serious voice and was less frequent in her intervention. She only had to look the student in the eye and he stopped misbehaving right away. As the saying goes, less is more. That's true also for expressing what you are angry about to the appropriate person. Stating the problem in a few words, making only one point at a time, and speaking in a straightforward, calm manner will go a long way toward diffusing anger and letting the other person know you are aiming for a peaceful resolution. Start teaching your teen the importance and power of expressing your feelings appropriately by modeling good tone, manner, and choice of words yourself.

* "The way that woman is expressing her anger is spoiling her chances of resolution, don't you think?"

* "Your tone of voice as well as your words tell the other person you are not out to beat him and that helps him be less defensive."

* "Jennifer, how do you feel you come across when you are telling Jeff what's upsetting you? In what ways do you do well? In what ways do you need to improve?"

* "'Express appropriately' means, of course, no yelling and screaming or calling names. It also means being focused, to the point, and succinct."

* "If you say something to hurt the other person, you may feel good that you 'got to him' for a little while, but you will not likely have a satisfying resolution."

* "State the problem and your feelings in resolvable terms. That means to put it in a way that offers hope that, between you, you could do something specific to change it."

Step 9. **Listen Actively.**
The art of listening isn't cultivated enough in our culture. You may think listening well means letting others convince you when you want to convince them. But listening well is not a loser's technique. Excellent listeners go far. It is a key attribute of successful politicians, physicians, therapists, bartenders, and parents. Listening while everyone else is mad and replying calmly can be dramatically disarming because other people aren't expecting you to really listen. Once you do, they are more likely to listen to you, so you're a winner.

Try really listening, actively listening, to your teen. Be a good model of what you're trying to teach.

* "Notice how Cliff [Bill Cosby] says, 'Now let me get this straight. You want me to. . . . ' It's funny the way he says it, but it also lets his kids know he's listening and gives them a chance to straighten out any misunderstandings."

* "Show you understand what the other person is saying. Repeat in your own words what he is telling you so you both know you truly see his point of view."

★ "When someone is trying to persuade you or push her ideas on you, the way to show you are a good listener is to ask the other person to clarify things, repeat what they said, and then ask for more elaboration or examples. Then summarize what they said. Of course, drawing out has to be sincerely done out of genuine desire to understand rather than as a patronizing act. And you don't have to sound like a sitcom therapist when you summarize; just say it naturally."

★ "Jennifer, when it comes to talking and listening, I can hear it's not going too well. I hear you interrupting so often, saying 'But . . . , but . . . ' along with yelling and crying. I know it's hard to control your emotions. But you need to agree to give each of you uninterrupted time to tell each other how you feel. Then while the other one talks, really listen. Don't plot what you are going to say in rebuttal. Instead, when he's finished, tell him what you understood him to say. He'll be so amazed, he'll settle down a lot. You can explain active listening to him also, asking him to listen well to you and tell you what you said to prove he really listened and understood. To break the old pattern you have been using, you probably have to agree to this pattern in advance."

Step 10. **Admit Fault.**

If people only knew what power admitting fault has! But generally most people don't like to take responsibility for their bad behavior. I recently heard that someone wanted to name the 90s the "don't blame me" decade. People want to blame other people: their parents, negligent teachers, and society at large. Also, they frequently blame their bad behavior on what tempted or provoked them.

The idea of acknowledging your part in the problem is not a unique idea, but often is not clearly taught, and it's rarely done spontaneously. People feel that admitting fault means giving up or losing. But admitting what you have done to contribute to the problem reduces your anger and often wins the other person's cooperation.

★ "I can see what got us off on the wrong foot. I started out whining because I was so upset and that made her defensive."

★ "I can see that Jerry is mainly the problem here, but Elaine also contributed to the fiasco by lying about what she said to his girlfriend."

★ "Can you think of anything you may have said or done that made him hostile and uncooperative?"

★ "Most problems are not all one person's fault. The word 'all' and 'fault' shouldn't appear together in the same sentence."

★ "Jennifer, since you can see now that your interrupting and yelling contributed to the intensity of your argument with Jeff, it would do a world of good for you to tell him you know your behavior contributed to the problem. Take some time out from telling him what he's doing wrong to acknowledge what you are doing wrong. I think you will see an immediate softening in his approach. He may admit that he was wrong in some way, too, and you'll be one step closer to resolution."

★ "If you admit what you were doing wrong and he doesn't, you can say, 'That's what I was doing wrong that made you more upset; it would help me to hear what you think you were doing that made me more upset.' It's so rare and difficult to admit fault that you may have to teach the other person by your example."

PART THREE: THE SOLVING STEPS

By the time you get to Part Three: The Solving Steps, you shouldn't be very mad anymore. Thinking, talking, and listening have had their positive effects. If you face a difficult situation and you're sure no one is angry, you can start the process with The Solving Steps as a form of conflict prevention. For example, if your teen is fifteen years and eleven months old, you could use this model as a way to set up driving and car use rules with his input. You could even make learning better conflict resolution a condition of having driving privileges.

Step 11. Brainstorm Solutions.
Brainstorming is a creative process. If your teen is a divergent thinker, she may be really good at brainstorming. Encourage her to throw on the table several ways to solve the problem without pointing out the flaws in anyone else's ideas.

Encourage her to mention anything she wants or thinks might work. You also throw in your wish list. Every now and then suggest an idea that might fly with her, too. Take your time. Show her how everything does-n't boil down to your way and her way, that there are lots of variations that don't feel half bad. Brainstorming might even be fun, but be careful not to tell your teen that.

A Negotiation Strategy

In family therapy, as the teen's "consultant," I help him structure a proposal to present to his parents. (The parents may be present but quiet.) I say to the kid: what do you think is a reasonable curfew? What do you think are reasonable places for you to be? What do you think should happen if you are five minutes late, and what should happen if you are a half-hour late? How many times a week on a weeknight do you think you should go out? On Friday or Saturday night what should be your curfew? The kid thinks. Usually, the curfew the kid suggests is a half-hour more than he has now. He states what he thinks are reasonable punishments.

Then the parents get together and discuss this proposal. They come to a consensus between them and say what parts they can agree with and what parts not. I go back with the kid and we redo the plan to something the parents might accept.

This negotiation gives the teen a greater sense of autonomy. It teaches him to plan for himself. Teens often make more reasonable proposals than you would imagine. At the same time, parents retain the position of final authority, and they retain enforcement rights because these are always built into the plan. Everyone has a structure to follow so they don't have to argue about every little thing over and over.

★ "You could have the car one evening each weekend, our choice, except on your most special occasions. Or you could have the car any evening we're not using it. Or you could have it five times a month. And you could lose the use of it if you got a traffic ticket, caused an accident, or failed a mid-term test at school. Or . . ."

★ "If you could have it your way, what would you suggest? Try me." (See "A Negotiation Strategy" in text box on left.)

★ "Jennifer, if you and Jeff are at an impasse and both of you seem to be miserable, maybe it's time to brainstorm. What have you got to lose? Both of you throw out ideas, and don't get upset if you don't like one. They don't all have to be good ones, but a few will be. You may be surprised at which ones are."

★ "Brainstorming is a technique widely used in business settings. It's a good thing to learn to do."

Step 12. **Pros and Cons.**
Exploring the pros and cons of the better brainstorming ideas is a little like troubleshooting beforehand. You're looking not only at the merits of each idea but at the likelihood that your teen and you will follow through. Will

your teen really do his part? Will you?

A valid con is "I won't take the time to do that." A valid pro is "I could easily check that off in the morning while I'm waiting for my bagel to toast."

* "Let's decide which ideas have the most merit and assess the good and bad points of each idea."

* "The main advantage, for us, of you having the car anytime we don't want it is that we have first choice. The disadvantage, for you, is that you only get the car if we don't want it. You wouldn't be able to plan until you knew what our plans were. We'd need to have some deadline for deciding our plans. That would cramp our spontaneity, wouldn't it?"

* "Give each idea a chance. Don't think about whose idea it was or why he said it. What advantage does it offer? What are the drawbacks?"

* "Jennifer, it's important not to freak out over his ideas. Give him some respect for his effort to brainstorm. He'll be more likely to see your point of view if you calmly point out both the good and bad points of his ideas."

Step 13. **Decide and Plan.**

If you have a teen, you've observed that planning is not their style. When they go out, they don't know where they're going, what they're going to do, or with whom. Whoever shows up will decide all that later. Spontaneity rules. So any step called "Decide and Plan" will likely be foreign territory.

Let your teen have as much say-so as is practical in the decision because he's more likely to follow through on his own plan. Also, if the conflict resolution has gotten this far, reinforce his cooperation by giving him some choice — maybe your plan two instead of plan one — if it's better than the current situation. Finally, if your teen chooses something that doesn't work, he may learn from his mistakes and choose better next time. But don't agree to something that's unlikely for you to follow through on. And of course, if he chooses anything outrageous, unsafe, or immoral, that's the time to exert your authority by vetoing it.

Choose the solution that has the best chance of working and that all sides "buy into." Plan how to put it into action and monitor it. Set a time to review its success.

★ "That's not my first choice, but if you like it and you're pretty sure it will work, let's give it a try."

★ "Letting you smoke outdoors but not indoors is not a compromise I can go along with. Smoking anywhere at your age is unlawful, and it's addictive and harmful to your health at any age. If you smoke to relieve tension, maybe you can think of other ways to relax."

★ "Jennifer, eliminate the ideas you can't live with. I guess breaking up is out of the question for you?"

★ "One way to decide is to choose the idea that offers the greatest advantage and then problem-solve the disadvantages."

Step 14. **Do It.**
Make a sincere effort to do what you have agreed to do and remind your teen in a constructive way to do her part of the plan. Keep track of progress. The success of the first conflict resolution process will influence whether she uses it again.

★ "Ahem." (. . . glancing toward the pile of dirty laundry.)

★ "Oh, phooey, I don't feel like calling Ethel tonight but I promised to make my weekend plans early so you'd know in advance if you could have the car or not."

★ "Let's see. You haven't had the car yet this weekend. Want to take it tonight? I'm bushed."

★ "Not tonight. A deal is a deal."

★ "Jennifer, if you'll tell me what you decided, I'll help in any way I can. For instance, I could answer all telephone calls so you wouldn't be tempted to talk to Jeff when you weren't in a good enough frame of mind to talk."

★ "Following through is one of the most important things in life. Employers always notice. There's a slot on every performance appraisal at work for 'following through.' That record really counts when it comes to a company keeping and promoting an employee."

Step 15. **Review/Revise.**
New Year's Eve resolutions, diets, and exercise plans are notoriously hard

to keep because you only promise yourself. People more often keep their promises to other people. You follow through not so much on personal resolve but on the expectations of others. That's why agreeing to a good plan with someone else has a better chance of success. Your teen needs to know there will be a day of review of her success with the plan, whether it's with you or someone else, and there will be a chance to change the plan if it's not working.

Get together and talk about how well your plan has worked. What changes do you need to make? If you've succeeded, celebrate your success.

* ★ "You've done your chores all this week, and don't you think I've cut you more slack on how you dress, as I agreed to do? So let's celebrate by going to an early movie, even though it is a weeknight, and bringing home some pizza afterwards."

* ★ "Back to the old drawing board."

* ★ "Is your deal with the coach going okay? If you don't know, ask him how it's going. A plan's no good unless it works. Check it out."

* ★ "Guess it's time for Plan B."

* ★ "Jennifer, it seemed like a good plan for you and Jeff to stay apart for two weeks to cool off and think things over before you tried to talk again. Sorry it turned out this way. Now that you know he used the two cooling-off weeks to date other girls, I guess that tells you something about what he really wanted. Too bad he didn't have the courage to tell you honestly himself. A resolution ends conflict. It's supposed to make both people feel better. In this case, it's going to take a while for you to feel better. In the long run, I think you'll decide it had to happen, and it was better not to go on arguing for months."

PUTTING THE STEPS TOGETHER: A SAMPLE CONFLICT RESOLUTION FROM BEGINNING TO END
High School Hostilities

Two boys, one a high school sophomore and one a junior, had gotten into fights at school. It began with rivalry over a girl and a position on the football team that they both wanted. Unnecessary roughness at spring training was followed by verbal jabs at each other in the hall and one fight at a party off school grounds. Then a serious fist fight on school grounds led to a two-day suspension for each of the boys.

When the boys returned to school, there were continued hostilities, mostly verbal, at football practice, and friends of both boys fed the rivalry by reporting everything one said about the other. The younger boy had supposedly made a fairly serious threat. The coach, unable to make much headway with the situation, reported the problem to Ms. Myer, the school counselor. He knew she was trained to mediate student conflicts.

First, the counselor talked to each of the boys separately. It came out in this discussion that Sam, the sophomore, had been dating a sophomore girl for about a year. They had broken up several times, but the last time, while Sam was hoping to patch things up, Jim, the junior, had asked her out and was now going with her. In addition, Jim and Sam were leading contenders for defensive backfield positions on the football team for next fall.

Sam's view was that he was the injured party, that the girl was dating him first, that they were going to patch up their relationship as they had before, and juniors had no business taking sophomore girls away from sophomore guys. As for the football rivalry, Sam thought he was a better player and deserved to start. Besides, he just didn't like Jim and his "rich, snobby friends" who thought they were better than other people. And if Jim was favored for the football position, it was only because he sucked up to the coach. "Everyone" (Sam's peers, that is) said that the older boy didn't have the raw talent and fight that the younger guy had.

Jim, on the other hand, reminded the counselor that Suzanne, the girl involved, represented herself as free at the time he started dating her. The starting positions on the football team were open to both of them, but he, as an equally talented but more experienced player, should have a starting position. As for the fighting, Jim claimed Sam was initiating it, and he was only defending himself.

Ms. Myer heard the boys' stories out. Then to each of them separately she said something like this:

MS. MYER: You have reasons to be angry at each other, but anger with fellow students, no matter what the reasons, doesn't justify name-calling, threats, and fighting. Those forms of expression are against school rules and completely unacceptable. It would be better for your development as young men to learn more mature ways of handling conflict. I know this idea of getting together to learn a conflict resolution model might sound awful, scary, corny, weird, or really unlikely to work, but I've seen it work before. Of course, it will work better if you have an open mind about it — give it a chance — have a good attitude. Besides, it's a requirement of school discipline rules and, if it fails, there are pretty serious consequences.

Ms. Myer presented to each boy a written copy of Part One: The Thinking Steps and discussed each step as follows:

MS. MYER: Let's first look at:

Step 1. Assess Emotions.

There might be other feelings that underlie your anger, including being hurt, being jealous, frightened, or embarrassed. Do you feel there are other emotions that affect your reactions and are part of the situation? Would it be appropriate to convey some of these feelings when you get your chance to talk? If it's too revealing or personal to discuss these, at least be aware that these could be part of your overall feelings.

Your assignment for Step One: Write a one- or two-paragraph statement about how you feel about your anger and what other feelings you may have experienced during the conflict.

Step 2. Accept Anger, Behave Well.

First reflexive thoughts are clearly important, and, once you respond to anger in a reflexive fashion, the other person is likely to also. What are your first reflexive thoughts? Are they retaliatory? Could you modify them quickly and tell yourself to react appropriately? What can you say to yourself to catch that first reflexive thought and get a better attitude?

Your assignment for Step Two: First, write down what you think your first thoughts usually are when [Sam/Jim] makes you angry. Then write down some things that are more appropriate to think and do when you first get angry.

Step 3. Gauge Intensity.

How strongly do you really feel about these anger-provoking confrontations? Gauge the intensity on a 10-point scale to see how strongly you feel.

Your assignment for Step Three: Write down where on the anger scale of 1 to 10 you were at the beginning and at the height of this conflict and where you are now.

Step 4. Who and What?

You said [Sam/Jim] was a jerk. That's just name-calling. It will be helpful to you to clarify what exactly you're angry about and state that in resolvable terms. That will be the focus of our discussion Monday. Think clearly about what it really is and who are all the people involved. Is it how the person has treated you directly that makes you angry? Or is it being embarrassed in front of your friends or is it more related to some other types of jealousies? Is it only the other boy you are angry with or is it the group of friends or Suzanne or someone else?

Your assignment for Step Four: State in writing the actual problem that needs solving as you see it now and whom you are angry at.

Step 5. Perspective Check.

It's useful to try to put this conflict in perspective. Compare it with other situations in your life. Ask yourself if your behavior was overreacting and whether there are times when you have dealt better with a similar situation. Is the other fellow's behavior really so bad or is it just the last straw? Is there another way to look at this that doesn't make you feel so hostile? When you look at other people who have competed for a spot on the team or have dated the same girl, are you reacting more strongly or the same? It would be useful to put yourself into the other person's shoes.

Your assignment for Step Five: Write an answer to these two questions — Was your reaction to the provocation in proportion to what the other guy did? And, looking at the issues from the other boy's point of view, why do you think he acted as he did?

Ms. Myer told the boys they must complete these written assignments to avoid further disciplinary action and bring them to a joint meeting the following Monday.

She also told the boys that she would check the assignments but not show them to anyone. She explained that the assignment was for the purpose of fostering a mindset conducive to resolution, and the answers would serve as a guide to each of the boys during the second and third parts of the resolution process.

She was sending copies of Part One of the conflict resolution model and the assignments to the boys' parents along with a letter of explanation. In it she encouraged the parents to discuss the materials with the boys but only after the boys had answered the questions for themselves.

MS. MYER: Hopefully these materials will serve as a springboard for discussions with your parents. I'm looking forward to a good resolution session on Monday. Please come well prepared.

The following Monday both boys showed up at the counselor's office with their parents, as directed. The counselor met with the boys together this time, and their parents were instructed to wait in the lobby or return in a half-hour.

Ms. Myer checked to see that both boys had made, in writing, at least a reasonable attempt at each of the assigned steps. She then gave them a handout showing Part Two: The Talk/Listen Steps and explained each of them. She pointed out how the steps of Part Two corresponded to The Thinking Steps of Part One, which hopefully had prepared the boys for talking and listening well. She was going to coach them through the procedure.

MS. MYER: I have taken care of the first two steps of Part Two for you. I have chosen the time and place and I have brought you here privately so there will be no others around taking sides today. That includes me. I'm going to help you do a better job of talking, listening, and coming up with a solution, but I'm going to be careful not to take sides on the main issues you are trying to resolve.

Step 8. Express Appropriately.

Sam, go first. Tell Jeff how you feel. Keep it rather brief. Just say it directly.

SAM: I'm upset because you stole Suzanne from me while we were going together. You had the car and the money. Besides we just had some problems for a few days, and we were going to work it out until you came along. And every time I come around you and her, you do something lovey-dovey just to bug me. Like you weren't even doing it and then you see me and you put your arm around her. And then you start stuff at football practice. And somebody told me you were calling me "that redneck." You said, "That redneck isn't going to get my place on the team." It's not your place for one thing; it's for the one who plays the best.

MS. MYER: How mad did that make you and how mad are you now, Sam? Remember gauging your anger?

SAM: I was mad like out of control just about every time I saw him. But, sure, when I was writing down this stuff, I was about a 4 or 5, but now when I start to talk about it, I get mad — like an 8 — all over again.

MS. MYER: So Jim, moving on to the next step for Sam, Active Listening. Can you repeat to Sam in your own words what he's feeling and why?

JIM: He's mad because Suzanne and I are dating even though we have a perfect right to. . . .

MS. MYER: Whoa! Just tell him what he told you. No editorial comment now. You can tell your point of view when it's your turn. For now, stick to showing him you understand what he said to you. And talk to him, don't talk to me.

JIM: (to Sam) You're mad, very mad, that Suzanne and I are dating and you didn't think you had quite broken up. And you think we try to rub it in whenever we see you. And you heard somebody say something about a "redneck."

MS. MYER: Is that a good representation of what you said, Sam?

SAM: Yeah, except I didn't just hear somebody say "redneck." It was you. And that's just what your big-shot crowd thinks, but you guys aren't any better than we are. And in fact, that's another thing that makes me mad: You think you and your buddies own the football team. Half the time you guys make the team because you kiss up to the coach. It ought to be about who plays the best.

JIM: Now wait a minute, if you think you can say. . . .

MS. MYER: Okay, I can see that tempers are flaring here. Can you two get down to where you can talk appropriately or am I going to have to send you home to think some more?

JIM: Okay. Let's get this over with.

MS. MYER: Just try to listen to and repeat what Sam is saying.

JIM: He seems to be mad at me for getting some attention from the coach.

MS. MYER: Say "you seem."

JIM: You seem to be mad at me getting the coach's attention. And about the "redneck" remark. And going with Suzanne, which I can understand.

MS. MYER: Okay, Sam? (Sam nods.) I want to make several points here. One is that maybe the best thing Jim said is "which I can understand." Showing sincerely that you understand is a very powerful thing. I just felt you relax a bit when Jim said that.

Also, remember in The Thinking Steps . . . and you wrote out your thoughts, didn't you? Sam, what emotion did you say you felt?

SAM: I was mad.

MS. MYER: And who did you write that you were mad at, Sam?

SAM: Him.

MS. MYER: I think I'm hearing some other feelings in here along with anger. I'm thinking maybe jealousy, maybe hurt, maybe embarrassment about name-calling. What do you think? (Sam shrugs grudging acknowledgment.) And also, it seems that some other people come into play here. Suzanne, for one. She chose to date Jim instead of you; it's not all Jim. And she participates in what you call "rubbing it in," doesn't she? And the name-calling — you said somebody else told you about it, right?"

SAM: But he said it.

MS. MYER: My point is that you are very angry, jealous, hurt, and embarrassed, and it seems you are turning all your anger on Jim. I see he's a big cause of your anger, but maybe only one part. I'm guessing you are also angry at Suzanne. And the guys in Jim's group seem to irritate you, too. "They" think they are better than you, you said. They repeated the insult to you. Peer groups often "egg on" people who are having a disagreement. They often run and tell you what the other side said. They feed the conflict. You look to them for approval, and, if someone seems to get the better of you, you are embarrassed in front of them. So it's important to note that if this were just between you and him, as it is right this moment, you might be able to work things out better than if you have a spectator group.

What do you think, Sam, about all the different feelings you have and the other people involved?

SAM: Yeah, his group is definitely part of it. I don't really feel so mad at Suzanne as. . . .

MS. MYER: . . . maybe hurt?

SAM: Well, yeah, of course I'm hurt. (He kicks at the legs of a nearby chair. The admission itself seems to make him angry.)

MS. MYER: Saying you're hurt is sometimes hard for guys. I'm not saying to run around announcing to everybody that you're hurt — and neither should Jim — but it's something you should be aware of in your own mind. It's something that, if you admit it to another person, brings you closer to that person.

The other thing is that, since you are feeling hurt, you are probably angry at Suzanne for hurting you. You're turning on Jim all those feelings as well as anger about name-calling and football stuff you two are dealing with. That's called displaced anger, when you don't direct your anger at the person you are really angry with but at someone else. Remember that Suzanne is an equal part of dating Jim. What do you think, Sam?

SAM: Yeah, well, my mom said last night that it was kind of an insult to women to say a guy "took a girl away" like she had no say in the matter. She left, that's all.

Sam looks at his shoes and everyone seems to know this is a turning point and a painful one for Sam. Ms. Myer quickly moves on.

MS. MYER: Jim, will you do your Step Eight and tell Sam what you are upset about and why.

SAM: I'm really not mad at him very much. . . .

MS. MYER: Talk to him. Say "I'm really not mad at you. . . ."

JIM: Honestly, I'm not really that mad except when you do something to me. I'm not sitting around my house thinking how I hate you. But when you elbow me on the field when we're not even part of the play, I get really mad. And I don't like it that you seem to follow Suzanne and me around. Maybe I do sometimes put my arm around her when I see you but it's not to get your goat, it's that I want to show you that you need to butt out. Then, of course, when you pull a swing, I'm up for a fight. Also, you say I called you a "redneck." Well, you called me and three or four of us "geeks" right to our faces. So what am I supposed to do? I told you I'd show you who was a geek on the football field. So then I had to do it. What am I supposed to do? Sure, I'm mad when you bug me, but I wouldn't be mad at all if you'd just stay out of my face. Your saying you were going to "get me" was especially bad. That's war, man.

MS. MYER: Sam, your turn to let him know you heard well and to clarify.

SAM: You don't like me hanging around you and Suzanne. You say you're just being defensive like you think I started it all.

MS. MYER: Jim?

JIM: That's about it.

MS. MYER: Okay. Do you both think you understand the position of the other person and that he understands yours? (The boys nod.)

Now the last of The Talk/Listen Steps is Admit Fault. For most people that's a hard one, but I think you two are mature enough to do this now that you've begun to see there are two sides of the situation. How about if you go first, Jim? What have you done to contribute to this rivalry?

JIM: Okay, I did say something about a "redneck," meaning you, but I didn't mean for you to hear about it. And, yeah, I got my licks in a time or two. I suppose I kind of show off with Suzanne when you're around.

MS. MYER: Your turn, Sam.

SAM: Well . . . I guess I blamed you too much for all this. Part of it was my just being mad about wanting to date Suzanne and just our natural competition for a spot on the starting team. I'm not saying I like everything you do or say any better than I did, but you're probably just doing what I would do in your place. I guess I've been too aggressive.

MS. MYER: I'm glad you can both see that you each have made a contribution to this problem. It's almost never just one person's fault entirely. In fact, both of you are being more reasonable and appropriate than I would have expected.

So now we're ready to go on to Part Three: The Solving Steps.

Ms. Myer gave out a sheet with Part Three of the conflict resolution model and explained that this is the part that helps keep the conflict from recurring. It is intended to solve both the content and the process problems.

MS. MYER: Part Three: The Solving Steps is an important part of any conflict resolution, and it's remarkable how much easier it is to do if the first two parts have been done well. It often is the most time-consuming part, but in this case I'm guessing we can do it fairly quickly.

First, in brainstorming, both of you just throw out ideas that will help you not get into any fights since you both know that behavior is so critical. We aren't expecting you to become best friends but we do expect no more fighting, name-calling, or threats. So do you have any ideas?

SAM: Well, we could just promise not to say anything to make each other mad. You know, just keep our mouths shut when we are around each other.

Jim nodded and offered nothing more.

MS. MYER: Since you have done Part Two of the conflict resolution model so well, it may be a bit cumbersome to go through the five Solving Steps of Part Three in detail, but do be specific about what you're going to do and not do and remember to provide a way to know if your solution is working or not so we can come back and rethink it if it's not. I can tell we all really want this to work.

JIM: Okay, let's also both promise not to use derogatory names about each other.

SAM: Or about each other's friends.

JIM: And, of course, we can't do any physical fighting even if we do get mad. Let's just agree to walk away but not call anybody a wimp for not fighting.

SAM: Right. I can agree to that.

JIM: It would be easier if we just weren't in each other's faces so much at football, but I guess that's impossible to change.

SAM: Maybe Ms. Myer could ask Coach not to put us in one-on-one drills against each other.

MS. MYER: I could do that. (When no one adds anything, she goes on.) Do you feel as if you have resolved this? One part of resolving is to solve the problem and the other is to feel better.

JIM: Speaking for myself, I feel better. I didn't have that much of a problem really.

SAM: We didn't exactly solve my problem but I guess I can accept it better. And if I make the team . . . who knows, maybe both of us could get starting positions if somebody drops out. Yeah, I feel better.

MS. MYER: Will your better feelings last?

SAM: I think so now, but let's get back to talking about our friends. They kind of expect me not to take any stuff off anyone.

JIM: Yeah, the other guys. We have to sort of get them to lay off.

SAM: Just tell them, hey, man, that's over. Forget it.

JIM: And let's promise not to say anything about what we said in this meeting. I think that's really important.

SAM: Yeah, I agree. Actually, it could be embarrassing, so I will try to say it wasn't worth it to keep up this feud.

MS. MYER: I'm glad you two are aware of how coalitions tend to feed a conflict. Remember Step Seven: Avoid Coalitions. We didn't talk much about that before. . . . And what if you get mad again?

SAM: Just think about all this stuff we've said.

MS. MYER: Do you think we need to meet again in a week to see how things are going?

SAM: Naw. Let's just say if either one of us thinks it's not going well, we can ask you for a meeting and the other one has to come.

Jim nods agreement.

MS. MYER: Do you think this model of conflict resolution has worked for you?

Boys nod and shrug.

MS. MYER: Now I'm going to call in the vice principal and your parents and summarize what we've done here, and I'm going to tell them what you all have resolved. I'm sure Mr. Reinquist will have something to say to you, also.

Ms. Myer told the parents and Mr. Reinquist that the boys had resolved the conflict for now and had agreed to discontinue verbal and physical attacks. She felt confident, she said, of their sincerity.

Mr. Reinquist felt obliged to restate for all of them that any recurrence of physical fighting or any verbal threats would result in a ten-day suspension with zeros for academic work missed.

It was clear to all involved that the remarks of the principal would be a deterrent but not the most powerful force keeping Sam and Jim on civil terms. The process itself gave them increased control over their own feelings and acts, a power more valuable than that of "winning" a fight.

CHAPTER 8

The Thinking Steps
for Adults

He said something, then you said something, then he said something else, and frankly you were upset. So you slammed the door and went out and got to thinking and you realized he was always saying things like that and you shouldn't have to put up with it. So you told him a thing or two under your breath, then you opened the door again and went back and told him that thing or two to his face and then wham, here it came: accusations, raised voices, hostile looks, counter-accusations, and if that's the way he felt about it you were outta here. Sure, you'd heard of negotiation and problem-solving and fair fighting, but that had to wait till you

> **See One, Do One, Teach One**
>
> There's an expression I heard frequently in medical school: "See one, do one, teach one." This meant that to really learn a medical procedure well we should see someone do it, do it ourselves, then teach it to someone else. We have to learn before we can teach, and when we teach we learn even more deeply. I hope the examples in this book will help you "see" a good conflict resolution model, and then you will "do one" yourself, and then you'll be able to teach it to your child.

got this out of your system! Besides, it's hard to do all that negotiation stuff when you are so-o-o-o mad.

Yes, adults are often just as prone to behaving badly in anger as children are. Most adults have heard there is a better way. They may even have disguised their angry behavior so it looks better: subtle put-downs instead of name-calling; sarcasm instead of shoves; the cold shoulder instead of a kick in the shins. But this kind of "civilized" war is destructive, too.

Adults are every bit as much in need of a model of conflict resolution as children. Unlike children, however, they may want to know more about what makes taking certain steps toward resolution so hard. They may want to know how they developed their reflex reaction to anger, a pattern that takes deliberate effort to change. They may want help in persuading a partner of the value of a better conflict resolution process.

The trouble is there's never a time when you get around to talking productively about your conflict because, every time the subject comes up, you get mad again and he gets nasty again and the negotiation goes out the window.

Well, you're right. It is hard to negotiate when you're too hot to think. That's why many conflict resolution methods fail — not because they are wrong in principle but because people who start out barely under control often lose control at about Step Two. Or, if they don't actually appear to lose control, they're not negotiating in good faith; they're not trying to solve the problem; they're trying to win or to punish or to make the other person look like the bad guy or just trying to get through the discussion so they can go away.

Going through the motions of conflict resolution is not enough.

BEETLE BAILEY reprinted with special permission of King Features Syndicate

Going through the motions in bad faith is usually counterproductive.
So how can you achieve an attitude that will make solving a conflict possible? I have observed that what you do before you talk about your conflict is as important as how you talk about it. Going through Part One, the five Thinking Steps, before you "talk it out" will help prevent the obstacles that have made your previous attempts at conflict resolution fail.

The Thinking Steps serve several purposes. One is simply to delay an impulsive response, whether physical, such as a slap, or verbal, such as an accusation that "gets to" your opponent, or some subtler signal of hostility like a disgusted sigh or rolling eyes or turning the music up full-blast. If delaying were all it took, however, "counting to ten" before you speak would be more successful than it actually is. The Thinking Steps are more than a delaying tactic. They should help you clarify important issues, improve your frame of mind, and then allow you to enter a discussion with a fair attitude.

The following Thinking Steps are numbered one through five, but it's not cheating to skip around. In fact, doing the second step may help you achieve the first one. You may be so good at number four that you do it easily and have no need to focus on it. For those of you who began reading this adult chapter first, I've given the steps numbers and short names to help you remember them:

PART ONE: THE THINKING STEPS

Step 1: ASSESS EMOTIONS.
Step 2: ACCEPT ANGER, BEHAVE WELL.
Step 3: GAUGE INTENSITY.
Step 4: WHO and WHAT.
Step 5: PERSPECTIVE CHECK.

Now let's take a look at the five steps one by one.

Step 1. **Assess Emotions.**
People usually think they can easily recognize anger and distinguish it from other emotions. But this task is not so simple. People make two common errors in identifying anger. The first is identifying anger while ignoring another negative emotion that preceded the anger. The second is to deny anger altogether or to identify it as some other feeling. It's easy to make these mistakes because anger, like many emotions, rarely comes in pure and simple form. It is often felt along with other complicating emotions. It's not so easy to know which is the primary emotion.

RECOGNIZING YOUR OTHER EMOTIONS

One occasion when anger pushes another emotion aside is the night when a teenager comes home late. Seventeen-year-old Adam came home one Saturday night almost an hour after his midnight curfew. The first ten minutes past midnight, his mother was annoyed. "Why does he do this? Why can't he follow a simple rule?" she asked herself. Then the "Why?" triggered a growing fear. Had something happened to Adam? Had he been in an automobile wreck? Had he been mugged? Adam's mother thought of how much she loved him, how precious he was to her, and how distressed she would be if anything happened to him. Her anxiety became so painful she couldn't sit down but paced back and forth for forty-five minutes, anxiously looking up the street for familiar headlights.

When at last, at almost 1:00 A.M., Adam's car pulled in the driveway, his mother felt a huge relief. But then other worries seized her. She strained her eyes to look out in the dark, trying to see Adam's face. Was there a sign of trouble, was the car damaged, was he sober?

When the kid hit the door and she saw he was whole and healthy as ever, anger flooded her. "Do you see what time it is!!??@#! You are going to be grounded so long you'll forget what sunshine looks like!" The kid identified her anger correctly. His mother was angry at him because he had caused her intense anxiety. Her anger was clearly understandable, and the greater her fear the more anger she felt. But she showed her anger only and she didn't stop to tell Adam she was frantic with worry for the full hour of lateness because she cared about him so much. He probably recognized the caring at some level but what he saw was almost all anger. He had difficulty not being defensive under attack.

Properly identifying and expressing the emotion masked or accompanied by anger can go a long way toward resolving the conflict. If Adam's mother had burst into tears of relief along with a reasonable degree of anger when Adam had arrived home safely, the boy would have understood her emotion primarily as caring. She could have said, "I'm glad you're okay, but I'm angry that you weren't more considerate of my feelings. It's miserable to be as anxious as I was for that long."

Seeing her also as caring and worried rather than just angry, he would be more likely to call her the next time he was out to say, "The movie is starting later than I thought and I don't want you to worry if I'm not home till one o'clock. Is that okay?" Many kids don't make the call home that would resolve the problem precisely because they fear their parents' anger.

Similarly, many people who initially have hurt feelings or anxiety about rejection quickly shift their emotional gears into anger. Beneath their obvious anger remains an underlying hurt or fear they don't identify or show.

For example, Ethel was angry because her husband, George, repeatedly came home from his job as a sales manager later than seemed reasonable to her. She greeted him at the door with flaming eyes and sharp words. "I'll bet you stay late at work because you like that new secretary," she accused him angrily, even though there was no indication he had ever even flirted with the secretary. George, in response, lashed out at her. As he strode angrily past her, he pushed her aside with his arm.

"I bet you don't push her aside like that," she said.

This kind of scene was repeated at least twice a week. Each of them knew they were really angry at each other. They certainly acted angry. But it soon became clear to her that Ethel didn't deep down inside really suspect George of anything improper with the secretary; instead, she was hurt that he didn't seem to want to spend his early evening time with her. She cheerfully allowed him his work time till five-thirty or six but after that she felt he was voluntarily giving away their time together to his job. Knowing that questioning the time he spent at work was a losing battle, she allowed her hurt to turn into anger. So she conjured up a suitable "crime" — hanging around with the secretary — to justify her anger. When he didn't even bother to deny her accusation, she began to believe it was true.

George, similarly, was hurt that Ethel mistrusted him. After all, he worked hard for his family and he couldn't believe she would come up with something like that. His anger was secondary; it stemmed largely from the hurt. If, instead of blasting George with angry accusations, Ethel had told George she was hurt because he seemed to choose to be away from home after official work hours instead of with her, he might have soothed her by saying, "I work long hours because my job requires it, but I would much prefer to be with you." They could have worked out a way for him to show her he meant it, like meeting her for lunch a couple times a week or spending more time one-on-one with her on the weekend.

And if, even in the face of her anger, instead of pushing Ethel aside, George had said, "I'm hurt that you don't trust me," then Ethel might have thought twice about the accusation for which she had no evidence. If they were both able to understand their own hurt and express it appropriately, they both would feel more sympathy for the other, and they could reach resolution more easily.

Denying Anger

Almost as often as people convert another painful emotion into anger, people deny or fail to identify basic anger even when it is crippling them.

Brenda suffered from unexplained tiredness and feelings of pressure on her chest. She feared there was something wrong with her heart. She would go to a doctor periodically only to be told there was nothing wrong. Finally, because her internist was aware that emotion often contributes to physical discomfort, he called for a psychiatric consultation.

It turned out that Brenda was experiencing a serious conflict with her husband in which she felt she had no power. She was very angry at her husband but was not expressing it openly. She repressed her anger so quickly that she was barely aware of the emotion of anger. Even a momentary thought of open conflict made her very anxious. That anxiety caused her to react in the way that brought on discomfort. In her therapy, Brenda learned to identify the source of her anxiety as repressed anger and fear of conflict and to take better control of this aspect of her life.

If you feel a little glimmer of anger, admit it to yourself. No one will hear you. Practice saying, "I'm angry" or "I'm a little angry" to yourself so you get used to the feel of it without repercussions.

When in a stressful situation, you hear yourself say, "I'm not angry, I'm just upset," are you avoiding acknowledging anger? When you hear yourself use words like "I'm concerned," does that mean you are worried about a problem or does it mean you are angry? We have a large lexicon of words to express negative feelings while avoiding statements of anger. Looking ahead to Step Two will help you admit to being angry when you really are.

In sum, determine whether you have a tendency to let anger mask other emotions or whether you go in the opposite direction and deny anger. When you feel anger, identify underlying or accompanying emotions. When you feel other negative emotions, ask yourself if you are angry as well.

Step 2. **Accept Anger, Behave Well.**
Your first reflexive thoughts after you are provoked often contribute significantly to the outcome of the conflict. That's why your first thoughts should be constructive ones. Too many people shout their first thoughts out loud, angering the other guy before they even know what's on his mind. Others act out their first thoughts. Just when they think, "I'll show

him!" they show him. Discussion after that is pretty negative.

But even if you don't act out your first angry thoughts, they often "set your attitude." You very likely need to reset your attitude to a resolving orientation instead of an angry one. For example, your first thought may be, "Boy, you make me so angry." Not too bad. You are correctly labeling your feeling of anger. Now's the time to go one step further. The ideal next reflexive thought would be, "Feeling angry is normal and okay; but it's how I behave that counts." This ideal may be unrealistic at first after years of angry responses, but at least you can now begin to catch yourself in those first thoughts and then move to change them.

Less-than-ideal first reflexive thoughts range from the mildly angry to the murderous. They may be disbelieving thoughts like "I can't believe you did that!" or "What the hell do you think you're doing?!" They may include overgeneralized labeling like "That's just like you," or "You always do that!" or "You bigot," or "You control freak!" Retaliatory thoughts come next on the hierarchy, but even they vary from the mild, "See if I speak to you again," or "You can't get away with that," to the truly dangerous, "I'll fix you," or "I'll make you wish you were never born," or "I'll punch your lights out," or worse.

In fact, it's useful to record your first thoughts the next few times you feel angry. What kinds of things do you most often immediately think when you get angry? What kinds of things do you most often do?

Recognizing your current first reflexive thought is an initial step towards learning a new first reflexive thought when angry. As soon as you have identified your anger (Step One), the second thing you should do, to set an attitude more likely to lead to resolution, is think: It's normal and okay to be angry about this; it's how I behave that counts.

When Anger Triggers Guilt and Anxiety

"Feeling angry is normal and okay" goes against what many of us have learned in the past. Maybe when we were children our family told us anger was wrong and we felt guilty about having the feeling, or maybe they showed us it was wrong by punishing every expression of anger. Now even the beginnings of anger bring conditioned anxiety and fear of some form of punishment . . . or a more ill-defined fear that something bad will happen . . . or conditioned guilt, a feeling that you are a bad person just for having that feeling.

Either way, such old lessons are hard to overcome. Anger may be tightly linked to guilt and anxiety long after our families have anything to say about it. The linking may be strong and largely beyond our awareness.

Nathan, for example, had an older brother with cerebral palsy. The brother was spoiled and demanding. When he took Nathan's belongings without asking and left them out in the rain or broke them, Nathan felt angry. But any time he expressed anger at his brother's negligence or refused to give him a toy, Nathan's parents said, "Nathan, be patient with Sherman. He doesn't get to have much fun. You have other things to play with. Why can't you let him play with the toy he wants? Just be grateful that you're not disabled." And so, in their understandable concern for Sherman, they belittled Nathan's complaint. Nathan felt guilty about his anger. He felt as if any negative feelings he ever had were unjustified because he had good legs. And so, throughout his life, anger and guilt were linked.

Many other people had parents who said in response to any complaint, justified or not: "Be grateful that you even have food," or "What's your problem? At least you have a roof over your head." This kind of reasoning discourages any direct expression of negative feelings. The linking of anger and guilt remains in adulthood.

Brenda, the woman whose tiredness and chest discomfort were caused by her inability to recognize and express anger, learned to deal with a link between anger and anxiety. When she reflects on her background, she realizes that in today's terms her father might have been considered abusive. On the few occasions when she brought up a matter about which she felt some anger, her father, who was prone to drinking, became red-faced, yelled, and sometimes knocked dishes off the table, saying he would not tolerate back talk or disrespect.

Brenda's mother "got on her" for upsetting her father. At the time, Brenda thought that was the normal way; only now did she realize her family had a problem and she did have a right to feel anger and voice her concerns as long as she did it appropriately.

Breaking the Links to Allow Healthy Anger

Being aware of how anger gets linked with other emotions is the first step in unlinking them. Another step in unlinking is achieving the sincere belief that "Feeling angry is normal and okay." Sometimes even what we accept intellectually we don't "believe" emotionally. You should repeat thoughtfully the words, "Feeling angry is normal and okay," until the thought sounds like your own idea. This device is part of cognitive therapy — changing your feelings by changing your thoughts. Saying "it's normal to be angry at this" and believing what you say works, but it may take time to unlink the feeling of anger from guilt and anxiety.

Another important step is actually to express anger appropriately and experience the situation turning out for the better. This way has the most power. Take the risk, identify and express anger, see that the world doesn't come to an end, move on to resolution. Then you can reflect on what benefits accrued from having allowed yourself to feel anger, to express it appropriately, and to manage it well.

It's important that this process works because if it doesn't, you will have resensitized yourself. That is why I recommend following the fifteen steps to conflict resolution rather carefully at first to guarantee success. Only later, when you are confident, you can skip or combine steps you are good at. If we risk confrontation, then fail to resolve, we just prove what we always believed — that resolution is impossible, that the other person is a jerk, that no one understands us or ever will.

In early risk-taking, some people express their desire for resolution so tentatively that they really get creamed, "proving" that their efforts are not worthwhile. When the other person shows a little of the usual defensiveness, the tentative person pulls back. Confrontation takes courage.

Does Your Anger Justify Retaliation?

Part of the reason it's okay to feel angry is because, as the second part of Step Two suggests, you're going to behave well. If you're not going to behave well, maybe it's not okay to feel angry.

Handling it well means resolution; handling it badly most often involves retaliation. Retaliation ranges from killing and injuring to obscene gestures, and to more subtle forms such as withholding affection and intimacy from a spouse, snide remarks, and even deliberate ignoring. Most of us, even though we would never kill or injure, must admit we have retaliated at one time or another in more subtle fashion.

We may find ourselves wondering: But isn't retaliation sometimes justified? We remember when the neighbor dumped his summer yard cuttings on our side of the property line so we blew our autumn leaves onto his property. We remember when someone manipulated us into doing something we didn't want to do, so we deliberately screwed up. Or we recall when someone made a joke at our expense, so we cut him down with a major stroke of wit. Wasn't our retaliation justified? Should we let these people get away with "murder"?

We justify retaliation by one of these kinds of thoughts:

* They deserved it.

* I'm going to teach him a lesson.

* I feel so angry, I can't help it.

They deserved it. Some people think that a crime justifies retaliation. This may even be a majority view. For example, where some people view incarceration of criminals as a way to keep them off the street or to act as a deterrent to others, many people find punishment a way to assuage their anger. Retaliation is justice. The perpetrator deserved it. Crime should not go unpunished. People differ greatly on how far they want to take justified retaliation for crime. Evidence of widely differing opinions lies in the ongoing debate about capital punishment and about what kind of comforts prisoners should be allowed, but in general society feels that crime justifies punishment.

Society's retaliation for crime, however, is usually not reflexive retaliation. Instead, it is limited in these ways: The victim does not determine the punishment or retaliation. The retaliation is decided on by a number of impartial people guided by a body of law and only after careful investigation and consideration. Lynchings and other forms of vigilante justice are not acceptable to most of modern society.

Even beyond criminal justice, the general idea that being wronged justifies retaliation pervades society. I was watching an amateur rugby game when I heard one player use an ugly profanity. I was not so much surprised at the outburst in this rough-and-tumble sport as I was to hear the captain protest, in the middle of a scrum, that such language was not tolerated in rugby. Then came the justification: "But he spit on me!"

One wrong deserved another.

Retaliation is "understandable." It may even be "justified." However, it is not very often constructive. Often what's wrong with retaliating, even when you have been truly wronged, is that it makes matters worse. Maybe "they deserve it." Even so, the person you retaliate against will retaliate against you, and you will be justified in retaliating back, and the matter may never end. This is how feuds work. This is how nations and peoples carry on wars against each other for hundreds of years. There is no way to stop a conflict until someone stops retaliating. Unfortunately, that one may have to suffer injustice for a very long time to make the point. Retaliation often precludes or at least hampers the process of conflict resolution.

I'm going to teach him a lesson. The following line of thinking is very compelling: "If he thinks he can get away with this, he will do it again. I have to show him I will not put up with this."

Yes, sometimes if you are persistently provoked and in spite of your efforts the other party is unwilling to resolve the problem, you might do something to teach him the lesson that you'll stand up for yourself. Sometimes retaliation brings persistent abuse to a halt, as one young man's story demonstrates:

Jason recalled that his older sister picked on him incessantly. She used physical force, ridicule, and manipulation. He cried and complained about this to their father. He often heard his father tell his sister, "You'd better watch out because one day Jason is going to be big enough to fight back."

That day came. Jason had grown taller and stronger. One day, when his sister was tormenting him, Jason punched her in the face. She ran to their father. The father told the sister, "I told you this would happen," and he told Jason, "Never, never hit a girl again."

Jason's sister left him alone after that. As a result of his act, he felt a surge of confidence, but he never had the desire to hit a girl again.

It should be noted that Jason's sister's abuse was repeated over a long period of time and that turning to a higher authority had not stopped it. Also, Jason waited until he was big enough to succeed. He also stopped hitting when the "lesson" worked.

If you choose to use a one-time retaliation to end repeated abuse, my advice is that you use an appropriate, measured retaliation — measured enough that you do not do permanent damage, measured enough that you won't feel guilty later — and that you are committed enough to follow through and strong enough not to get clobbered. Sometimes it works and sometimes it doesn't.

Almost any physical retaliation can do serious damage, even when not intended. People slip and fall, jump back and crash into something, lose an eye or a tooth from what was intended to be a minor blow with an object, suffer broken bones, and many other regrettable results. Both parties are at risk.

One teenager, Mandy, failed in fighting back because she was not strong enough. Her older brother tormented her physically but always behind their parents' backs. He pinched or poked her every time he walked by and swung his fist in her face, making her flinch and jump back, even though he stopped the punch a fraction of an inch away. The parents saw nothing; all they heard were Mandy's complaints, which they considered whiny and annoying. Often the father told her, "Hit him back."

Overhearing this advice, her brother stood leering, daring her to do it. After years of cowering, she finally hit him as hard as she could in the chest. Then he completely overwhelmed her, striking her with his fists until she huddled in the corner with her arms covering her head. Obviously the "sticking up for herself" did no good. It had the result she had expected, and she only did it because she thought she should give her father's advice a try. Now she resents that her father did not support her more constructively. The moral of the story is, if you want to "teach someone a lesson," you have to be in a position where your retaliation will do some good. Lack of a protective authority is a huge disadvantage.

Lack of commitment to fighting back is demonstrated daily by battered women who call the police to stop the abuse. They often lose courage as they picture what will happen to them later either at the hand of the abusive man or without the financial support of the man. So when the police arrive, the women recant, fail to press charges, even testify on the abusive man's behalf. The abuse then repeats itself or even redoubles.

Thus, while sometimes retaliation puts abuse to a stop, it usually fails and escalates the conflict.

I feel so angry. I can't help it. Even though retaliation rarely leads to resolution, there is some logic in the first two reasons for feeling entitled to retaliate. The third reason, however, is less logical than emotional. At the other end of the spectrum from people who feel guilt or anxiety about anger, there are those for whom the feeling of anger and entitlement are linked. They feel no guilt or anxiety about anger. They believe anger itself entitles them to hurtful behavior. They feel retaliation is justified by anger. They think they have the right to say hurtful things, to retaliate physically, to reject or abuse someone. They tell themselves, "I can't help it because I am so angry," as a justification for bad behavior.

On the hierarchy of behavior resulting from the link between anger and entitlement, among the worst is the physically abusive spouse (sometimes the wife, more often the husband) who thinks his feelings of anger over major or minor annoyances entitle him to hit her. He relieves his bad feelings temporarily by demonstrating his power over her. The common excuse, "She asked for it," demonstrates the link between anger and feelings of entitlement.

While the link between anger and entitlement occasionally results in a retaliatory crime, more often it takes the form of minor abuse. For example, a man in line at a bakery shop felt angry at another shopper ahead of him who bought the last doughnut. The shopper who got the last doughnut happened to be an overweight woman. So the man who missed out on a doughnut yelled derisively after the woman, "Like you need another doughnut!" The man's disappointment was expected; even his anger may be somewhat understandable. But even the most addicted doughnut lover should realize that he was not justified in retaliating verbally against the woman who bought the last one. Some people, however, don't thoughtfully consider the wrong done them; they consider the feeling of anger itself to be justification enough for retaliation. Anger in such a person's mind is linked with entitlement to express anger in any old way he feels like it.

Another example is an abusive athletic coach who humiliates, embarrasses, or even physically strikes players. He yells angrily on and off the court. He throws things. He threatens the referees. Zippo control. He seems to enjoy his reputation. He's not trying to learn how to deal with his anger better. He appears to feel entitled to his behavior, perhaps, because of his success on the scoreboard. Much of the public seems to have accepted this kind of tantrum, also. Public and official acceptance of abusive behavior by a few coaches tightens the link of entitlement.

One of the most common situations where people feel entitled to exhibit retaliatory behavior is on the road. For example, in traffic, if you are cut off by a lane darter, it's natural to feel a couple of seconds of anger. If you roar after the offender, pull up beside him and give him the finger, however, you are behaving inappropriately and dangerously. Hitting your brakes in front of tailgaters, honking at little old ladies who are going too slowly, and yelling at people who won't let you change lanes are retaliatory behaviors fraught with danger for all around you. If you cause an accident by retaliating, you can't undo the harm by saying, "Well, it served him right." The fact that anger is understandable doesn't mean you are entitled to retaliation.

Other forms of inappropriate behavior to which people sometimes feel entitled are serious verbal attacks, snide remarks and "the silent treatment." A serious verbal attack might destroy the other person's self-esteem by hitting on an area of known insecurity, for example, "If you weren't so fat, you might not need a ride; you could get there by yourself," or "No wonder you don't have any friends; you're so pushy." Snide remarks might include comments like, "When will you ever learn?" or "You're a fine one to talk." Even silence can be hurtful and humiliating. While sometimes silence indicates that a person is tired of an issue or unwilling to or afraid to deal with it anymore, at other times silence has a retaliatory intent. You're going to punish someone with your withdrawal. Silence announced with a time limit is usually a deliberate retaliation: "I'm not going to speak to you for a week!" or "I'm not going to speak to you until you apologize." But any prolonged silence may be a retaliation.

One of the most common ways of expressing the link between anger and entitlement is "I was so mad I couldn't help it." Sometimes you *are* so mad "you can't help it." Most of us have had the experience of doing something because we were "so mad we couldn't help it." But there is a difference between occasionally slipping up and regretting it later and habitually linking anger and entitlement. Every now and then any person may lose his temper and do something inappropriate. I know. As a coach of a youth basketball team myself, I remember rushing out on the court once and yelling at a player on the other team who intentionally slammed the head of a player on my team against the floor. My anger was understandable. It was normal and okay to feel angry. My reaction as a coach, however, was not appropriate. There were referees to take care of the problem, and I soon regretted that I handled the situation poorly. (I am not alone in my regret; see the attached sidebar.)

Excerpted from the *Atlanta Journal/Constitution*

A guy on my team — not my son, mind you — had been emulating our idolized pros, engaging in a little "trash talk," prompting an opposing dad to saunter menacingly over to our dugout.

"If that kid says another word to my son, I'm going to come inside that dugout and break both his legs," the man spat, his lips curled in trembling fury.

I told him to chill out, to walk back to his team's side, and that I'd talk to our boy. I did. Then I looked up, and the opposing dad was still there, making threatening gestures — taking off his sweatshirt, as if he'd decided to come after our player.

Here was a grown man acting nuts — threatening to break a kid's legs. So how did I react? I went nuts, naturally.

I yelled, letting loose with a torrent of words that would've made a sailor blush. And then I told the boys on my team to find the biggest bat in the dugout, just in case I might need it.

Happily, the guy walked away. Obviously, I should have asked for one of the many cellular phones in the bleachers and called the cops. But that didn't enter my barbaric mind until my fight-or-flight hormones had skedaddled.

As an old newspaperman, I've seen dead bodies left over from such silly squabbles.

— Bill Hendrick

How does the attitude that anger justifies destructive behavior happen? It's usually learned from a parent or other person who served as a model. It's reinforced by experience. If you are someone who generally behaves badly in anger, an entitled attitude probably got you something you wanted in the past. You may like the energizing surge of power that sometimes accompanies anger.

Unlinking Anger and Entitlement

If you are one of those people who habitually behaves badly in anger, you need to concentrate on the second half of Step Two: Accept Anger, Behave Well. Tell yourself, "It's how I handle it that counts."

To unlink anger and entitlement:

1. Understand how you absorbed the attitude that entitles you to retaliation.

2. Tell yourself, "The feeling of anger does not give me the right to retaliate," until it feels like your own idea.

3. Prove to yourself that resolution works better than retaliation. Use the

fifteen steps to conflict resolution and see how much better you feel than you did in the old retaliation cycle.

4. Seek appropriate therapy if necessary.

Step 3. **Gauge Intensity.**

We all know the famous count-to-ten tactic for delaying an angry reaction. True, counting to ten delays, but mere counting doesn't change your attitude. Instead of counting to ten, visualize a scale of 1 to 10 and gauge your anger or other emotion on it. Sometimes the act of measuring itself reduces anger, but there are several more important reasons for doing this step.

Weighing Your Anger

How angry did your spouse make you at dinner yesterday? Were you just annoyed or completely infuriated? Did your teenager merely aggravate you or did she send you through the roof?

Are you angry or are you . . . aggravated, annoyed, bent out of shape, boiling, cross, displeased, distraught, enraged, fit to be tied, flaming mad, freaked out, ****!@!#,** fuming, furious, galled, heated, hot, huffy, hysterical, incensed, indignant, infuriated, irate, irritated, livid, mad, offended, peeved, p.o.'d, put out, resentful, riled, seeing red, sore, steamed, surly, teed off, testy, ticked off, touchy, up in arms, or vexed?

Will you lose your cool? Blow your top? Go through the roof? Explode? Like totally lose it?

It's very useful to put the intensity of our anger on a scale so that we can talk about it and compare it. We can measure and compare our anger today with our anger yesterday, our anger at the beginning of an argument with our anger at the end, our anger over one issue with our anger over another issue, etc. Words, however, although varied in nuance, don't seem to be very accurate in comparing our states of anger. Though a thesaurus's words that describe anger range from "irritated" to "livid" in intensity and from "bitter" to "hysterical" in quality, they seem to mean different things to different people. Are you "peeved" or "surly" or "ticked off"? Is it worse to be "irate" or "incensed"? Which is more angry, "resentment" or "wrath"?

To show how little agreement there is about the amount of anger indicated by various words, I have asked groups to tell me which word expresses more intensity, *mad* or *angry*. Some people say the words are equal in intensity. Other people insist one is greater than the other but disagree on which word is more intense. The same people will always agree that four is more than two and five is less than eight. That's one reason that I use a number scale from 1 to 10, with 10 being the greatest level of anger, as a reference that everyone understands and can use somewhat consistently.

Moreover, people are generally more honest with numbers than with words. Some people, while seething with anger, will say, "I'm concerned that . . ." while other people who are mildly and temporarily put out will say dramatically, "I'm furious that. . . ." These people know the difference in the meaning of the words but they differ in their willingness to express anger. Some people are raised to feel different levels of histrionics are appropriate. In some families, dinner table conversation may sound like war, but everyone goes away happy. In other families, deep resentments are expressed in low-key remarks between the blessing and passing the salt. A number scale seems to bridge the gap between the styles. Those who are reluctant to admit anger may never name a 10 or even a 9 on the scale but they are likely to be consistent within the range of intensity they allow themselves.

To Weigh It Helps You Say It

Deciding how intense your feelings are on a scale of 1 to 10 prepares you to convey to another person how important you think an issue is. Sometimes you are really furious and your partner persists in thinking you are expressing a trivial annoyance.

Style Stings

In certain families and even cultural groups, people will have an "expressive" style, that is, they raise their voices a lot and exchange insults and wave their arms around. Yet it's understood in the family that the apparent anger is not too serious and they get over it quickly. The amplitude of their expression is stylistic and family members adjust to it; they understand that their anger may not be greater than the anger in a less expressive family where, though it is expressed more "coolly," it may even be more hurtful.

While I understand this stylistic difference certainly exists, I want to point out that even where "everybody" understands the anger is "not serious" there may be a sensitive child in their midst who may not feel safe. I see people in therapy who saw their family's expression of anger as normal but still found it hurtful. I also see families whose children do not feel safe, who are afraid of anger, their own and other people's.

Margie, for example, told her husband several times that she was upset by the way his mother treated her during her lengthy visits to their home. The husband shrugged off Margie's comments. Finally, during one particularly trying visit, Margie left the room, went into the bathroom, and threw up. Her husband was concerned and asked her what was the matter. Margie told him she was ill because of the things his mother was saying. The husband, in apparent surprise, said, "We've always been so close. Why haven't we talked about this?"

A wife shouldn't have to throw up to get her husband's attention. Mild-mannered Margie had evidently not gotten through to her husband on this matter. If Margie and her husband had established the 1 to 10 scale, she could have said, "Remember how upset I was when our neighbor cussed out our son over nothing?"

"Yeah, you were an 8!"

"Well, this time I'm a 9½ with your mother and heading for a 7 with you for not taking my problem seriously."

"We'd better do something about this quick."

Conversely, sometimes a person interprets another's sharp look as serious anger when it's not. Giving your partner or friend a number can help both of you respond appropriately.

These numbers take on meaning as you become accustomed to using them. But first you have to practice gauging your emotion accurately by yourself.

Are You Overreacting,
Or Is Someone Taking Advantage of You?

Do you hit a 9 when you discover your teenager left a used glass in the den instead of taking it to the kitchen? If so, where would you go on the scale if a burglar hit your mother on the head and took her purse? Maybe you haven't explored the full range of your anger and your scale needs adjusting. Or maybe you are overreacting to the glass left in the den.

On the other hand, suppose your friend is forty-five minutes late meeting you for a movie for the umpteenth time and you're at a 1 on the anger scale. You're saying, "That's just Mabel. She can't help the way she is." Maybe you're underreacting. Maybe you need to move up to a 3 on the scale and tell Mabel it's time for a talk because you're not waiting outside past the opening credits again. Letting people take advantage of you is no healthier than getting too angry too quick.

If a 1 is mild annoyance and a 10 is blinding rage, most of your issues of anger should fall in the mid-range where they are most resolvable. If your emotion is not proportional to its importance, there's probably a larger underlying issue that makes you react too much or too little. Putting your emotion on a scale allows you to identify your hot buttons and/or cold feet.

When Do You Confront?

1

2   Forget it. No need to talk.

3

4

5   Resolve it. Okay to talk/listen now.

6

7

8

9   First cool it. Talk/listen later.

10

The most important purpose of gauging your emotion on a scale of 1 to 10 is to determine if you are ready for conflict resolution. Once you gauge your anger, you can decide what to do about it.

The low end is a 1 and 2; this is the "forget it" end. The high end, from 8 through 10, is the "cool it" end. Let's look at these ends first.

Forget It

When your anger is a 1 or 2 and has never been higher, forget about it, let it slide, don't make an issue out of it. Why? For one thing, if everyone brought up every little annoyance, think what a mess it would be. For another thing, if a person at a 1 or 2 goes into a full-fledged analysis of his anger (who am I mad at and why?, etc.), he may work himself into a 3 or 4 by overthinking it. Also, dealing with every 1 or 2 annoyance may make other people around you go straight to a 3 or more!

In general, a 1- or 2-level annoyance that has no underlying problem and has never been above a 2 will soon go away on its own. A small annoyance that does have an underlying larger problem or one that is repeated over and over will soon hit a 3 or 4 on the scale anyway.

Cool It

People make the most common process errors at 8 to 10 (yelling and screaming, not listening, saying things they don't mean, blaming). If you are at an 8 to 10, don't say or do anything about it now. Stop. Cool down. In the 8 to 10 range, conflict resolution steps are not likely to be successful. Don't try to resolve your conflict until you are down to a 7 or below.

Of course, the other person can probably see you are angry. So that she doesn't think you are just walking off, you might have to say you are too angry to talk now. Say, "Let me cool down first. I'll talk about it later." At 8 to 10, you cool off, but you are *obligated* to go back later and resolve the issue.

For some people, just waiting will allow their anger to cool. For others, waiting just heats them up. They need to engage in some activity that helps bring their emotion down. See if any of these activities would work for you:

* Physical release such as taking a walk, running, aerobics, hitting a tennis ball, shooting baskets, or raking leaves; displacing anger on an inanimate object such as a pillow or punching bag, or, again, by hitting a tennis ball.

* Distraction: listening to or playing music, reading, watching TV, daydreaming, baking bread, doing any kind of work, deliberately seeking humor, or doing something silly.

* Analyzing: thinking through your situation, writing out your feelings on paper and filing the paper or throwing it away, talking about the problem with someone not involved. (Analyze as a cooling-down tactic

only if it works for you. Some people at this level of anger get even madder when they analyze.)

Caution: Avoid negative forms of cooling-down activities such as driving a car too fast, running in traffic, punching the wall, throwing breakable objects, eating junk food, getting drunk, mailing what you wrote while your judgment was still clouded with anger, etc.

Sometimes your 8 to 10 can be legitimate given the provocation. If you're facing a bad enough situation, such as someone beating up your child, it deserves an 8 to 10. It's not "bad" to be that angry, but, unless it's an emergency, you will still be more effective if you bring your emotion down.

The Rise and Fall of Anger

Using the scale also allows you to see patterns. Some people engaging in a conflict start out at a 7 or 8 and in thirty seconds reach a 9. Others start out at a 3 and it takes ten or fifteen minutes of argument for them to get up to an 8. Others never get over a 5 but stay there day in and day out. Recognizing your anger patterns helps you learn what triggers your anger and what soothes it.

Here, for example, is one couple's argument with the rise and fall of anger noted:

Sue and Rob were studying together. They were pretty good at getting down to doing the work and took pleasure in the proximity of the other one. Then one day Sue found Rob's chewing gum was bothering her a little. (She was 1 on the anger gauge.) She began to think about the rhythm of the chomps and the occasional pop and got a little irritated. (She went to 2 on the scale.) She decided to say something matter-of-fact about the problem: "Rob, could you study without the gum, please, or maybe close your mouth when you chew?"

"Oh, okay."

Sue appreciated his stopping and got on with her work. (0)

Rob soon started chewing again with his mouth open, Sue noted with a sigh. (Back to 2)

"Rob, you're doing it again."

"What?"

"The gum."

"Oh. Sorry."

One minute passed and the gum began again.

"Rob!" (3)

"Hey, what's the big deal? So it's a little noise!" (Now Rob is at 3 on the scale.)

Sue was annoyed (by now at 4) because it seemed Rob not only wasn't controlling the chewing, he didn't take her complaint seriously.

Now it was time to begin resolving this problem.

"Are you making chewing noises on purpose?"

"No. I just forgot about it, but now that you make such a big deal of it, I feel like doing it on purpose just to serve you right." (Rob is also at 4.)

"What do you mean 'serve me right'? (5) It was a perfectly reasonable request."

At this point, both Sue and Rob were feeling a 4 or a 5 on the scale. If Rob will quickly throw away the gum, Sue's anger will drop rapidly below the "need to resolve" level. Rob's will probably drift away, too. If on the other hand he pulls out a second piece of gum and starts chewing it with great vigor and Sue gets mad (4 or 5) again, it's a sure sign of something that needs resolving — Rob's desire not to be "controlled" or Sue's having to have everything just the way she wants it . . . or his liking to tease and her being too serious to accept teasing. The anger may rise and then level off as they discuss the issues and then think of ways to solve the original problem. There may be a simple solution — Rob moves farther away so his chewing is not in Sue's ear or Sue puts on a Walkman to replace the chewing sound with music. With the resolution, their annoyance should sink to a 0.

No, I do not expect Sue and Rob or you and your family to take out a paper and pencil and start writing down numbers on a scale every time you get annoyed. But the concept of noting rising and falling levels of anger may actually help you recognize what is really making you angry.

Gauging Progress

The number scale will show improvement or failure over the long term. If a recurring issue brings two people to a rapid 7 and the way they deal with it gets them to a screaming 9, it's obvious they are not resolving the problem well. If they learn to do conflict resolution and then find that their initial annoyance is somewhat lower, say a 5, and they rarely get above a 7, that's progress and should be appreciated. It's a sign that future attempts at conflict resolution should soon bring the matter to a less troublesome level. If, on the other hand, hashing the issue over and over is leading to the same or worse level of anger, things are not improving and a new direction may be in order.

Again, you do not necessarily have to plot all your disagreements on paper. Do whatever it takes to get the concept. However, you'll find literally plotting the ups and downs of your conflict resolution successes useful, at times, especially when teaching a child.

Step 4. Who and What?

You may think you always know who and what made you angry, but this step often proves to be harder than it seems at first glance.

Displaced Anger

Sometimes you feel angry at one person when you are really angry at another. This error is called displacement or displaced anger. For example, a teenager may be angry at her parents because they put her on restriction so she picks on her little brother. Or a grown woman may be angry that her own parents are telling her what to do. She then snaps at her husband who makes some innocent remark that reminds her of her conflict with her parents.

Similarly, a man may be angry at his staff for failing to take important deadlines seriously, and then he yells at his wife for not having dinner ready when he got home. "Why can't you do anything on time?" he yells. His wife is hurt and bewildered because she didn't know there was any urgency at all about dinner. And there wasn't. His anger was displaced.

This scene is so familiar that it has given rise to the following oft-told joke: The man of the house is angry at his secretary for not getting a letter out so he comes home and yells at his wife for not picking up shirts from the laundry. His wife is angry for being chastised, so she yells at her oldest son for talking too long on the telephone. The son slams down the phone and picks on his little brother. The little brother is mad about that so he kicks the dog. The wife finally says to her husband, "Why don't you just come home and kick the dog?"

When a father comes home from work and says, "I'm in a bad mood, just leave me alone," he's probably protecting himself and his family from the possibility of his displaced anger. At least he recognizes the possibility.

He's a step ahead of the guy who acts out displaced anger, but he still needs to work on not feeling angry towards the wrong people.

Using the coming-home-from-work model, here's a hierarchy of facing possible displaced anger, beginning with the least healthy and moving towards the ideal:

1. A man comes home angry about a problem at work and displaces his anger. He feels entitled to display his anger toward his family and expects them to deal with it and not be angry back.

2. The man comes home angry about something at the office and clearly displaces his anger but recognizes his family is not to blame for his anger. He feels some remorse for taking it out on his family.

3. The man feels displaced anger at his family because of a problem at the office but is aware his anger is displaced. He expects the family to adapt to his needs. He makes them be quiet, turn off the music, and leave him alone.

4. The man feels angry about work, and he does not displace at all, but he wants to be alone after work. He goes to his own space rather than impose silence on his family in the living area of their home.

5. The man is angry about something at the office and uses his family as a support system, telling them what happened and why he is angry.

6. The ideal is the man who resolves the problem at the office or at least leaves it there to resolve at the earliest opportunity and comes home in a genuine good humor.

Sometimes when you displace your anger toward the wrong person, there is no right person. You might just be angry because you can't have what you want. The computer has locked up, the weather has canceled your camping plans, or you're out of milk for your morning cereal. You get in a bad mood and snarl at people.

The trouble with these generalized bad moods is they can be punitive; they are often contagious; they can make the other person feel guilty or sad or angry even though your anger is misdirected. It's unfair to expect someone else to deal with your bad moods, especially when your anger-based bad mood has nothing to do with them.

Sometimes the person you are really angry at is yourself for screwing up. This is one of the most uncomfortable feelings; we'd much prefer to be mad at someone else. We look around for someone on which to displace our anger and we usually can find him.

Overgeneralized Anger

Often you feel angry at a whole bunch of people like your family or your office staff or the whole world. The problem with global anger is you don't know with whom to resolve your conflict. Group resolution is harder than one-on-one. Global anger affects everyone around you negatively and does not invite resolution.

Racial/Cultural Prejudice as Overgeneralized Anger

People often displace their anger toward one or two "bad eggs" in a group to all the members of that group. Or they overgeneralize the characteristics of a small minority to include the whole group. This is a root of racial and cultural prejudice. Hate towards a certain profession, racial prejudice, clan rivalry, and family feuds are all based on overgeneralized animosity. Gangs harm an innocent member of a group to "pay back" an injury committed by another member of the same group. Store personnel search all teenagers in a store because some teenagers shoplift. A teacher treats a child unfairly because his older brother was a discipline problem. Often general attitudes about groups are based on the behavior of a minority of that group. The majority thus suffers from the overgeneralization.

What Are You Angry about?

Sometimes we know well what we are angry at. If someone has harmed us or our family or has misused our possessions or inconvenienced us or otherwise done us wrong, we can recite the reasons for our anger chapter and verse. Many arguments, however, arise over some event or remark that both parties will later realize was inconsequential. Then why were they arguing over it? The answer is: the minor remark or event was probably not the real issue that was bothering them.

IDENTIFYING THE BASIC ISSUE

Take the case of Frank and Elaine. Every morning Elaine complained to her husband Frank that he always left his dirty clothes on the floor and he never put the coffee can away after he had measured the coffee out into the percolator. Every morning the sight of these objects made her blood boil.

Some people have genuine concerns about messiness, of course, but in Elaine's case it turned out that she was mad every morning because she had spent another night without any sign of her husband's affection. If he had wanted to be intimate the evening before, the dirty clothes on the floor and the coffee can left out would have been no problem. She would have been happy to have gathered up the clothes and set the coffee can on the shelf herself. Her misidentification of the cause of her anger kept Elaine from discussing the real issue with Frank and resulted in much unfruitful argument about dirty clothes and coffee cans.

Frank and Elaine did not deal with their basic issue, the withholding of affection. The failure to deal with it and the subsequent carryover into unrelated areas meant the issue was too big, too touchy, too long-standing, and too scary to deal with.

Another way you might miss the basic issue involves getting angry at a little thing that is symbolic of or reminds you of the issue. Or you get angry about a small example of a larger issue. The little trigger issue may not be troublesome in itself, but the larger issue is worth resolving.

For example, a teenager who had asked for some new sneakers balks when his mother tells him, "Hurry up and get ready. We're leaving for the mall in five minutes." He acts angry even though he wants to go buy the shoes. His mother finally says, "If you are going to act that way, we won't even go." Then the teen is angry because they are not going.

The problem here was that the mother's well-intentioned "Hurry up" directive was an old familiar refrain of control, something she had said to him when he was two and three years old. "Hurry up" had become a trigger for anger over being controlled like a child.

A man walks by his wife who is painting the woodwork. "Don't hold your brush that way. Let me show you how to hold it," he tells his wife, taking the brush from her hand. One small thing, but the woman put the brush down, snapped the paint can shut, and walked angrily away from the painting job. The husband was trying to be helpful, but it was one more example of how he was always telling her how to do things and when to do them. Again, a major control issue was touched off by a small interference.

An important way to help correctly identify what you are angry at is to remember accurately when your anger first arose. Who were you with? What were you doing? What did he or she say when you felt that first flicker of anger? Eventually, you may be able to be aware of rising anger at the moment it happens instead of in retrospect. This is where Step One: Assess Emotion comes in, also, because you have to recognize anger to know when it started. Step Two: Accept Anger, Behave Well may kick in, too, because if you don't accept your anger as normal, you may not be willing to admit it even to help yourself.

This is a good time to enlist the help of trusted bystanders like your spouse or good friend. For example, when you are having an argument with your mother over the phone, you might ask your spouse when she first heard anger in your voice. Your spouse might say, "I knew you were angry in the first minute of the conversation when I heard you say, 'I was not out all day, I was here for six hours straight!" As an observer, your spouse may have helped you identify what button your mother pushed: her expectation that you be home awaiting her call, her need for frequent attention.

A second way to know what issue you are really angry about is to recognize the theme of the argument rather than the particulars. Many people argue over and over about the same theme; only the details differ. Recognizing each new argument as really the same old theme helps you identify what you will work on in conflict resolution.

Some themes that cause conflict and anger are more common than others. Look over the following very common themes and see if any of them ring a bell with you:

* ★ rejection

* ★ feeling controlled

* ★ not feeling listened to

* ★ jealousy

* ★ "I'm angry at you because you're angry at me."

* ★ misinterpretation of your motives

* ★ being treated unfairly

* ★ not being trusted

How many of your conflicts over "little things" seem to fit into these big categories?

Overgeneralizing the What

What did this person or these people do to you to make you so angry? "They just get on my nerves," you may say. Or "He's such a jerk," or "It's too complicated to explain."

If it's too complicated to explain, it may be too complicated to resolve. But don't give up. You can break the issue down into parts and state them in ways that invite resolution.

Ways of stating an issue in terms too global to be solved include:

★ "You're impossible to talk to."

★ "Why are you always so selfish?"

★ "Mom, you're never nice to me."

Ways to state the same issue in resolvable form:

★ "It seems you don't really listen when I talk to you."

★ "It makes me mad when you spend a lot of money on clothes for yourself and so little on clothes for me and the kids."

★ "I get hurt and angry when you won't trust me and let me go out with my friends."

Step 5. **Perspective Check.**
Something is making you angry. You've already given your feelings a number value on the intensity scale; your number typically correlates with the intensity of your response. But are you overreacting? Underreacting? Is your anger justified? Will your reaction get you in trouble? What would be the "normal" reaction to this provocation? How would other people react? Take the time to compare the importance of the anger-producing issue with the degree of your response. Putting the issue into perspective is a key to controlling your reaction.

How big a deal is this anyway? For example, if you found an empty glass in the den when your household rules say no dishes in the den, how angry would the rest of the world be compared to how you feel? What would you think of an adult who picked up the glass and threw it across the room, smashing it into a million pieces against the fireplace? What would you think of the adult who picked up the glass and put it in the dishwasher and never said a word to anyone?

Without a doubt, people react in anger with a wide range of intensity from underreaction to overreaction. Which of the following styles seems to be yours?

Underreacting

People who underreact are generally people who are more fearful of anger and more guilt-driven. They don't like to feel anger so they suppress it or talk themselves out of it. These people are generally thought of as "nice" and "easy to get along with."

The downside of being underreactive is that the underreactive person may build resentment over time concerning recurrent issues. The resentment (unresolved anger) results in emotional distancing, falling out of love, depression, feelings of inadequacy, hurt feelings, feeling walked on, feelings of powerlessness. A relationship that fails to allow assertive expression of anger with a spouse, parent, or child leads to passive-aggressive behavior — for example, not talking, withholding attention and intimacy, invoking guilt by acting the martyr, stalling, changing the subject, "accidentally" damaging someone's things.

Assertiveness means honestly, straightforwardly, and reasonably stating your feelings or your needs and allowing the other person to respond truthfully.

It is, of course, part of socialization to be able to restrain anger appropriately. But if you are underreactive most of the time, you should work on allowing yourself to feel anger, label it, and then react assertively. Some of the thought processes recommended later in this step that relate to overreaction could also make the underreactive person wake up and be more confrontative.

Overreacting

Some people are thought to be, by temperament, biologically predisposed to quick reaction and fast-mounting anger. Also, overreaction is often part of identifiable syndromes such as Attention Deficit Hyperactivity Disorder (ADHD) or the manic phase of Bipolar (Manic-Depressive) Disorder.

However, one of the biggest causes of overreacting is a process called **accumulation**, or what I call the "last-straw syndrome." It occurs over a relatively short period of time.

As an example of short-term accumulation, take the case of Robert and his older brother Jay. Jay picked on Robert in different little ways all one Saturday afternoon. It was nothing much — jumping ahead of Robert in line at the movies, taking his last piece of bubblegum, using his baseball glove without asking, getting it muddy and not cleaning it off, switching computer games when Robert glanced away from the screen. Robert just sighed at each of these provocations. As the family gathered for dinner that night, Jay walked by Robert and snatched his cap off, saying, "No hats at the table." Robert grabbed at the hat and Jay kept it out of reach. Then Robert blew his top and ran into Jay's room and started flailing at Jay's airplane models, breaking several of them. Their father, who came late on the scene, confronted Robert, saying, "What did he do to you?"

"He . . . he . . . he . . . ," Robert stammered, pointing at Jay and realizing already how small the provocation would sound. "He grabbed my cap off my head." And then to emphasize that, though the provocation was slight, his feelings were huge, he added, "I hate him."

Even Robert didn't know why the hat incident made him so mad. He didn't catch on to the fact that his anger had been mounting all afternoon and that the hat snatch was the last straw. The annoyances in accumulation are often unrelated; they are cumulative only because they occur close together without cooling-off time or resolution in between.

In short-term accumulation, someone blows his top over some little thing because they did not react to a whole succession of recent small things and now they have had it. The answer to the last-straw syndrome is to resolve each conflict as you go along so that issues do not build up.

Sensitization is another process that often results in overreaction. Sensitization comes from a build-up of instances of a particular issue over a long period of time or, occasionally, a severe one-time trauma. A person experiences sensitization when he has not resolved the old issue or recovered from the trauma. He becomes sensitized to that issue and its symbols. Later, when the issue comes up, no matter how small its manifestation, he blows up.

An example is Rhonda, an attractive young mother who was disturbed by what she admitted was her own tendency to overreaction. She had most recently been on vacation with her husband Ted and their three small children. She had been enjoying the time and feeling quite loving. They were all relaxing by the pool one afternoon when friends of her husband stopped by and asked him to make a foursome for a game of golf. He agreed and was happily going off to get his clubs when Rhonda burst into tears. In fact, she did not get over her anger that week and spent the remainder of the vacation making them both very miserable. Her husband and she agreed she was overreacting. Still, she found it difficult to get over her hurt and angry feelings.

Rhonda and Ted were generally happily married, and Ted was a good husband in most ways. He was loving and generous to her, and they went out often as a couple. He was, however, not a lot of help with the children; this was something of a recognized issue but not an overwhelming one.

What was so bad, then, about this particular vacation game of golf? Golf! Rhonda became agitated at the very word. She remembered several occasions, for example, when she sat by the bedside of a child with an earache listening to the sound of Ted putting on the carpet. Ted would play golf while she was tied down to the sickbed of their children. Golf was beginning to represent his absence when the children were particularly demanding. Her sensitization to golf as the culprit became more intense near the birth of their third child, due in October. Ted had been practicing all summer for the big club championship tournament in September. He had been lifting weights more consistently and his drive was longer than ever. He felt more focused than he ever had in all his years of playing golf and he thought he had a shot at winning the club cup this year. His name would be displayed on the plaque in the front hall of the clubhouse where not only his friends but his children could see it for years to come.

Rhonda was having some contractions that month. The doctor called them "false labor" pains and nothing to worry about. She was having a particularly hard pain when Ted left for the tournament.

"I don't know, Ted. This doesn't feel like it's 'false.' This feels like the real thing." She saw him blink slowly as if trying to make what she had said go away.

"I want to watch you play, but I don't know if I am up to dragging the kids over to the club."

"I'll take Toby with me," he said. "See if you can get your mother to keep Sarah."

"Maybe I'd better stay here just in case. . . ."

"Just in case what?"

Just in case the baby comes, stupid, what else? she felt like saying. Instead, she sighed. "Oh, it's probably nothing. Just go on. I'll deal with it." Then she kissed him, wished him luck, and said she'd be over if she could, and he left.

Rhonda's pains soon grew more intense and by the time Ted would have been on the fourth or fifth green, she knew this was labor. She called her mother and lay down on the floor, frightened and in intense pain, Toby and little Sarah hovering over her, until her mother got there. She delivered a four-pound baby girl minutes after they arrived at the hospital. The club steward got the news when Ted was one stroke behind going into the eighteenth hole, but his tee shot put him on the green in one stroke. The steward let Ted finish the hole before he told him the news.

Ted brought the trophy to the hospital. Rhonda turned her head away from it.

"I thought you'd be happy," he said.

"I would have been happy if you'd been with me when the baby was born."

"I didn't know the baby was coming."

"You saw how bad the pain was."

"You told me to go ahead."

"Oh, sure, what else could I say?"

The topic recurred for months and Ted was more defensive than apologetic. Rhonda felt he had never recognized her original disappointment; he had never validated her feelings.

Golf. That was the fire that lighted her anger and her fuse had become a lot shorter that very day. She was sensitized to the whole activity of golf, and, whenever Ted indicated he was headed for the course, she felt resentment even though at that particular time she might not have needed his presence. So on their most recent vacation, when everyone felt relaxed and the children were playing happily and the responsibility for them was not particularly burdensome, an appropriate game of golf triggered Rhonda's anger and she overreacted.

In this case, when Ted decided to leave the pool with his golfing buddies, Rhonda knew she was overreacting and knew why. She just needed to know how to control her feelings. Other people may not know when they are overreacting and may not recognize sensitization.

To recognize sensitization, look at what made you mad and ask yourself if it was really so bad in itself. Is it appropriate to be mad at this one instance? To help put the issue and your anger into perspective, check with friends, a therapist, a parent, or any other person with an objective opinion. Ask them how they would feel. If they don't see the issue as important, their opinion may help you put an incident into perspective.

Making the Headlines

Every day newspapers print accounts of acts of anger. Often the story includes hints of the reasons for overreaction as in the case below. I have added the italics to show how the letter carrier felt entitled to retaliate and was sensitized to the event by previous experience. (Names have been changed upon request.)

Mailman faces charges

A letter carrier has been accused of using his mailbag to smash a windshield in a car operated by a student driver.

Sgt. Josh Stuart will seek a complaint against Jim Cantrell for malicious damage to property, according to police reports.

Bruce Wilson, who owns Wilson's Driving School, told the *Times* this morning that he was giving a driving lesson to a 16-year-old girl on Maplewood Avenue around 2:50 p.m. yesterday.

Wilson said he was in the process of telling the girl about stopping for pedestrians as they approached a mailman who was crossing the street. When the girl saw the mail carrier, she slowed down, but thought the carrier was letting her go by, Wilson said.

As she approached Cantrell, who was halfway across the road, he suddenly wound up his heavy sack and threw it at the car, Wilson said. It shattered the windshield, showering glass on Wilson and the girl, who received a small cut on her thigh.

Wilson said the postal carrier walked away after the incident, saying "I had the right of way."

Stuart reported he spoke with Cantrell, *who said he became angry when the car did not stop at a place where he had almost been hit several times before.*

Cantrell "could have blinded or even killed us," Wilson said. "The 16-year-old is scared to death. She may never drive again."

Gloucester (Mass.) Daily Times

On the other hand, you may find that 90 percent of the world feels you should not be angry but you still are. So that's when you ask yourself why.

What is your hot button?

The hot button is what you are sensitized to. Here are different kinds of hot buttons:

★ a tone of voice or facial expression from a person with whom you have frequent conflict

★ certain processes or tactics like changing the subject when an issue is brought up

★ yelling — it scared you when you were young

★ a particular person — anything negative that person does

★ a specific issue, usually related to a current relationship or to a relationship you had when you were growing up. For example, you may be sensitized and overreacting to people telling you how you feel or how you should feel, guessing your motives, or that all-time favorite — saying you are overreacting. Either because of the repetition of the issue or the trauma of it, it never feels resolved.

Issues to which you are sensitized need to be resolved to the point of genuine forgiveness.

Perspective Check Techniques

One way to put an issue into perspective is what I call the "Whoa, wait" technique. When anger strikes, stop, say to yourself: "Whoa, wait! Is there another way of looking at this?"

Here are some questions that will help you consider alternative perspectives:

★ "How many possible motives can I think of for the other person's behavior besides the one I thought of first?"

★ "If I put myself in their shoes, what would I be thinking?"

★ "What was I doing wrong to contribute to this problem?"

If you can ask yourself these questions, you'll probably gain empathy for the other person. The questions help you understand the other person's behavior and why the other person may not take your issue seriously.

How Many Possible Motives?

Whitney, a tired mother, was reading a bedtime story to her small son late at night to get him finally to sleep. She was angered when her husband Tom came home late and walked into the bedroom, stirring up the child and further delaying his sleep. When the father first entered the room, Whitney shot him a look that could kill and it was downhill from there.

If Whitney had withheld her dirty look a few seconds and asked herself why Tom was coming into the room, she might have found other reasons at least as plausible as the explanation that came first to mind. She thought that Tom was thoughtless, at least, and probably selfish, and he didn't care how much trouble he caused her. Here are some additional ideas, some equally negative, some more benign.

* He was jealous and wanted more "daddy time" to compete with her "mommy time."

* He was jealous and wanted more of her time and attention for himself. "She should be cooking my dinner."

* He was oblivious to her difficulty with a late bedtime and just came in without thinking.

* He was a nice, loving dad who wanted to kiss his son goodnight.

* He intended to be helpful, to help lull the child to sleep. He might even have felt guilty that he was not home earlier to help.

* He was mistakenly mind-reading that she wanted him to come in and speak and not ignore her when he came in late.

Any of the last four thoughts would have made Whitney less angry than her original thought. Some of them might actually have calmed her down. Taking the few seconds to generate such possibilities before she reacted would probably have cooled her intense anger and kept her from glaring at Tom who, in turn, reacted in anger. She would have seen the need to wait until she had more data and to talk and listen to find out what he was up to.

As for Tom, when he saw Whitney's punishing glare, he might have given some thought to her possible motives, too: She's tired. It's been a long day. Getting this child to bed is a real challenge and it's not surprising she was upset when he was stirred up again.

If I Were in His Shoes, What Would I Be Thinking?

Let's look again at Rhonda, the wife of Ted, the golf champion. If she put herself in Ted's shoes she would begin to empathize. Here's what she might think:

★ It was the club championship and he had practiced so much and this was his best shot at winning.

★ If Ted had really known she was going to give birth that afternoon, he would never have gone.

★ Ted probably felt terrible about it but just couldn't show it verbally. He was simply being defensive.

What Did I Do Wrong to Contribute to This Problem?

When Rhonda had felt a few labor pains, she said to Ted, "Go ahead and play golf," but she was miffed when he got ready to go. He took it as her usual "miffed" over golf, not a special "miffed." She didn't communicate and then blamed him for not reading her mind. So she can see his behavior was a little bit her fault.

If, through this sort of reasoning, Rhonda had been able to forgive Ted for his absence at the birth of their child, she would not have been so sensitized forever after to his leaving her to play golf.

We often bring data into our minds on "grooved perceptual pathways" based on our past experience (with that person or even another person). Grooved perceptual pathways are assumptions that may have once been true or may never have been true but are now habitual thoughts that cause anger. Looking at the situation in a new way and broadening the possibilities from our first assumption are ways to reduce anger, to listen better, to empathize, and to resolve the issue.

A sincere effort at The Thinking Steps should leave you better prepared not only to bring your own emotion under reasonable control but ready to talk and listen during The Talk/Listen Steps.

CHAPTER 9

The Talk/Listen Steps
for Adults

It's time to talk. Are you ready to get in your best shot and start persuading, outconvincing, outmaneuvering the other person with logic?

If that's what you're here for, you'd better go back to The Thinking Steps and try again.

Remember, resolving conflict is not about who's right and who's wrong, but how to solve the problem so you can feel close again. You are trying to clarify your own position by stating it well and being candid and open. The rationale for the label "The Talk/Listen Steps," however, is that I want to put talking and listening on a par with each other. You don't just talk. Think of the Talk/Listen part of conflict resolution not only as an opportunity to communicate your feelings, but as a discovery process where you try to ascertain what's really going on and understand the other person's feelings.

To begin the Talk/Listen part, a lot of people will have to overcome hesitancy and anxiety about moving ahead. They may suppress and avoid talking out of fear. Or they may have been used to punishing, pouting, or "losing it," and they're not sure they can do any differently.

Or it's the other person they worry about. The history may be that the other person pouts, punishes, or attacks in the most vulnerable spot. They feel intimidated by the expected intensity of the other's hostile response or discouraged by previous lack of success. There's also the fear that talking will become a confrontation that will threaten the stability of the relationship and lead to a downward spiral instead of a positive one.

STONE SOUP reprinted with permission of Universal Press

All that may have been true in the past. And it will probably not change dramatically the first time you try your new approach unless the other person has agreed to use a new and better approach as well. So be prepared to persevere through several attempts, taking comfort in the fact that you are doing the mature thing. After the other person experiences your more mature approach, he may gradually lose his defensiveness and respond with a more cooperative spirit. Don't respond to his inappropriate behavior in kind. You have to be "bigger" than he is for a while and maintain your confidence.

Tell yourself optimistic thoughts like, "If I do it well, it could work this time." Coach yourself. If the other person is at all reasonable, have some trust and optimism that he will be reasonable this time and that the confrontation could turn out okay. Trust and optimism can be self-fulfilling. In the meantime, practicing good conflict resolution skills offers an opportunity for more personal growth than is usually attainable through reading, listening to lectures, and other passive learning experiences.

If you are at a 3 or above on the anger gauge, don't hang back from starting the conflict resolution process. When people hang back on big issues or repeatedly on the same small issue, they often get so angry that it eventually shows anyway: they usually become overreactive, increasing the chance of scary retaliation from the other. So avoiding the issue ultimately lessens the chance of overall resolution.

The Talk/Listen Steps, like The Thinking Steps, could be fairly short, a matter of minutes — five to fifteen or so, especially if you make your statements fairly short and in a calm tone and if you stick to one main issue at a time. A more intense, lengthy, unfocused discussion might confuse the issues or cause additional anger over the process itself.

Here's a quick review of the steps in Part Two:

PART TWO: THE TALK/LISTEN STEPS

Step 6. TIME and PLACE.
Step 7. AVOID COALITIONS.
Step 8. EXPRESS APPROPRIATELY.
Step 9. LISTEN ACTIVELY.
Step 10. ADMIT FAULT.

Step 6. Time and Place.

This step seems like one of the easier steps, and sometimes it is. You choose a time and place when you think a good discussion could get somewhere, even if complete resolution may take several more sessions. Unless this is an emergency conflict resolution, you want to optimize your chance of success — so you allow enough time to talk, catch both parties in a decent frame of mind, expect few distractions, and give little opportunity for interruption. Don't choose the morning rush or a day when there's a deadline approaching or wait till the last moment of the evening when the other person wants to go to sleep. Find a place where there's privacy for those involved, for example, behind closed doors. If you need to do a thorough resolution with a child, rather than incidental teaching, don't pick a time when there's homework to be done or a place by the window where he can see his friends outside waiting for him. This is all common sense.

Think both of your needs and the other fellow's needs. Ask him for his input. If the other person participates in choosing the time and place, he may be more likely to come "to the table" with a good attitude.

At times I'm asked, should you tell the other person the issue before the time you actually agree to talk? It's the polite thing to do, and you may get greater cooperation. Not knowing the issue may make the person fear the worst or crank up some defensive anger over imagined conflicts that aren't the issue at all. So you may want to tell the general topic so the other person can mentally prepare, hopefully with a good attitude.

Another frequent question about setting time and place is whether the dinner table is a good place to resolve a conflict. It's true that dinner may be the time and place a family is most likely to be together. Dinnertime is convenient, but think twice before you use it for resolving a conflict that may be difficult. The process affects the family's together time as well as their eating habits and, if the conflict generates anxiety, people may not want to eat together. Dinnertime attempts at resolution may associate anxiety with eating and may even lead to psychological eating difficulties. There is also much opportunity for coalitioning (Step Seven). In summary, I lean toward not doing conflict resolution at dinner. Give conflict resolution its own time.

How about resolving conflicts in cars? We're in the car often enough; why waste it? Let's look at the parameters of car diplomacy. When the trip ends, the conflict resolution process may end, so decide if there's time. Also, you are in close quarters and it's hard to walk away. That might be good for someone who avoids beginning or seeing resolution through. It might be bad for someone who is very afraid of confrontation and cannot discuss a subject without a way to exit afterwards. Also, resolving a conflict in the car might distract the driver. But if the trip length is right and the confinement not an undue stress factor, and the conflict is not too touchy or heated, a car trip might be the right time and place.

What about starting a conflict resolution while a spontaneous argument is in progress and anger is in the air? Sometimes you must — for example, when someone has made a pressing demand on you or when the real world requires an immediate decision. But if you have a choice, what then?

Especially when you are an 8 to 10 on the anger scale, wait to settle down and find a time and place where everyone is likely to be more logical and reasonable.

On the other hand, a good goal is to develop enough confidence, flexibility, and self-control to deal with issues on the spot so you don't stew in your anger but, rather, clear the air quickly. Setting another time and place diminishes spontaneity and allows greater avoidance behavior. You may not have enough emotional pressure to bring the subject up later. Ultimately, whether to talk now or later is a judgment call.

The adage "Don't sleep on your anger" or "Don't go to bed mad" has merit. It seems to be a reasonable goal to solve most conflicts in the same day. If not possible, consider that an early promise to talk might soften anger enough to go on until the next day. Just don't promise and neglect to talk.

If the Time and Place step is easy for you, so much the better. You will spend little time and energy on it. For some people, however, this step is hard.

One man complained his wife brought up difficult subjects just as he was leaving for work and didn't have time to do the subject justice. He also didn't want to arrive at work agitated, should it come to that.

His wife admitted that she did choose this time intentionally, although she just then realized why: She was afraid of confrontation and was bringing up difficult issues when there was only time for her short statement of the issue and a short reply. She was limiting the time available so they wouldn't get into an upsetting argument. She needed to get the issue out, but she feared he would out-talk her once again if she gave him time.

In another situation, when a woman approached her husband about an issue, he would say, "Not now, can't you see I'm watching TV?" or "Why do you start up when I've just gotten home? I need some time to unwind and relax." When she brought up an issue at dinner, he said, "Can't we just eat and do this later?" When she approached him in the evening smoking in the yard, he said, "I come out here to be alone. Isn't there some place I can be by myself?" He worked long hours, and there never was a right time to deal with problematic issues. When his wife said, "Okay, not now, but when?" he said, "I don't know; just quit pressuring me."

So, while finding the right time and place is a matter of simple courtesy for some, it's the gateway to dreaded confrontation for others who will inevitably have trouble getting through it. When finding the right time and place is a major obstacle, the issue is probably not actually time and place but an unwillingness to try to resolve the conflict at all or a fear-based avoidance. Hopefully, resolving a few simple disputes successfully with the conflict resolution model will make you more willing and less fearful to try it as often as needed. At some point, try bringing up this "real" (process) issue as the substance (content) of a conflict resolution.

Step 7. Avoid Coalitions.

Rod is a very articulate, highly analytical, dominant, competitive person. He says he enjoys serving as an expert witness in litigation in his field, for example, because it's like a challenging sport. His wife Ellie is plenty sharp but seemingly no match for Rod in an argument.

One evening Rod and Ellie were out dining with another couple when

a disagreement arose between them. At first, Rod and Ellie said things to each other like "You don't ever tell me in time," or "Half the time you're not even listening." They occasionally made explanatory remarks to the other couple as if to fill them in on the drama.

Finally, Ellie made a strong point against Rod's position, and he was momentarily at a loss for a good comeback. So he quickly turned to the other couple and said, "She's not making any sense. Does she make any sense to you?"

The wife of the hitherto uninvolved couple, offended by Rod's belittling of his wife's calmly stated point, said, "Yes, she makes sense to me."

Rod had not only failed to make an ally, he had lost some of the power he was accustomed to having, so he dropped the subject. But Ellie, having inadvertently gained an ally, picked up the topic again. Soon the people at the next table were calling the waiter to ask to be moved to a table on the other side of the room.

Was Rod and Ellie's conflict resolved by this coalition? I think not.

Although coalitioning is almost always harmful and destructive to good process, it's less well known as a process error than other aspects of poor conflict resolution such as yelling, screaming, and threatening. Moreover, forming coalitions rarely causes the initiator embarrassment and shame. She often feels successful and clever when gaining an ally.

Coalitioning is destructive to overall resolution. If you gain an ally, you are more likely to be stubborn in your position instead of seeking a middle ground. Or you will be emboldened emotionally and be more on the attack. That makes it harder to listen to the other side.

If, on the other hand, someone uses an ally against you, you are more likely to get angry not only because of the issue but because people are "ganging up" on you. Or, if you feel forced by a coalition to accept a solution you think is unfair, and if you give in without true emotional resolution, you will feel even more defensive or resentful over time.

Some people deliberately bring up conflicts in front of others to embarrass their adversary or to gain leverage and power or because the other person won't dare come back at them too hard in front of their friends.

Blatant coalitioning might involve directly inviting another person to take your side, asking others who agree with you to give their opinion, or pointing out that the opponent similarly mistreats another person in hopes that the person will agree and join forces. Subtle coalitioning might involve knowing glances or a hint to encourage someone else to chime in.

If you have a hard time engaging in conflict resolution without seeking a coalition, it may be because you grew up in a family where people regularly took sides.

Coalitioning sometimes permeates family structure. Family therapists assess who is close to whom, who has conflict with whom, and then try to intervene in a way to help the family eventually move to a more appropriate structure. Dr. Salvadore Minuchin developed "Structural Family Therapy" and created "maps" of dysfunctional family units. These patterns are useful in understanding families in general.

According to Minuchin, a ***stable coalition*** involves a child in a close relationship with one parent, where there is marital conflict, allied against the other parent in terms of loyalty. The alienated parent either vies for this child's support or gives up and "disengages" from the relationship.

A stable coalition is not as dysfunctional as ***triangulation***, in which the child is suspended between two parents, dancing back and forth between the two, trying to win the favor of first one and then the other. He may also try to avoid being disloyal to either, to support both, always flip-flopping. Kids in a triangulation pattern are often really anxious and suffering.

Another dysfunctional pattern is ***detouring***, a situation where parents are in conflict and the child becomes needy, sometimes ill, drawing the couple together over him, distracting them from their problem so they don't solve it. The parents subvert the conflict to their child's needs — a detouring protective system. Or the child "acts out" and the parents again are distracted from their own conflict to angrily confront the child — a detouring attacking system.

If you were raised in such a family, coalitioning may seem to be the norm. Choosing up sides may seem to be a smart strategy. Understand, however, that it does not favor real resolution in either a practical or emotional sense.

It's good to discipline yourself and discourage your child from seeking to build coalitions as a way of dealing with one-on-one conflicts. Select a time and place for conflict resolution so that you can avoid coalitioning. For example, you might not pick a time when in-laws are visiting to have a discussion with your spouse or talk to a teen when his friends are there.

Moreover, when an issue comes up with a child, such as how much phone time is allowed or what is a reasonable curfew or how severe a punishment for shoplifting should be, and you differ with your spouse on certain points, you and your spouse almost always should go behind closed doors, work on it, and try to be of a common mind. It's unhealthy for one parent and a child to be in coalition against the other parent unless the other parent is clearly abusive and damaging. Occasionally, an older child is mature enough to understand his parents have different value systems in certain areas.

However, it's good to have some objective person hear both sides and martial some expertise or judgment, especially about process. When a parent mediates between siblings, to teach the process well, it might look like the parent is taking sides. When one child is being more inappropriate than the other or is using inappropriate power, a mediating parent may seem to be in coalition "against" one side, but you really are "for" both your children. At such times, the children must acquiesce to your judgment, and they feel ultimately more secure because of it.

At times, there is a subtle difference between coalitioning and seeking advice or emotional support from a friend or therapist. If you are discussing a conflict with a friend or therapist in order to gain better perspective or to embolden yourself to be appropriately assertive in your attempt at conflict resolution, that is appropriate; it doesn't meet my definition of coalitioning. Seeking advice or support from a person who will not be involved in the confrontation is not gaining unfair advantage unless your primary argument is that the outside person agrees with you. Coalitioning involves taking unfair advantage by bringing "an outsider" into the confrontation. It's the spirit of the thing.

Step 8. **Express Appropriately.**

CATHY reprinted with permission of Universal Press

Here we are halfway through the conflict resolution model, and we realize this is where many of us generally start. We start a discussion or argument without any previous thinking, without having analyzed our own feelings or considered the other fellow's, without having clarified the issue and chosen the right time, place, and person or people to express it to. What a difference seven steps make!

For those who have done the previous seven steps well, the eighth step may be as smooth as chocolate pudding. But for others there may still be lumps.

There are those who think ventilating and getting angry feelings off your chest is healthy, normal human behavior — the essence of dealing with anger well. They feel entitled to behave any way they want. The point is, if you have decided to learn to resolve conflict well, then you should do what works. The danger with ventilating or "spilling your guts" is that the ones who are yelled at usually retaliate (internally or externally). When they counterattack or escape your wrath in fear, resolution never has a chance. At best, the other person is angry himself and doesn't cooperate. Dumping your whole load on someone simply doesn't work very often.

Others who have trouble with this step are still fearful, but perhaps they don't realize how fear is affecting them. Perhaps they have suppressed their emotions so well that they say they don't need to bring an issue up anymore. It's resolved. Yet if the issue comes up over and over, it's not resolved.

One woman, who generally communicated well with others, reluctantly brought up certain problem issues with her husband, but she always approached the subject indirectly. She had trouble getting to the point. She drowned the main point in details and asides. She omitted key ideas and downplayed important parts that might displease him. She wanted to say what she meant, but she didn't want him to notice. And so she obscured her real meaning. If the subject ever came up later, she would say, "But I told you. . . ." Only when she talked about her fear in therapy did she realize what she was doing. Even then her habit of veiling the issues wasn't easy to change. She eventually learned to express her concerns appropriately by writing down points in clear wording and then sticking to her script. She actually felt more confident speaking from notes than she had when she skirted the issue. Her husband's response was better, too.

"You Get on My Nerves"

Find the courage to bring up a conflictual issue clearly and the self-control to say it appropriately. Be focused and state your complaint in resolvable terms. What behavior could the other person change to please you if you only say something vague like, "You get on my nerves"?

Instead, specifically identify the behavior you don't like. "I feel as if I have no privacy or space of my own. . . . I don't like you to read all my e-mail over my shoulder. And I don't like you to change the radio station or the heat and air-conditioning settings when you ride in my car. It would help if you would at least ask first."

The number of things that you bring up is important. Pick the most annoying thing only or the most resolvable of the serious issues. You can write out a statement describing your feelings and briefly name the event that triggered your anger and other emotions. Give no more than several paragraphs to the cause of your anger.

Use as near to a conversational tone as possible. Be honest, straightforward, sincere, reasonable, assertive. Don't yell, scream, threaten, or get physical. Don't be sarcastic, condescending, superior, or manipulative. Avoid also being pleading, whining, apologetic, unsure, flip-floppy, mushy, or syrupy.

Of course, all this is much easier said than done. Now is not the time to be a perfectionist. You shouldn't expect your initial statement of anger to be perfect. You also hope other people are mature enough to accept a slip or two. What's important is to move in the general direction of improved conflict resolution skills.

Step 9. **Listen Actively.**
Listening actively is like a mirror image of the last step, expressing appropriately. You are the listener you wish you had when it was your turn to talk. As I sometimes tell kids, become one of the "world's best listeners" — a real expert. Take pride in being a good listener and approach it with genuine curiosity. Having a clearer understanding of what's going on is always an advantage.

Listen so intently and well that you can paraphrase back, showing you understand. Say things like, "Let me show you that I understand what you're saying," and "Let me be sure I'm clearly hearing what you're saying." Then repeat in your own words what you understood the other person to say. Give her a chance to verify what you've said.

Another way to listen better is to pick up the last thing the person said and repeat it in a way to signal him to continue. Ask him to repeat what he said if you didn't process something.

Let the person know you're listening. Subvocalize what they are saying, repeating points to yourself. Most people do better looking at the person speaking, nodding their head, saying occasionally, "I understand." Some even take notes. Try to avoid planning your counterattack; people can often sense there are words of rebuttal sitting on the end of your tongue.

Listening actively is difficult. It's a skill you have to learn just like riding a bike or sewing; it doesn't always come naturally.

Sometimes it's hard to listen well because the other person isn't expressing herself appropriately. For example, her tone may be annoying, and she may be insulting you. She may not be working towards harmony or practicing self-control. She may want the power of being able to "get to you."

Often the person's tone and language affect you so much that you miss the content and become defensive. Try to ignore bad tone and insults — for now. (These process errors can be brought up as a content issue that needs resolution later.) Try to pick out the facts and issues, and repeat these to her. When she realizes the insults are lost on you, she may settle down. In any case, what you do as a listener will affect what she does as a talker.

Just being listened to can lead to some feeling of resolution, especially if there's no practical solution necessary or possible. For example, one member of a couple might be more liberal politically than another, and just understanding the other's point of view might lead to more mutual respect. The same is true with different religious views. Both people need to be able to express themselves freely. Being listened to generates good will and allows solution-oriented thinking.

Step 10. **Admit Fault.**

A couple in therapy in my office were at each other's throats most of the time. One day I said I wanted to do something different in this session. I wanted each of them to spend the time talking *only* about what he himself contributed to their conflicts and, therefore, not to be critical of each other at all for this one session.

Normally, they were articulate and persuasive, but this time they could barely talk. These people who were so good and clever at finding fault could find no fault with themselves.

Their "brains were trained" to think only along certain channels. Their immediate reflexive thoughts were the critical, I'm-being-treated-unfairly, why-are-you-doing-this-to-me, can't-you-understand, we-would-get-along-fine-if-only-you-didn't kinds of thoughts.

They did very little wait-a-minute, maybe-I-did, or let-me-think-what-I-must-have-done kind of thinking.

The experience was very instructive to this couple. You, too, could try

SALLY FORTH/ by Greg Howard

SALLY FORTH reprinted with special permission of King Features Syndicate

this technique at home and see what you learn.

Admitting fault allows you room for personal growth — you're aware you need to change. It also generates good will. If you can genuinely admit fault, it's contagious, and the other person may respond in kind.

Nobody said admitting fault was easy. You often see how tricky it is in political life where taking credit and denying blame is the rule. If politicians do accept blame for misbehavior, it can be problematic.

We live increasingly in a climate of individual irresponsibility, not accepting responsibility. Our judgmental, performance-oriented society leads us to reflexive defensiveness. One result in the public arena is frivolous lawsuits. Another is overusing various psychiatric reasons for defense in legal cases. In our take-care-of-yourself culture, people fight off acceptance of any fault in family/friendship situations. This is natural. Admitting fault produces uncomfortable feelings of guilt. It may give the other person leverage over you. Some people will pounce on your admission and use it as a weapon, unless admitting fault is a mutual effort. Also, it isn't fun to have someone justifiably angry at you. So, for all these reasons, admitting fault is not a step that comes naturally or easily to many people.

Scapegoating is a common pattern of dealing with conflict in families. Scapegoating is akin to displacement (discussed under Step Four: Who and What). When people can't face the appropriate person, they displace anger on a convenient other person. A couple may make scapegoats of their children. People make scapegoats of "them" — other races, religions, or other groups such as "the townies," "teenaged hoodlums," people from the other side of the tracks, or anyone in a government uniform. Blaming "them" keeps people from having to look at what they did to get into this mess.

Even when people do admit fault, they often do so by agreeing to the other's complaint with a nod, shrug, or "maybe you're right." It would be more helpful to resolution and to yourself if you would approach your admission of fault with an open mind, as a discovery process. The result would be contrition, remorse, and growth. In other words, admitting fault is more than lip service, and some actual emotional pain may result.

The key to growth through admitting fault is taking the time to really soul search and asking yourself, what am I doing wrong in this situation? What if you still feel it was not at all your fault, or you were misperceived, or the facts were wrong or the other person is truly unbalanced? My answer is that the distribution of fault is very rarely 100 percent to 0 percent. Seeing it as 100 percent the other person's fault might be your biggest fault. Even if it's 80 percent to 20 percent, you can still grapple with what your 20 percent might be. You can say you don't feel it's mostly your fault while still admitting some fault. Remember that the words *all, never,* and *none* don't belong in the same sentence with *fault.* "It's not my fault" and "It's all your fault" are reflexive statements as adverse to conflict resolution as any I can think of.

Occasionally I ask couples to do a global fault analysis, not just of one particular argument but of the overall fault in their relationship troubles. Often people split the fault 60 percent/40 percent or 70 percent/30 percent, giving themselves the lesser amount, or 50/50 to be politic. Yet many who sincerely give themselves more of the fault than their spouse still appear to blame the other when they talk. How much fault do you actually attribute to yourself and how much to the other person? And how does that compare to the blame you communicate to the other person?

When done well, these five Talk/Listen Steps offer ways to come to a consensus about what the resolvable problem is. It may be content; it may be process; it may be both. It may be an isolated event; it may be a pattern. Once two (or more) people recognize the problem as one they can and want to resolve, they have created a positive momentum that will carry them into Part Three: The Solving Steps.

CHAPTER 10

The Solving Steps
for Adults

Of the three parts of the conflict resolution model, Part Three usually takes the most time — the most time to do, the least time to describe. Now that you're here, having gone through the other steps productively, you should have less negative emotion and more optimism about resolving a conflict. So, not being angry anymore or feeling content about the process up to this point, some people skip The Solving Steps. That's usually a poor idea because slipshod planning or no planning at all can allow the issue to recur. Besides, being less angry and more optimistic, you should enjoy The Solving Steps and will likely do a good job of problem-solving.

Occasionally, however, a conflict is caused by pure misinterpretation, a misunderstanding that, once straightened out, doesn't require the next five steps. Someone admits a mistake or someone agrees to try not to make a certain mistake again, now that it has been called to his attention. A good percentage of conflicts result from process errors, and the major challenge is to follow a more ideal process. For example, if displacement of anger is the problem and that is recognized, the content issue may become a non-issue. Those are all valid reasons for shaking hands right here and calling it a day.

In some cases, people may actually begin with Part Three — where there has been no anger and both parties agree there's a clear and resolvable problem (thus condensing Part Two until it's unrecognizable), or when they foresee the possibility of a disagreement up ahead and they decide to do conflict prevention.

Here's a review of Part Three:

PART THREE: THE SOLVING STEPS

Step 11. BRAINSTORM SOLUTIONS.
Step 12. PROS and CONS.
Step 13. DECIDE and PLAN.
Step 14. DO IT.
Step 15. REVIEW/REVISE.

Step 11. **Brainstorm Solutions.**
To brainstorm, let your mind go free to think of any idea or plan that might be helpful to solve the problem. Try not to censor ideas at this stage. Let ideas flow.

A brainstorming session ends when no one can think of any additional ideas, and suggestions have been made that have a good chance of working.

A couple, for example, tried to problem-solve as a way to prevent conflict in their financial matters. They came up with these ideas for handling money:

* have separate pots where each spends only what he contributed.

* have a common pot and sit down together to pay the bills from the pot.

* jointly put money in a common pot for obligatory bills and split the rest into separate equal accounts for discretionary purchases.

* design a budget and have someone write the checks according to the plan, just as a secretarial job.

* have no formal plan but have anyone making a big purchase, spending more than a certain amount, get the other's consent.

All of these suggestions were rather ordinary; there were no off-the-wall ideas. But don't be afraid to throw in imaginative, untried solutions just to shake up your thinking. Some of the best solutions have been modifications of someone's "wild idea."

Often people very quickly censor their own ideas before they have even expressed them. This premature judgment inhibits creativity. Inhibition comes from a pessimistic overview, a general lack of confidence in their intellect or creativity, or from not wanting to feel the sting of the other person's judgment. Judgmental remarks about ideas can shut down the creative process and make people mad again. The rule of brainstorming is: no criticism of ideas at this time. Leave that to the next step.

Sensitivity to the ultimate judgment of an idea is greater for those who are wedded to "their" idea. So, in the brainstorming step, it's useful to offer a variety of ideas at the extremes of the spectrum, setting some up for rejection. For example, if the problem concerns doing an unwanted job, suggest Sue will do it all or Bob will do it all when clearly there should be some division of labor. Even kids will see that the answer is somewhere in the middle of the spectrum. Similarly, offer one very strict solution and one very liberal solution and encourage suggestions between the two. In short, show you're not afraid to offer an idea you know is far out and will be shot down later.

Paying attention to whose idea is whose, whose idea is best, and whose idea will be chosen nourishes the competitive spirit born in the original conflict. It may make someone defend and justify his idea beyond objective reason.

Both self-censorship and concern about the judgment of others often keep us dignified, suggesting only conservative solutions. Don't be afraid to be silly. Encourage humor in the brainstorming process. Do you remember the two siblings who were arguing over how to share play time with the family cat? In their brainstorming session, the family came up with the possibilities of drawing straws, flipping coins, assigning each child a alternate hour, day, week, etc., to play with the cat. Get another cat and have two, a child said. Get rid of the cat and have none, a parent said. Let the cat decide, someone said, and everybody laughed. The laughter totally transformed the argument into a family joke instead of a conflict. People who laugh together rarely resent each other.

To encourage creativity, you might give some credit to the one who came up with a highly original idea, whether or not it was ultimately chosen. In fact, the idea that finally comes out of brainstorming is often a blend of ideas, the "reasonable middle ground." Acknowledge and reinforce the teamwork that is forged in brainstorming, for it will prove to be valuable in the next step.

Step 12. **Pros and Cons.**

Pick several of the best ideas to "pro and con," that is, tell the advantages and disadvantages of each. In the case of adults, each can choose a top two or three. A parent with a child can give his best two or three and invite the child to pick his two or three favorites. If a child's idea is really too far out, give a quick reason that it won't work, and ask for another choice.

Depending on the severity, longevity, or importance of the problem, you might jot down some of the pros and cons on paper. If it's of lesser importance, writing them down might seem an exaggerated response.

Here are some important parameters to consider:

* likelihood of a solution being carried through. Is this plan too hard or too unrealistic?

* excitement, motivation, or personal commitment that each person can marshal to the idea

* reinforcement strategies that can be applied to the plan such as charts or rewards

* monetary cost of materials or rewards

* degree of difference between the new plan and the old, entrenched behavior patterns

* how much the plan fits the family value system

Step 13. **Decide and Plan.**

By the time all the ideas have been analyzed for pros and cons, it's usually fairly obvious which solution is the best. One idea just seems to have more going for it or more support than the others, even without being weighted and tallied. Sometimes, however, there's a tie or deadlock. What should you do?

In practice, the decision usually goes the way of the more dominant person. In certain authority-based structures this is appropriate: the military, for example. There are better methods for deciding, however.

One factor to consider is that the enthusiasm one has for the chosen plan affects the outcome. So if one person is more committed to his favorite idea than the other person is to hers, perhaps you ought to go with that one. Ask how committed each participant is on a scale of 1 to 10. If the husband cares at about the level of a 6 and the wife feels as strongly as an 8, go with the wife's choice, assuming she is being honest and not manipulative.

Another principle for breaking a deadlock concerns domain or expertise: If the conflict has to do with child-rearing and if the wife spent more time with children, she might make the final decision. If the conflict had to do with the car or the roof and the husband was more responsible for the cars and the roof, he'd have more say.

"You had your choice last time; now it's my turn," is a time-honored principle that might also help break a deadlock peaceably. And there's nothing wrong with a loving spouse voting in favor of doing what he knows the other one wants, unless it will be a cause of resentment later. ("I gave in last time.")

Hammering Out the Details

At this point, you may still need to work out the details of the conflict resolution plan. In the plan, do the following:

* ★ note the responsible parties for each duty.
* ★ establish criteria for following through.
* ★ set up checkpoints along the way.
* ★ set up reminders and reinforcement.
* ★ agree to a time to review and revise.

Settle who may remind whom. It's best to remind yourself. If the other person reminds you, it can cause resentment to flare. If you're sure you can accept a reminder from the other person, say, "Remind me if I slip." If you can't, consider asking a third person to remind you: "I'm trying to remember not to interrupt. Will you signal me if you catch me doing it?" Resolve not to remind the other person unless invited to do so.

Set up a reinforcement system in your plan. In training, I heard an example of a negative reinforcement program called "The Guaranteed Cure." Someone swore off a bad habit or promised a new better behavior. He also agreed to the following reinforcement plan: Each time he failed, he had to set his alarm for the middle of the night, and, when it went off, he had to get up and do a number of push-ups as punishment. The number increased exponentially so that further failures to "cure" the habit demanded much more punishment. The person was almost forced to meet his own goal. Granted, self-reinforcement of this kind requires almost as much discipline as changing the original behavior.

More effective in many cases is positive reinforcement. You can reward yourself for fulfilling a promise by doing something pleasurable. You might, for example, play a relaxing round of solitaire on the computer. Some might see this as a waste of time, but it's not as harmful as having a sweet, a drink, or a smoke if you are successful in a habit-changing plan. You can have breakfast when you've made your bed; you can use the phone after you've done your homework; you can watch TV after you've made all your calls. These are forms of positive reinforcement. The pleasurable activity is a reward for following through on your own plan. It can simply be for yourself or part of a negotiated resolution.

Should you put the plan down on paper? Writing concretizes a plan better, clarifies thinking, makes the plan more definitive, serves as something to refer to if memory fails. On the other hand, some people object that writing is unnatural, makes too big a deal of smaller issues, or seems obsessive. It's a matter of individual preference and, especially, what works.

One final word on planning: Devise a plan that doesn't set people up to overpromise and underdeliver. If anything, you should probably underpromise and overdeliver.

Step 14. **Do It.**
The Nike Corporation knew what it was doing when it came up with the slogan "Just do it." Taking a new positive action is easy to contemplate and to promise but hard to do. "Just do it" is about all you can say. The rest is in the doing.

People know well the failed diets, failed exercise regimes, and failed attempts to kick bad habits, along with the unfulfilled promises, convenient forgetting, and simple failing to follow through on a plan.

"Do it" is the bottom-line step. Suppose you went all this way and then didn't follow through. How frustrating! Each of the people involved owes it to the other to make it work.

Suppose the process error that you have agreed to reduce or eliminate is interrupting people who are talking. You promise to quit . . . but how to do it? You can ask someone to remind you every time you interrupt. You can put reminder signs on your mirror. You could post the rationale for quitting on your desk to review just before having a meeting where interrupting may be a problem.

Expectations should not be perfectionist. If you have backsliding, it's not the end of the world. You know the dieter who eats properly all week and then slips and eats some forbidden butter on his bread or a sworn-off brownie. So, having failed, he eats the whole loaf or the whole pan. Don't let one slip make you give up on the whole plan. Behavior often improves in a sawtooth pattern — up a ways, down a bit, then up some more — with an overall upward slope. Avoid saying, after a downward slip, "I knew it would never work." Say instead, "This is just a bad day," or "This is just a temporary setback. I'll do better next time." Remember the progress you have made since the very beginning of the plan.

Step 15. **Review/Revise.**

As Robert Burns once said, the best-laid plans of mice and men often go awry. I can't speak about the plans of mice, but the plans of men can often be put back on track with a little review and revision.

In reviewing the outcome of your plan together, be objective, state your position appropriately, draw the other person out, and listen actively.

Answer the positive question first:

★ What aspects of the plan are working out well? Should you keep those aspects?

Then, ask what aspects are not working out well:

★ Are there times when the plan was working well, and how did those times differ from now?

★ Are there unforeseen external forces or stresses influencing the execution of the plan?

Review your own role before you review the other person's part. Ask others for feedback: "Am I less controlling?" or "I am trying to do. . . . How do you think I'm doing?"

The more specific the behavior you are trying to change, the easier it

is to review. For example, you can count the number of times you interrupt; you can less easily quantify how much less controlling you may be.

If you find you haven't done your part of the plan, do Step Ten: Admit
Fault.

All of this is best when done as a reciprocal process, but if you are the
only one familiar with the conflict resolution model, ask your partner
whether he's disappointed in how the plan is working and how he thinks
he's doing. Lead him through the process, and give him equal input into
deciding how to put the plan back on track.

Ask yourself if there's something about the problem that you are still
angry about. If so, you'd do well to go back through all three parts of the
model.

If you're not angry but there seem to be some mistaken assumptions
or misunderstandings, begin with Part Two: The Talk/Listen Steps. If you
think you're on the right track and just need to alter your plan, go back to
the beginning of Part Three: The Solving Steps.

If it was a simple, casual plan with no documentation required, you
might decide to do it more formally with more structure, documentation,
and reinforcements. If it was a successful plan, fully documented, and
you're getting tired of keeping track, you might decide to discontinue documentation and just keep up the good work.

Reviewing and revising may be as simple as "no change needed" or a
quick adjustment made in passing. With deeper-seated or global issues,
reviewing and revising a plan could go on throughout a lifetime. The
problematic issue might recur despite good intentions. Or, as age and cir-
cumstance change, the situation could change.

I think of Connie, who had dated Brad for several years, reluctant
to marry him for fear of losing her independence. Eventually they went
through a process to resolve her concerns including brainstorming and
deciding on a plan. They agreed she would pay half of everything to maintain equality. Thus reassured, they married.

The agreement worked for the first few years when both were very
poor. Gradually, however, his income went up significantly above hers.
They still lived in a small apartment because she couldn't pay for half of
something better. He wanted to live in a nicer place and was happy to pay
more than half, but she didn't want to move because it destroyed her con-

cept of taking care of herself.

When they eventually decided to have a child, they reviewed the plan, and Connie agreed to revise it. They moved into an attractive house in a nice neighborhood. In the new plan, Brad had to do half the child care, half of everything, so Connie could continue her career, bring in an income, and have an equal shot at job opportunities. That worked for just about nine months. Then the reality of parenting set in, and they reviewed and revised the plan again. Connie traded off Brad's extra income for her extra child care. It worked, at least for a while.

Then they went overseas, where Connie was not legally allowed to work at all. Connie felt dependent, and she and Brad argued about money. This difficult time ended when they moved back to the States.

When their child and the one that followed were old enough to be in school most of the day, they reviewed and revised their plan again. Brad does more for the children than he used to, and Connie has resumed her career. In time, they may review and revise again.

THE PAYOFF

Accepting your feelings, behaving appropriately, being open-minded to the other person's point of view, understanding the problem, putting the problem into perspective, expressing yourself appropriately, and coming to a practical solution — if it all came naturally, you wouldn't need this book, and you wouldn't need to teach your children. But look around. Gunshots ring out in our schools, marriages fail, couples live in constant states of resentment, children lash out at their parents, parents abuse their children, clerks snap at customers, drivers rage in traffic, bombs express social dissent. And who wins? The only ones who win are the ones who can control their emotions long enough and well enough to resolve conflict. Teach your family to be winners.

Frequently Asked Questions

Some of the following questions I have been asked by others; some I've felt compelled to ask myself along the way in an effort to clarify my thinking. The answers all draw from the same model for conflict resolution, but the questions all have a special "twist."

Q: What are your opinions about "bullying" behavior?

A: Bullying is a broad topic, and it's important not to overgeneralize. Each child is different; what motivates him and what influences have affected him are different. The questions I would ask about a bully are these:

★ What type of modeling has he seen in his parents?

★ Has the child been neglected or abused?

★ How has violence in the media affected him?

★ Is he modeling the behavior of older siblings or older kids he's trying to impress?

★ Is his bullying behavior part of a group aggression mentality such as gang rituals or other types of unhealthy peer bonding?

★ Is it for "macho" status — to be perceived as the meanest and toughest?

★ Is his behavior chosen to impress the opposite sex?

★ Could it represent displaced anger — anger displaced from family conflict, problems at school, or being bullied himself by someone higher up on the aggression chain?

★ Is he compensating for feelings of inadequacy or trying to find some avenue to self-esteem?

★ Is his bullying behavior part of an overall psychiatric disorder such as Bipolar Disorder, ADHD, Conduct Disorder, Intermittent Explosive Disorder, or Depression?

★ Is it because of his own severe intolerance for being teased or his perception that certain individuals or groups look down on him?

★ Is it because he sincerely believes that the victim of his bullying deserves the aggression?

★ Is it pure revenge?

★ Does he perceive his behavior as humorous and enjoy making his friends laugh at the vulnerable child's expense?

★ Is it for monetary or material gain?

★ Is he sadistic, having somehow learned to enjoy the power and feeling of hurting other people?

Any combination or all of the above may help explain bullying behavior. Whatever the motive, however, bullying is serious and intolerable. None of the factors above should rise to the level of an excuse. All bullying behavior requires firm discipline; serious and persistent cases merit professional evaluation and therapy.

Some parents may deliberately support and encourage bullying behavior at times, allowing their child to act out their own aggressive desires. Other parents, moreover, refuse to acknowledge the seriousness of their child's behavior and unwittingly reinforce his aggressive tendencies by blindly taking his side. Hopefully, parents will recognize that bullying behavior requires serious attention.

If it's your child who's exhibiting bullying behavior, you need to understand the frequency and seriousness of the behavior and his motivation. If he's motivated by displaced anger, then you can teach him the whole conflict resolution method so he can deal better with his anger overall.

If he's more of a show-off and bullies to impress his friends or if he's feeling inadequate, work on improving his feelings of adequacy. That means not only showing appreciation for his good behavior and accomplishments but helping him actually become more adequate. Introduce him to something he can be good at, and give him experiences that will enhance social skills.

If he's supersensitive and can't tolerate anyone teasing or making fun of him and bullying is his way of getting people back, work on Step Five: Perspective Check with him. Try to convince him that defending himself by being more disengaged works best as in the anti-get-your-goat technique in Chapter Three.

If your child is not the bully but the victim of the bully, I also recommend the anti-get-your-goat technique. But if the bullying is serious and physical or threatening serious harm, teach your child it's okay and not cowardly to seek help from authorities at school and elsewhere. Let him know you will back him up. You should also help him avoid contact with the bully and be protective in other ways.

Q: What about someone who really relishes anger, feels empowered by it, and therefore looks for opportunities to become angry?

A: As a recipient of this kind of anger, you aren't able to deal directly with this motive very well, but if you understand the pattern, you might be able to take the other person's anger less seriously or personally. If the person who gets high on anger is your equal on the power curve, you could make her recreational anger the subject of a conflict resolution. Tell the person she seems to take advantage of you and hurts you by using you in that way. If it's a person with legitimate power over you, such as a boss, this is a good place to use the diffusion strategy discussed in the defensiveness section of Chapter Three. When she screams an accusation at you, draw her out, ask her to clarify the problem. Get her to put her accusation in concrete, specific, and resolvable terms. If she can't, your request may make her sheepish and quiet her down. If she can do this, you can gently initiate a conflict resolution. If there is some legitimacy in her anger, show you are willing to admit your faults and deal with them. That puts you both on an even plane and shows your maturity. Then push toward resolution.

Maybe you are the person who feels inappropriately energized and empowered by anger. You feel better when you've really vented; why can't the other person just accept that? In this case, you need to do some developmental analysis of how you got anger and power linked up. Was it because anger made you feel more powerful as you were growing up with your parents or peers? Did anger help compensate for some inadequacy? Did losing your temper help you win in your neighborhood? Are you modeling after your parents? Did they vent their angry feelings, and after it was all over they didn't seem to have any bad consequences? Maybe they kissed and made up. Maybe your father vented, and your mother handled it well (or vice versa). They didn't get a divorce, and one did what the other one wanted. Ask yourself, is this what you want long term? If you ventilate, get your way, and feel better, your victory might be a momentary one and ruin your long-term relationships. Do you want everyone to be afraid to approach you? Do you want to raise a child who won't talk to you? Or is intimacy one of your ultimate goals? If so, is scaring or hurting someone with your temper a step toward intimacy? Do you suffer from guilt and remorse later when you stop and think about your outbursts of anger? Such extreme expressions of enjoyed anger may seem to work short term, but ultimately they may work against you. Try the conflict resolution steps, and see if it's not more satisfying to resolve than to win.

Q: I answer the phone for a company, and people dump a lot of anger and blame on me that I don't deserve. It makes me furious, but I'm not allowed to react angrily. How can I deal with my anger?

A: People in customer service positions have to keep their cool even when provoked by the public. Stick to the content issues that people bring up. Just give the facts. On the process side, recognize that anger is not directed at you personally but at a product, company, or political position of your boss. Use the diffusion technique, draw the person out, take notes, make a few comments such as, "I understand the issue is upsetting." Explain the organization's policy. If you are a manager, say you have to make a final decision based on the policy — no money back after thirty days — for example, instead of making an angry retort. Keep a businesslike voice and be straightforward, not wimpy, scared, or defensive. Your own mature behavior will probably make you feel less angry. If, over time, you are getting increasingly sensitized instead of desensitized to angry calls, you may want to consider another job.

Q: Whenever I bring up a problem, my spouse apologizes immediately just to end the discussion, and so we don't get to finish resolving the problem. Then it comes up again. I don't think the apology is sincere, but I look like a jerk if I question it.

A: Saying, "You're right, I'm sorry" too quickly may be insincere, a move made to avoid conflict or keep a resolution from happening. A good response to this might be, "I'm better educated now about conflict, and I'm aware of process issues. I'm aware that resolution is more than just an apology and I want to continue our discussion, each of us stating our side of the problem and listening well. I appreciate your recognizing that you hurt me and are apologetic. But, you know, I might have made some mistakes too, and I feel a need to get a better resolution — one that will last." To his insistence that "It's no big deal, let's just drop it, I won't do it again," just go on, redefine the problem, and ask for active listening. Make reference to the fact that quick apology in the past has not been very useful because the issue keeps coming up again. Then try brainstorming ways to prevent it. It's not that you're trying to exact a pound of flesh, but you're trying to get a better solution than just an apology.

Q: Sometimes I'm mad, and I don't want to find a solution. I want to be mad, and I want people to really know it. I want them to fight back so I won't feel guilty when I want to pound on them. Is there any hope for me?

A: Most people honestly have this feeling at times, and it's good to admit it. It's an understandable feeling. However, it has very poor consequences if you feel this way too often or too intensely. You probably revisit frequently the wrong done to you to keep anger alive. When your anger gets to a 2 or 3 on the intensity scale, you may go over the affront in your mind again until you get back to a 6 or 7. Your question shows you understand very well what you're doing. It boils down to a decision you have to make: Do you want to continue this self-indulgent habit or do you want a better relationship for the future? If you sincerely choose the latter, substitute a different focus whenever you find yourself thinking about what made you angry. Instead of rehashing the source of your anger, reread and recommit to The Thinking Steps. Then give The Talk/Listen Steps and The Solving Steps a chance, and see if that doesn't feel better in the long run.

Q: Nice guys finish last, right? If I negotiate when I think I'm right and should win, won't I always get the short end? I'll never get what I deserve.

A: The conflict resolution model redefines winning. Winning is not proving you're right or getting your way. Nor is it walking away from the fight. Good conflict resolution means walking away feeling better afterwards. A lot of people "prove they're right" and "get their way" but still go away mad or with a ruined relationship or feeling guilty. Talking it through is often the only way to get anything from a bad situation. You're actually more likely to get your way through the less threatening process of conflict resolution than through expressing anger inappropriately. Showing you can resolve conflict will also get you more of what you want in the future because positive momentum makes the next conflict more likely to be resolved.

Perhaps you remember the old saw, "What's mine is mine; what's yours is negotiable." Be aware that conflict resolution and negotiation are not necessarily synonymous terms. When someone wants to "negotiate" with you to get what is rightfully yours, that's not true conflict resolution. You would go away resentful instead of feeling better. That would be giving in to a bully. In good conflict resolution, the problem is solved or improved and both people feel better.

Q: My child gets so mad at the computer, he snarls, growls, and pounds on the keyboard. I'm worried about him and the computer. Also, I think he's just like his father, who does the same thing in bad traffic or other situations outside of his control. It's scary. They aren't angry at a person they can resolve something with. What can I do about this?

A: Recognize that it's normal to be somewhat frustrated or angry about a carton that won't open or a computer that won't perform. A little bit of ventilation may not hurt anything. If their anger remains sustained and intense, however, your son and husband may have a problem. Do they pound on uncooperative machines until they break? That's harmful to man and machine. If every day in traffic your husband is angry for most of the trip, that's unhealthy for him and probably for others. He may displace his anger on other people and disrupt his own body chemistry so that he's prone to stress-related disease.

If the problem is frequent and its intensity is disturbing, approach your husband and your child saying that their behavior is a problem for you: "I'm upset about your outbursts and nervous about the level of tension when the computer (traffic, whatever) doesn't do the way you want it to." Point out that sometimes anger involves a problem that has no solution within our reach like bad traffic, balky machines and people you can't talk to. Instead of road rage and computer conniptions, ask them to do a perspective check (how big a deal is this anyway, probably "no biggy piggy") and then move toward acceptance thinking, that is, realizing that if there's nothing they can really do, dwelling on it is harmful to their health and the happiness of others around them. Ask your son to leave the computer for a while when it's causing him to lose his temper. Give him time to cool down, and let him return to the task when he's better able to deal with it. (The computer also behaves better sometimes if you turn it off and turn it on again later.)

Suggest to your husband that he focus on something else when traffic holds him up. For example, a person enraged by traffic tie-ups could listen to a book-on-tape or soothing music.

Q: What if I can't identify what I'm mad at? I'm mad at everything.

A: First, ask yourself when this generalized anger started. What were you thinking or what was going on at that time? Try to figure out triggering situations. Then look for themes. (Review the list of common themes under Step Four: Who and What? in Chapter Eight.) You can also ask people close to you to help you with it. Ask if they remember an event or recognized early signs. Generalized anger might be a symptom of depression, PMS, or other physical illness; check with your doctor about these possibilities as well. If these efforts fail, consider psychotherapy.

Q: How do I know whether my expression of anger will be so unwelcome that it will ruin my whole relationship with the other person?

A: First ask yourself if the person is really that sensitive to your anger. If so, it probably means there's a problem with the general fragile nature of the relationship. You may have been storing the anger for a long time. I suggest you not let it out all at once but little by little. When expressing your feelings (Step Seven: Express Appropriately), don't use words like "angry" or "mad." Say "a problem area" or a "disagreement" or "something I'm sensitive to" or "something I'm worried about" to soften the problem enough to have a good discussion. Be extra careful to choose the right time and place (Step Six), bring the issue up only when you have fully thought it out, and enter softly into the resolution process.

If you are very hesitant to bring the problem up, very deliberately revisit Step Five: Perspective Check. With one patient, I realized she was so fearful of being angry that I told her a good goal for her would be to be "sweetly assertive" to make the idea of assertiveness more palatable. On the other hand, your fear may mean you know you aren't being (or won't be) entirely appropriate yourself.

Q: My father, who lives with us, is a bad role model for handling anger. I don't want to teach our children disrespect for their grandfather, but I don't like them to see me just accepting his outbursts without co ment. What should I do?

A: By being a good example yourself and using good teaching techniques with your children (as in Chapter Two), hopefully you will overcome the influence of a bad role model. Another possibility is to try to work on conflict resolution with the grandfather. Ask him not to say certain words in front of the children, raise his voice, or otherwise behave inappropriately. If that's not judicious or doesn't work in spite of your persistent efforts, consider using the grandfather's inappropriate behavior as an incidental lesson. Depending on the age and sophistication of the child, say something like this: "I don't like the way Granddad handles anger. He has a lot of good qualities, but that particular behavior is not good for us and not good for him either." Does your father have a condition like Alzheimer's disease, depression or alcoholism? Consider those possibilities and help your children understand what's going on by learning about the disease.

Q: What if my child just won't listen?

A: Approach her at an appropriate time, when she's in a reasonable mood, and carefully get her attention first. Draw her out so that, as a result of your listening to her well, she'll be in a better frame of mind to listen to you. Ask her to listen actively, explaining back to you what you have told her (Step Eight).

Children who habitually don't listen sometimes have attention deficit disorder (ADD), a central auditory processing deficit, or hearing loss. You may also be talking over her head.

Children who don't listen are often defensive, expressing their defensiveness passively. Try rereading the section on defensiveness in Chapter Three.

If the problem is severe and persistent, after you have ruled out or solved any medical problems, seek professional help from a child psychiatrist or licensed clinical mental health professional.

Q: When I yell to show my children I'm serious, it seems to work. And what about spanking? That's what my parents did, and it got results.

A: Your children at times need firm, serious discipline that is memorable. It lets them know that you are in control and develops respect and appropriate fear of the consequences if their behavior is egregious. Such discipline also helps them develop an appropriate internalized guilty conscience. "Firm and serious" do not necessarily equate with yelling and spanking. Generally, I advise against these techniques. Yet I don't feel that all parents who occasionally yell or spank are bad parents. Many thoughtful and caring parents with whom I have worked have, at times, yelled or spanked and have regretted it. It may have been what caused them to seek therapy. If you do these parental behaviors, it's important to consider the following points:

Frequency is an issue. The more frequent the yelling or spanking, the more likely it is to lose efficacy. After a while you have to yell louder and spank harder to have the same disciplinary impact. Often this escalating pattern produces children who are neurotically fearful, hostile "power strugglers," resentful and difficult, or resentful and distant. Resentful children make promises to themselves that someday they will get back at you. They may not act on these promises, but their feelings remain a barrier to intimacy with you or respect for you. They may also become overly dependent and turn to whoever or whatever is more reassuring: an inappropriate boy/girl friend or substances like alcohol and drugs.

If you yell and spank frequently or too intensely, you should do some self-examination. Does your yelling or spanking correlate with the severity of what your child did or is it displacement — a reaction to your anger about something else misdirected to your child? If the intensity of your anger reflects another problem not related to your child, it's not only unfair, it's confusing.

Very infrequent yelling or spanking that is not abusive does have impact; the child sees that your behavior is out of character and is shocked. He knows that what he did is a more serious matter, and he wants things back the way they were. So he may make amends and resolve to do better. A firm spanking when a toddler runs into the street or your child beats up a younger sibling may be okay. Such spanking hurts a child's feelings more than his bottom. However, in such a situation I still prefer the parent use a very somber, disappointed tone and have a profound talk about the consequences of the child's act and then develop a serious punishment that requires thinking on the child's part. This type of discipline will more likely have lasting positive impact than yelling and spanking.

Another negative aspect of yelling and spanking is that it often lets the kid off the hook too quickly. After a spanking or tirade, he has been punished, he's paid his debt, and he doesn't have to think about it anymore. Moreover, yelling and spanking are models of aggression. When a child sees his parents being aggressive, he doesn't blame himself so much. A parent's bad behavior actually relieves his guilt. Spanking also may border on abuse and put the parent under appropriate scrutiny.

Q: What if this conflict resolution method doesn't work?

A: That depends on your definition of "doesn't work." Does that mean the method, conscientiously studied and applied over time, didn't work even a little, or does it mean it didn't get instant, dramatic results? If the problem is serious and you studied and used the method conscientiously but it didn't help at all, seek the help of a professional. If partly worked, that's success because some improvement often stops a downward spiral and can begin an upward spiral. Don't expect perfection on the first try. Try, try again. Each time you reread and study the book, you'll change a little bit more and internalize another point that you can teach your child. Together you will grow towards greater and lasting harmony.

Afterword and Acknowledgments

The model of conflict resolution and other ideas in this book have evolved over my twenty-two years of clinical family psychiatry practice. New steps (for example, the most recent, Perspective Check) or new ways to describe a problematic process (for example, "defensiveness disorder") have come to me during the process of clinical observation and while trying to explain to families with unresolved conflict logical ways to set goals and learn necessary skills.

I have also taught this model to child psychiatry residents and various other groups over the years. The feedback I have frequently received is that they have heard some of these ideas elsewhere but never seen them all put together in this organized and comprehensive way. They often say that the model is easily understood, practical, makes common sense, and has been a helpful schema to refer to as we work together. Many have encouraged me to write this book.

I am grateful to many patients — parents and children — and students for their questioning, commentary, and encouragement. Special thanks to those who are the basis for the illustrative stories in the book. Their names and story details have been altered to protect their confidentiality, although I have tried my best to maintain the integrity of the point made by the examples. The long dialogues representing sample conflict resolutions from beginning to end have been created or recreated for illustrative purposes.

Theories, research findings, and psychological and psychiatric literature have generally contributed to these ideas, but my training background in cognitive therapy, especially under Aaron T. Beck, M.D., and in structural family therapy under Salvadore Minuchin, M.D., deserve special mention. After the model was developed, it was reassuring that many of the principles that met the tests of common sense and clinical judgment were supported by the research-based conclusions regarding anger explained in Daniel Goleman's recent excellent book, *Emotional Intelligence*.

I recognize the difficulties and limitations of doing research on the effectiveness of teaching this model, but I would welcome it, with the caveat that individual steps should not be studied in isolation from one another, especially if the outcome measures are global improvement in conflict resolution. Many of the individual steps, if poorly done, can undermine eventual resolution.

I also gratefully acknowledge:

My colleagues through the years, especially those at the Atlanta Area Family Psychiatry Clinic, for their friendship and intellectual stimulation, and the staff for their daily help in keeping me "together."

Longstreet Press, especially Sherry Wade for her great editorial help and Chuck Perry for allowing me this opportunity and for being so supportive.

Letitia Sweitzer, who deserves special praise. Her knowledge, talent, dedication, and insight have made this book possible. She is not only an excellent collaborator and wordsmith, but also contributed substantively with good questions, ideas, and examples.

Finally, I much appreciate the patience, encouragement, and support of my wife, Sherry, who has generated almost no conflict over my messy piles of papers and periods of inattention during the creation of this book.

Bibliography

Covey, Stephen, *Seven Habits of Highly Effective People*; Simon and Schuster, NY, 1989.

Goleman, Daniel, *Emotional Intelligence*; Bantam Books, NY, 1995.

Hoban, Russell, *Harvey's Hideout*; Parents Magazine Press, NY, 1969.

Leichman, Seymour, *Rumplestiltskin*; Random House, NY, 1977.

Lewis, Melvin, ed., *Child and Adolescent Psychiatry: A Comprehensive Textbook*; Williams & Wilkins, Baltimore, 1991.
Chapter 19, "Infancy," Michael E. Lamb, et al., pp. 222–256.
Chapter 20, "Development of School Age Children," Lee Combrinck-Graham, M.D., pp. 257–266.
Chapter 21, "Normal Adolescent Development: Empirical Research Findings," Daniel Offer, M.D., and Andrew M. Boxer, Ph.D., pp. 266–278.